Children, Courts, and Custody

Interdisciplinary Models for Divorcing Families

Andrew I. Schepard

Hofstra University

CAMBRIDGE
UNIVERSITY PRESS

PUBLISHED BY THE PRESS SYNDICATE OF THE UNIVERSITY OF CAMBRIDGE
The Pitt Building, Trumpington Street, Cambridge, United Kingdom

CAMBRIDGE UNIVERSITY PRESS
The Edinburgh Building, Cambridge CB2 2RU, UK
40 West 20th Street, New York, NY 10011–4211, USA
477 Williamstown Road, Port Melbourne, VIC 3207, Australia
Ruiz de Alarcón 13, 28014 Madrid, Spain
Dock House, The Waterfront, Cape Town 8001, South Africa

http://www.cambridge.org

First published 2004

Printed in the United States of America

Typeface Palatino 9.75/12 pt.   *System* LATEX 2$_\varepsilon$ [TB]

A catalog record for this book is available from the British Library.

Library of Congress Cataloging in Publication Data

Schepard, Andrew, 1948–
Children, courts, and custody : interdisciplinary models for divorcing
families / Andrew I. Schepard.
    p. cm.
Includes bibliographical references and index.
ISBN 0-521-82201-7 (hb.) ISBN 0-521-52930-1 (pb.)
1. Custody of children – United States.   2. Divorce mediation – United States.
3. Children of divorced parents – United States – Psychology.   4. Divorced
parents – United States – Psychology.   I. Title.
KF547.S33   2004
346.7301′73–dc21   2003053224

ISBN 0 521 82201 7 hardback
ISBN 0 521 52930 1 paperback

Contents

List of Figures

Acknowledgments

As described in the Preface, this book has been germinating for a long time, and many people have been gracious enough to touch and affect it.

Linda Silberman first nurtured my interest in mediation and child custody law, and has continued to do so for years.

Jay Folberg and Vivian Berger have both been deeply supportive of my work for a long time, and I am grateful to them.

Judge Sondra Miller has been a long-time source of wisdom and advice and a model of what a great family court judge should be. I am grateful to her for encouraging me to begin the Law and Children column for the *New York Law Journal*, which has been a regular forum for my developing thoughts about how courts can best process child custody disputes.

Mike Asimow inspired me to write the chapter on *Kramer vs. Kramer* with his wonderful article on the subject reflecting his long-time passion for integrating the study of law with the study of popular culture.

The role of the Association of Family and Conciliation Courts (AFCC) in developing my thinking and in providing a forum for interdisciplinary dialogue with judges, professors, lawyers, mediators, and mental health professionals cannot be overstated. I have been privileged to serve as editor of AFCC's academic and research journal, the *Family Court Review*, for several years, and have thus been fortunate to work with like-minded academics and practitioners from all over the world.

Ann Milne and Peter Salem are the center of a marvelous group of interdisciplinary professional colleagues who provide a welcoming, supportive environment for all interested in the constructive resolution of family conflict through the court system. Peter supported my efforts to develop P.E.A.C.E., a model court-affiliated parent education program, and Ann supported the development of the *Model Standards of Practice for Family and Divorce Mediation* for which I served as Reporter. I am grateful to both of them for all I learned because of our work together.

A number of friends and colleagues read all or some of the book in draft and provided valuable comments. Eric Freedman gave me an overall edit with his usual high standards of scholarly rigor. Sheila Schwartz, one of the outside reviewers commissioned by Cambridge University Press, did an admirable and helpful job in commenting on the entire manuscript. Woody Mosten, Phil Stahl, Greg Firestone, Joanne Pedro-Carroll, Jan Johnston, Linda Elrod, Marsha Klein Pruett, Elayne Greenberg, Naomi Kauffman, Theo Liebmann, and John Gregory all provided me with valuable insights, which found their way into the book and for which I thank them. They are not responsible for any errors or omissions, which are mine alone.

Julia Hough of Cambridge University Press was a deeply supportive first editor of this book. She believed in the project and in me. Without her, there would be no book. Phil Laughlin of Cambridge gracefully picked up the editing of this book when Julia was transferred to other duties. The anonymous reviewers Cambridge selected for both the book proposal and the text helped sharpen my thinking about the nature and purposes of the book.

Ronald Cohen helped reduce the anxiety of this first-time book author by editing each page of the manuscript with great care and competence and graciously sharing his years of experience with me.

Dean David Yellen and Vice Dean Marshall Tracht of Hofstra Law School provided a leave and a grant for this book that provided precious time for research, reflection, and writing. Lisa Spar of the Hofstra Library responded to my every research request with imagination and vigor. I do not know how anyone can write a book without the support of such an excellent librarian. Betty Leonardo, my long-time secretary at Hofstra, suffered almost as much as I did through the development of this book.

Bill Howe is the model of what a divorce lawyer should be, and his leadership role in reforming Oregon's divorce system is an inspiration for many of the ideas in this book.

Sandra Kaplan, Alan Cohen, Naomi Adler, Paul Meller, and Lisa Berman – my colleagues at the Hofstra University-North Shore-Long Island Jewish Health System Center for Children, Families and the Law – provided ideas and support that found their way into this book. We have had a fine interdisciplinary collaboration over the years to the benefit of our students, thinking, and research, and hopefully to the benefit of children and families in court.

I also thank Reggie Bullock of the Legal Department of North Shore-Long Island Jewish Health System Center for helping to arrange permission for the use of the Center's logo on the cover of this book.

My Hofstra Law School students over the years have been a source of dialogue and discussion and increasing insight on the issues this book addresses. I am especially grateful to the present and former student staff members of the *Family Court Review* for their hard work and dedication. Michelle Aulivola, Olga Batsedis Kimberly DiConza, Roland Estevez, Lisa Flesch, Thomas Foley, Christopher Graziano, Matthew Melnick, Gallit Moskowitz, Jennifer Spina, and Kevin Thurman, members of the class of 2003 or 2004, helped with the cite checking for the sources for this book, for which I am also grateful. Joi Kohlhagen provided valuable research help on the evaluation of parent education programs.

Jim Bozzomo, Hofstra Law School class of 2003, was an invaluable research assistant over the last two years. His excellent research help, editing, and insistence on rigorous analysis immeasurably improved this book. He graciously allowed me to adapt his Harry, Wendy, and Cindy example from his recently published law review note for use as a case study to compare New York's and California's child custody system in Chapter VII.

Nadeen Agour, Columbia Law School class of 2005, helped immeasurably with the final work on this manuscript.

I have been working on the topic of child custody law and dispute resolution for two decades. Although this book contains a great deal of new material, it also draws on earlier writings. Earlier versions of some of the chapters of this book appeared in articles in the *Texas Law Review, University of Arkansas at Little Rock Law Review, University of Michigan Journal of Law Reform, Family Court Review, Family Law Quarterly, Hofstra Law Review, Nova Law Review, Family Advocate, Practical Litigator,* and my bi-monthly *Law and Children* column in the *New York Law Journal.* All previous writings have been substantially revised and updated for this book.

I have saved the most important acknowledgments and thanks for the end. My sons David and Eric contributed materially to the book. David, a law student at Columbia, came up with the title, read over drafts, prepared the figures, and rescued me from computer disasters. Eric, a recent graduate of Amherst College, edited every word and made sure that my prose was coherent. I am grateful to them for this help but above all for being wonderful, loving children – the kind every parent should be blessed with.

Debra, my wife of more than thirty years, encouraged me to write this book and kept me focused on the end result on my down days. Without her love and support, this book would never have appeared.

Preface

[E]ach divorce is the death of a small civilization.[1]

This book was inspired by an experience in an urban courtroom a long time ago. I was a young law professor supervising a law school clinic in which my students represented children with the help of faculty and students from the university's medical and social work schools. The clinic was assigned to represent a physically disabled ten-year-old boy whom the relevant social welfare agency believed was ready to be released from foster care back to his family. The problem was that the agency did not know which parent should have custody of the child after his release from care.

The mother and the father were in the middle of a bitter divorce, and each of them wanted the child released to his or her custody. The precipitating event for the divorce was the mother's affair with a neighbor, which she claimed resulted from the father's long-term neglect of her needs. The parents were poor and could not afford expensive private treatment. When the father lost his job, the family lost its home. The parents voluntarily placed their child in foster care, and the agency arranged for treatment for the boy that the parents could not otherwise afford. They both visited their son regularly, and he did well in the program in which he was placed. Foster care is not supposed to be a long-term alternative to a family for a child. The agency said he was ready to go home, but the parent's custody dispute was holding up the child's release.

Detailed investigation and mental health assessments conducted by the clinic revealed that both parents were fundamentally decent people, but each had a dreadful view of the other. Each parent tried desperately to convince the boy to tell the court and us that he wanted to live with them. The boy refused to favor either parent. He wanted nothing more than his parents to stop fighting. He loved them both and wanted to live with both of them.

Our clinic made a variety of proposals for what we would today call a parenting plan for joint custody (a term not then in general use). The parents' lawyers rejected our proposals (ethically, we could not talk to the parents without their lawyers present). Both were sure their client was going to win sole custody and both blocked any attempt at what we regarded as a rational compromise in our client's best interests.

So the court scheduled a hearing. On the appointed day, we sat with our client in the middle of a horseshoe-shaped waiting room in the family court building. The mother and her court-appointed lawyer were at one end of the horseshoe and the father and his lawyer at the other. Both parents stared at their son. The boy looked away from them. We had told him that the judge would probably ask to talk to him as part of the judge's decision about his future. He kept saying to us over and over, "I don't want to tell the judge anything." The boy was terrified that the judge would use whatever he said to give custody to one parent or the other. When the time came for the case to be called, the boy simply refused to walk into the courtroom with us. He stood outside and screamed, "I won't go in, I won't go in, I won't go in."

We persuaded the judge not to interview the boy because of the emotional damage we feared it would do him. We were concerned that he would blame himself no matter what the judge decided. We then participated in a trial of bitter accusations, counter-accusations, and mental health testimony, some of which we initiated in the interests of getting all the facts before the judge. The judge never attempted to get the parents to agree on a parenting plan voluntarily, probably assuming that if we could not broker a settlement, neither could he. Eventually the judge ordered sole custody to the mother, with visitation rights to the father. His decision was based on our recommendation to him as the child's lawyer. When the court told the father that he had lost custody, I saw a pained and haunted look in his eyes, the first of many I would see when a parent was told something similar. The father looked at my students and me and the judge with hatred and despair.

When we told our client the result, he cried, and worried about his father incessantly. What would happen to him, he wondered? Would his father visit? Would his mother move away to spite his father (she had made some statements about a desire to relocate)? We had no answers for him, only hope that his father's love would motivate him to come to terms with the decision and stay involved in his life. We never had serious contact with the family again.

After the case was over, my students and I and the mental health professionals discussed the result, and asked ourselves whether we had done our client any good. We concluded that we had performed our duties as lawyers well. We shielded our client from having to choose between his parents before a judge. We presented valuable information and perspective to the court, and the court adopted what we thought were our well-reasoned recommendations.

I was still dissatisfied. The boy was right – the judge's decision embittered the father and damaged the parent-child relationship. Our client had come close to breaking down at the prospect of having to choose between his parents, or thinking he had to. He loved and needed both parents. Why should the court even suggest that he should make a choice between the two most emotionally important adults in his life?

The parents' experience in the child custody court taught them nothing but bitterness and anger toward each other. It was highly doubtful that they would ever speak to each other civilly again, much less consult each other about future decisions in their child's life. Their lawyers, though doing their jobs, fueled the parents' hatred through courtroom advocacy that demonized the other parent, magnifying his or her faults and minimizing his or her strengths. The victorious parent would surely lord the court order over the vanquished parent.

I wondered whether the adversary process might have done the parents and the child more harm than good. Interestingly, the mental health professionals, who I thought would be supportive of the boy's need to have relationships with both parents, told me we had done the best we could for our client. Citing psychoanalytic theory, the mental health professionals said that the parents, while both normal and fit, were in hopeless conflict and could not be trusted to cooperate for the benefit of their son. They felt the court had to choose one of them. The boy needed the stability of knowing which parent he was responsible to.

I would not accept that analysis. I just could not believe that a civilized society had to put children and their parents through so much distress because their parents could not agree. They both had a great deal to give their son, but they could not see what each other had to offer. I wondered whether there was some way we had not tried that the parents could have been encouraged to reach an agreement. Before the trial began, no one had made any serious attempt to educate the parents about what their conflict was doing to the child they both loved. The settlement conversations we had with the parents' lawyers seemed stilted and full of posturing about what was going to happen in court when one parent or the other testified. Something was missing somewhere. I kept asking myself whether the court really had to choose between the parents. Surely the court could have ordered them into some kind of joint therapy before doing so.

In the luxury of my academic environment, I began to explore whether there was any other way of resolving child custody disputes. I was fortunate because at that time the New York State Law Revision Commission wanted to conduct a study of joint custody and mediation in child custody disputes, reforms that had recently been enacted in California. A wonderful colleague and I were appointed as consultants for that study,[2] and came in contact with many people around the country active in seeking alternatives to the adversarial system for child custody disputes.

This book is the result of more than twenty years of research, arguing court cases, law reform projects, classes, discussions, field trips, and conference presentations that followed my experience representing that tormented young boy in the child custody court. It is my perspective on the evolution of the child custody court as an institution and the policies and social problems that have motivated its recent development.

The book's aim is to provide an accessible overview of the court's evolution to help readers understand how and why it functions at the beginning of the twenty-first century. The book also seeks to identify the policy challenges that the child custody court faces as it seeks to promote the best interests of the children of divorce, and to identify an agenda for its future reform and development. It is thus aimed at policymakers for the child custody court – legislators, governors, court administrators, citizens, and voters. We all have a stake in the effective functioning and future evolution of the child custody court. Even if we are not directly involved in disputes filed there, our employees, relatives, friends, and colleagues are.

Parents who are litigants in the child custody court are not criminals. They are doctors, lawyers, accountants, teachers, nurses, construction workers, police officers – parents from all walks of life and of all ethnic and religious backgrounds. These otherwise productive and usually sensible members of society have lost their moorings as parents because of their divorce, and need court intervention to get their and their children's lives back onto a rational track. Their productivity and humanity are greatly affected by the child custody court. As citizens we have a great interest in the quality of an institution that so vitally affects the welfare of our next generation.

The modern child custody court is an interdisciplinary enterprise, and this book is aimed at an interdisciplinary professional audience. It takes a village inhabited by different professionals to raise a child of divorce, and child custody court is the village's command center. Different professions have to work together to serve the best interests of children. Mental health professionals, mediators, parent educators, social service and community agencies, and court administrators play a central role working alongside judges and lawyers in the modern child custody court's operations. The book documents the way the administration and procedures of the child custody court have evolved beyond the adversary process to include education and mediation that promote parental agreements and responsible conflict management. It also looks at the roles of key players in the custody court – the judges, lawyers, mediators, educators, and evaluators who work under its auspices – and asks how they can help divorcing parents help their children.

The overall message that parents should get from this book is that conflict between them is a key but controllable factor in how well their child will cope with this time of difficult emotions and transitions. Parents make their children's lives better by keeping them out of the middle of conflict. The best gift a divorcing parent can give a child is the right to continue to love the other parent. The modern child custody court encourages parents to adopt that philosophy. Only parents can decide whether they will hear the message, as difficult as it is to surmount the anger and pain they experience in divorce. Everyone who hears that message gives his or her child a great gift.

The conflicts that divorce creates for children and parents are not going to go away anytime soon, and someone has to resolve them. What the child custody court can do is provide a rational framework for resolving parenting disputes expeditiously – a framework that encourages parents to manage their conflicts responsibly and devise their own parenting plans and allows their child to have a meaningful relationship with both of them safely. The court can require parents to participate in programs of education, mediation, evaluation, supervised visitation, and therapy that will help them and their children. It can also ensure that the providers of these services are competent and accountable. It can encourage lawyers to work with parents to de-escalate rather than inflame conflict about their children. It can recognize the dangers of violence between family members and take steps to protect vulnerable family members from such danger. The child custody court can better perform its mission of placing children at the center of the agenda of divorcing parents if concerned citizens understand the court's importance and support its growth and development. It is to that end that this book is dedicated.

How the Book Is Organized

Chapter I is an overview of the themes of the book.

Chapter II describes the sole custody/adversary system of the child custody court around 1980 by using the Academy Award–winning movie *Kramer v. Kramer* as a case study.

Chapter III summarizes what we know about divorce, its effects on children and parents, and the caseload of the child custody court.

Chapter IV describes the post-1980 evolution of joint custody and parenting plans as an alternative to sole custody.

Chapter V summarizes the parallel growth and development of alternative dispute resolution, especially mediation, in the child custody court.

Chapter VI discusses court-affiliated education for divorcing parents and children.

Chapter VII compares and contrasts the child custody courts of California and New York, two states with very different visions of how a child custody court can best meet the needs of parents and children.

Chapter VIII discusses family violence, the most serious problem facing the child custody court in promoting children's post-divorce relationships with both parents.

Chapter IX describes Differentiated Case Management, an emerging theory of judicial administration under which the child custody court uses a triage system for cases and devotes more-intensive resources to more deeply troubled families.

Chapters X, XI, and XII address the role of key professional actors in the child custody court: lawyers for parents (Chapter X); lawyers for children, the child's voice, and the alienated child in custody disputes (Chapter XI); and court-appointed neutral mental health evaluators (Chapter XII). These chapters identify current problems in the roles these professionals play, and analyze the way they are changing in light of the changes in the child custody court's mission.

Chapter XIII focuses on what legal standard courts should use to decide contested child custody cases by comparing the "best interests of the child test" with its principal competitors – the "approximation" presumption and a mandated presumption of equal physical custody. It also discusses the question of whether divorce should be made more difficult for parents because of the emotional, economic, and educational problems that divorce creates for many children.

Chapter XIV summarizes the themes of the book (1) by describing interdisciplinary coalitions that support efforts to reform the child custody court, and (2) by identifying key goals that policymakers for the court should try to achieve to meet the needs of divorcing parents and children in the 21st century.

I Overview

What Is the Child Custody Court?

This book is about the policies and practices of the institution that American society charges with the responsibility of supervising the reorganization of parent-child relationships after divorce – the child custody court. The child custody court essentially determines which divorced parent gets the right to make decisions for the child and how much time each parent gets to spend with the child, two different ideas that the legal system groups together as "custody."

All states have child custody courts. Often, however, they cannot be easily located on an organizational chart of the federal or state court system. American custody law is highly decentralized. The United States does not have a uniform national divorce and custody law as do Australia, England, and Canada. The power to determine custody is left to each state. A national law establishing parental rights and responsibilities after divorce is part of what makes those countries unified political and social entities. The child custody courts in Sydney and Melbourne are essentially the same.[3] In contrast, as described in Chapter VII, New York's child custody court is very different from San Francisco's.

There are fifty different state systems that administer child custody courts and create the substantive law that those courts apply. Even within a single state, child custody courts are often organized on a county basis, and different courts use principles of local autonomy to implement the same statutes differently. Court organization, procedures, and funding differ from state to state and between counties within a state.

No court anywhere is labeled a "child custody following divorce" court on an organization chart. In some states, the court that makes a child custody determination for divorcing parents is part of a unified family court that hears all legal matters relating to families (e.g., child abuse and neglect cases, foster-care review proceedings, juvenile delinquency petitions) in addition to divorce and custody.[4] In others, the court responsible for child custody

1

decisions for divorcing parents might be colloquially labeled the "divorce court," but is more formally labeled the "superior court." The superior court is usually a state's trial (first level) court of "general jurisdiction" and hears everything from contract disputes to auto accident cases and divorces. The superior court may have a special division that hears divorce and custody cases.

To illustrate how confusing identifying the proper court for child custody cases can become, consider court organization in New York State. There, the superior court is misleadingly called the "supreme court," which is not New York's highest court but its highest trial court. Only the supreme court can grant parents a divorce, and in the process of doing so, decides their child custody disputes. New York also has a family court. The New York family court, however, has no power to grant a divorce, but deals with most other kinds of family disputes. Many of those disputes heard in the family court are post-divorce, and are initiated by parents who want to change the custody arrangement they either agreed to or the supreme court ordered when the marriage was dissolved.

To avoid confusion, "child custody court" as used in this book refers to all these differently labeled courts throughout the United States that perform the profoundly important function of determining parenting arrangements for a child of divorce.

An Evolving Mission

Traditionally, courts define their role in civil cases such as contract disputes or claims for damages arising from an automobile accident as that of an umpire rather than as a proactive force to improve the lives of the parties to the dispute. An umpire (the judge) resolves disputes between the players according to the rule book. Sometimes, umpires have to interpret rules. They do not have an obligation to teach the players (the parties and their lawyers) the rules of the game or compensate for a player's weakness on the playing field by awarding one team extra points, nor do they warn players about the harm that the game can cause them. If a dispute arises, the parties present their evidence, and the umpire decides. A judge makes little effort to help the players resolve the dispute themselves, focusing instead on gathering evidence to make a decision. A judge's efforts to promote a settlement traditionally have been seen as inconsistent with the judge's role as a neutral umpire. In recent years, as we will see in Chapter V, courts have actively supported mediation and other alternatives to litigation designed to promote a settlement.

Child custody disputes are like most other civil cases in that the parties to it are private citizens. The private citizens who are parties to the child custody dispute are in court, not because of commercial relationships, but because they have a unique and special status – they are parents. Child custody disputes are thus not like auto accident or contract cases. In most civil cases, courts reconstruct a past event – Who went through the red light? Why were the goods defective? – and then assess blame or damage for that event. In a child custody case, in contrast, a court reconstructs past events concerning family relationships for the purpose of making a prediction about the future: What kind of post-divorce parenting arrangement is in the child's best interests? That prediction is not made to assess blame or damage but to make an educated guess about what will happen to the child if the court orders one custody arrangement or the other.

Historically, courts that resolve disputes involving children other than custody following divorce have adopted a different operational philosophy from courts that resolve contracts or auto accidents. Instead of defining their mission solely as that of umpiring, courts for children try to promote positive change in the problems that brought the family to court in the first place. This proactive philosophy for families in court has its clearest expression in the juvenile court movement. The juvenile court was created as a special court for young offenders, mobilizing community resources and working with parents to help rehabilitate them.[5] The first specialized juvenile court was established in Chicago in 1899, and the practice spread across the country. Numerous questions have been raised subsequently about whether the juvenile court actually fulfills its rehabilitative function,[6] and recently, the goal of the juvenile court has shifted somewhat from rehabilitation to punishment. Nonetheless, rehabilitation of the child with the support of the family and community remains a major goal of juvenile courts.

Child protection courts, which decide disputes when parents are accused by the state of abusing or neglecting their children, also have a proactive rehabilitative mandate. They order the use of services to help parents and children (e.g., counseling, homemaking help, participation in drug programs). They terminate parental rights, and free the child for adoption only if these rehabilitative efforts fail.[7]

For a long time, courts that decided child custody disputes arising from divorce followed an umpiring rather than a rehabilitative model. They functioned more like traditional courts in disputes between private parties, deciding contract cases or awarding damages from auto accidents, than juvenile or child protection courts. Disputes between parents over custody were private matters that were in court only because the parents could not agree on how the child should be brought up. Each parent argued that he or she promised a better future for the child. The court used the same adversary procedure as in other civil cases – accusation and counter-accusation, direct and cross-examination to probe the historical facts on which predictions were based. The court's function was to resolve the parents' dispute by choosing one or the other as the custodial parent and awarding the other parent visitation. Divorce was the death of a family. The legal system believed that divorcing couples should make a "clean break" from each other without further dealings. The court had to choose between parents because the child could not be left in emotional limbo, subject to continuous disputes, not knowing where he or she lived or which parent could make a decision about which doctor could treat him or her.

It took the advent of mass divorce and much research and time to understand that these underlying philosophical premises were incompatible with the needs of most children. For children, divorce is a time of reorganizing emotional relationships with parents, not ending them with one or the other. As will be discussed in later chapters, most children of divorce are better off if they are placed in a demilitarized zone between their parents. And, also as discussed in later chapters, they are also better off if, consistent with safety, they have a meaningful relationship with both parents.

The operating philosophy of the child custody court over the last twenty-five years has evolved toward a rehabilitative model closer to that of the juvenile and child protection courts. The child custody court has redefined its mission from deciding *which* parent should receive custody after divorce to determining *how* to involve both parents in the life of the child safely. The modern child custody court sees parental conflict in most families as modifiable and manageable through coordinated interventions. Instead of relying on courtroom combat, the modern custody court mandates educational programs and mediation to encourage parents to put their children's interests first and to negotiate their own parenting plans.

The evolution of the modern child custody court parallels the continuing movement to create unified family courts in which a single judge and a single interdisciplinary support team are assigned to a family regardless of whether the case arrives in court as a result of a charge of juvenile delinquency, violence between the parents, abuse or neglect of the child, divorce, or other trauma to the family. The first family court was established in Cincinnati in 1914, and the idea has been adopted in other states since. In the words of the great legal scholar Roscoe Pound, the logic behind the unified family court movement is

to put an end to the waste of time, energy, money, and the interests of the litigants in a system, or rather lack of system, in which as many as eight separate and unrelated proceedings may be trying unsystematically and frequently at cross-purposes to adjust the relations and order the conduct of a family which has ceased to function.[8]

The modern child custody court is also part of the movement for "therapeutic justice." Therapeutic justice evaluates the legal system by applying mental health criteria. When persistent social problems such as child abuse, domestic violence, drug addiction, and, more recently, parental conflict following divorce, appear on court dockets, therapeutic justice asks whether legal interventions are likely to produce net benefits or burdens for the mental health of the litigants. It weighs those benefits and burdens against other critical values such as due process of law.[9]

Therapeutic-justice values support the child custody court's evolution from umpire to proactive problem-solver. Mediation and education have helped thousands of parents to maintain a meaningful relationship with their children after divorce and settle their own disputes rather than having a judge impose a solution on them. But significant challenges remain in the court's continuing evolution toward providing effective therapeutic justice.

Differential Diagnosis and Treatment

A major benefit of a child custody court's adopting a proactive philosophy is that it can require parents and children to attend education, mediation, and mental health evaluation and treatment. The problem is that once the court defines its role as a family problem-solver, it must figure out what services it should order in a particular case. It must also have the services available to parents of all income levels and backgrounds. The millions of divorcing parents and children range from cooperative to combative, from functional to violent. The modern child custody court must carefully match available services with family needs and resources. It must use limited resources wisely by ensuring that families are not enmeshed in interventions they do not need. Modern custody courts have to make these difficult classification decisions, and often need help from the mental health and social service professions to do so.

A useful way of thinking about the challenge facing the modern child custody court is by way of a medical analogy – the emergency room of a major hospital. The child custody court needs to evolve, in many ways, into an emergency room for parenting disputes. In the same way they go to the emergency room, parents go to the child custody court when the symptoms of conflict become acute and need immediate treatment. The child custody court needs methods of triaging cases, stabilizing parents and children, and diagnosing whether further and more comprehensive treatment is necessary. It needs to devise procedures to carefully plan, coordinate, and evaluate the family's care. This planning can only be accomplished with the help of interdisciplinary professionals to develop a workable scheme for services for the family that the court ensures parents and children adhere to.

Protecting Safety

An abusive, neglectful, or violent parent is a serious risk to the safety of children and the other parent, whose protection justifies restrictions on a violent parent's relationship with the children. The child custody court's first challenge is to distinguish cases in which the fear of violence or neglect is documented and credible from those in which it is exaggerated or imagined for emotional reasons or is deliberately falsified for tactical advantage. A second challenge is to devise appropriate remedial plans for families in which a parent is violent. All violence in a family is deplorable. Violence, however, differs in degree and context – from a one-time slap expressing anger when one spouse learns the other has committed adultery, to an escalating pattern of assault, inflicted by a controlling batterer as part of a pattern of physical, financial, and emotional control over his or her victim, to continuing sexual abuse of a child. Child custody courts need help from the mental health community in making these kinds of distinctions and in devising restrictions on the relationship between the violent parent and his or her child that is proportionate to the actual risk to safety the parent presents.

Ensuring Accountability

The relationship between parents and children is not only emotionally precious; it is also a constitutionally recognized value. The Constitution does not explicitly mention the words "parent," "child," or "family." The U.S. Supreme Court has nonetheless held that parental rights are entitled to procedural protection as part of the "liberty" protected by the due process clause, and cannot be terminated without a hearing.[10] In the context of a grandparent visitation dispute, the Supreme Court recently held in *Troxel v. Granville* that a parent has a constitutional right to control the upbringing of his or her child as part of due process of law.[11] The deference to parents' decisions that *Troxel* seems to require signifies that parental rights have a substantive meaning as well. Other courts have described a constitutional right to family integrity that cannot be violated by government action absent a "compelling" state interest in, for example, the protection of children.[12]

Procedural protections such as cross-examination of witnesses and reliance on the rules of evidence to restrict the information that a court can consider put a brake on the power of courts to make arbitrary decisions in child custody disputes that affect these constitutionally protected interests. The high value we place on parental and family rights requires that elected or appointed judges, accountable public officials, make custody decisions if parents contest.

The modern child custody court nonetheless relies heavily on non-judicial personnel such as mediators, neutral mental health evaluators, and guardians for the child. These professionals can be extremely helpful to the court, parents, and children. But they are not elected or appointed public officials. The training and practices of these important professionals have not yet been standardized. The child custody court faces a challenge to ensure that these non-judicial professionals are qualified and accountable, do not coerce parents into uninformed, involuntary agreements, or supplant the role of the judge in making ultimate determinations that affect the parent-child relationship.

Redefining the Role of Lawyers

A related problem is defining the appropriate role of lawyers in the modern child custody court. Most parents and children who come before the child custody court are not represented by counsel, but desperately need legal information and advice. On the other hand, the modern child custody court emphasizes parental cooperation and planning, whereas some lawyers believe that the ethical responsibilities of the profession require them to be contentious and adversarial. For the modern child custody court to realize its mission, it will have to encourage lawyers to engage in more collaborative, problem-solving behavior and clarify their professional responsibility obligations to take the welfare of the children into account.

Ensuring Efficiency and Access to Justice and Services

Child custody disputes have significant economic costs both to society and the parents involved. Taxpayers pay for the courts and the education, mediation, evaluation, and therapeutic services connected to the court that help process and resolve them. Parents who are not eligible for legal aid have to pay the costs of private counsel and other mandated services. These costs can be substantial, especially in very contentious cases. A small number of parents with means can afford these costs; more and more of the parents who seek the help of the child custody court to resolve their disputes cannot. At a minimum, the child custody court must be careful to ensure that mandated services are necessary and are provided efficiently and expeditiously. More broadly, the same services that benefit wealthier parents and children should be available to all families regardless of income.

Public Support and Research and Development

There is no single magic solution to the challenge the child custody court faces from too many cases and too few resources. The court needs a plan and public support to help it meet the needs of parents and children. Lawyers, judges, mediators, parent educators, mental health professionals, and concerned citizens need to join forces in an interdisciplinary coalition to create support for the development of a truly family-friendly child custody court. A coordinated national and interdisciplinary program of research and development that can be shared by all child custody courts would help fill in the significant gaps in our knowledge about how to best serve children and parents. It would also provide a laboratory to develop the best practices for courts everywhere.

II   *Kramer vs. Kramer* Revisited

The Sole Custody/Adversary System Paradigm

This chapter describes the philosophy and assumptions of the child custody court before the 1980s – sole custody and the adversary system. The vehicle for the description is a well-known motion picture released in 1979, a time of ferment and change in the basic premises of child custody disputes. Based on the novel by Avery Corman,[13] *Kramer vs. Kramer*[14] won the Academy Award® for the best picture of that year. A leading scholar of law and popular culture describes it as "an outstanding and definitive film that treats all the elements of the divorce process seriously and which pointed the way for divorce-related films of the present."[15]

Kramer vs. Kramer is centered on a child custody dispute. The movie is intended for a mass audience. As a result, its portrayal of the child custody dispute resolution system is emotionally powerful, but not always entirely realistic. Because it is so well known and respected, *Kramer vs. Kramer* is a useful place to begin in order to understand the rapid changes in the child custody court from the time of the film's release until today. Indeed, the movie may well have had a significant influence on those changes, since it popularized and promoted the goals of gender equality in custody determinations and the notion that parents should forgo legal advantage, put aside their anger, and reach their own agreements in their child's best interests.

The Story

The movie begins with Ted Kramer (Dustin Hoffman) – a self-centered and materialistic advertising agent – arriving home in a celebratory mood after receiving a promotion. Joanna Kramer (Meryl Streep) is Ted's well-educated and intelligent wife. She devotes herself to raising their six-year-old, Billy, in their Manhattan apartment. Joanna feels unfulfilled and stifled, describing herself as "somebody's daughter or somebody's wife." She wants to work outside the home, but Ted is indifferent to her desires for self-fulfillment.

Joanna decides to leave Ted and Billy. Joanna's friend Margaret (Jane Alexander) supports her decision. Joanna is in the midst of walking out when Ted arrives home with news of his promotion. When Joanna says she is leaving, Ted seems more upset that she is spoiling his moment of professional success than he is about the seeming end of their marriage. He tries to stop her, but she goes out of the apartment and leaves Billy in Ted's care. Joanna moves to California and occasionally sends Billy letters.

Ted now has to learn to be a single parent to Billy, and Billy has to become accustomed to Ted as the nurturing and supportive figure in his life. Billy is deeply hurt and bewildered by Joanna's absence. Ted is angry with Joanna for leaving him in this situation and initially resentful of having to care for Billy. Father and son have emotionally powerful encounters where they learn more about each other and adjust to their differences and to Joanna's departure. Ted gradually becomes a much more attentive parent, taking Billy to school, cooking his meals, and taking him to the park. Ted receives emotional satisfaction from his involvement with Billy, comes to understand his son's needs and fears, and begins to put being a parent above professional success.

Joanna and Ted are presumably divorced in an uncontested action in which Ted gains custody of Billy in their divorce decree. The details of the legal dissolution of their marriage are not made clear on screen.

Ted forms a platonic but emotionally important and supportive friendship with Margaret, who is also a single parent. One day at the playground, Billy falls from the monkey bars and cuts himself. Ted frantically carries him to a nearby hospital where Billy is successfully treated.

Joanna returns to New York a year and a half after her departure. She too has evolved. She has a good job as a sportswear designer. She is in therapy and feels she is becoming stronger emotionally.

Joanna arranges a meeting with Ted in a restaurant. The discussion begins warmly. Then, Joanna says that "she wants [her] son" and an argument ensues. Ted accuses Joanna of abandoning Billy. She states that she has her life together and never stopped loving Billy. In anger, Ted breaks a glass against a wall. As he departs, he tells Joanna that she should "do what she has to do" and so will he.

Ted consults a lawyer, John Shaunessy (Howard Keel). It is not clear at the time of their initial interview whether any legal action has been taken to change Billy's custody, though the tone of the discussion suggests that a court case has been filed or is likely to be filed in the very near future.

Ted states that he thinks he has a strong case, as Joanna abandoned Billy. The following dialogue ensues:

Attorney Shaunessy: "Well, uh, first Mr. Kramer, there is no such thing as an open and shut case where custody is involved. While I'm willing to bet your ex-wife has already found a lawyer and he has advised her to move back to New York to establish residency, the burden is on us to prove your ex-wife is an unfit mother. And that means that..."

Ted: "Yes..."

Shaunessy: "Now, how old is the child again?"

Ted: "My son is 7."

Shaunessy: "Uh, huh." [with a skeptical tone]

Ted: "Why?"

Shaunessy: "That's tough. Well, in most cases involving a child that young the court tends to side with the mother."

Ted: "But she signed over custody!"

Shaunessy: "I'm not saying we don't have a shot. But it won't be easy...."

Shaunessy ends their interview by informing Ted that fighting Joanna for Billy's custody will cost him $15,000, a figure that obviously shocks Ted. Shaunessy tells Ted to go home and make a list of the pros and cons of a custody fight. A subsequent scene shows Ted making a list with many cons but no pros. Nonetheless, he decides to fight for custody, and retains Shaunessy.

Ted and Joanna have no pretrial settlement discussions in the movie. Their lawyers, however, apparently do have some communication, as evidenced by the following dialogue:

Attorney Shaunessy: "I just got a call from your wife's lawyer. She wants to see the kid."

Ted: "She wants what?"

Shaunessy: "Huh, she's the mother. That means she's within her legal rights..."

Ted: "All right just wait a minute now. I'm not so sure about her mental health."

Shaunessy: "What do you mean by that?"

Ted: "She told me she was seeing a shrink – a psychiatrist or something."

Shaunessy: "Well, did you ever see her talk to the walls?"

Ted: "No, but I'm just saying, you know..."

Shaunessy: "And I'm just saying that you don't have a choice. Have Billy at the boat pond in Central Park Saturday at ten o'clock."

Billy runs into Joanna's arms at that first visit. Additional visits are not portrayed on screen. Meanwhile, Ted's devotion to Billy interferes with his work. Ted misses important business meetings because of parenting obligations, and is ultimately fired during the Christmas holidays. Just at that time, a court date is scheduled. Shaunessy tells Ted that he doesn't have a "hope in hell" of winning the custody case unless he has a job.

Ted tells Shaunessy he will have a job in twenty-four hours. He lands a new job the day before Christmas by aggressively displaying his talent and using "take it or leave it" tactics on his potential new employer at a holiday party. The new job, however, is at lower pay and a lower professional status than his old one.

A custody hearing before Judge Atkins in a New York courtroom follows. Joanna is the first witness. She explains that she left Ted and Billy because she did not feel emotionally strong enough to care for Billy and was no longer in love with Ted, who was not responsive to her emotional needs. She feels she is much stronger now because of therapy and increasing insight. Joanna states, "I am not saying he doesn't need his father, but he needs me more." Ted learns during Joanna's testimony that she is actually making more money than he is. A report from Joanna's therapist is received into evidence over Shaunessy's objection, but not explored in depth.

Shaunessy's cross-examination of Joanna first establishes that Ted never beat or abused her or Billy, and he provided for her. Shaunessy asks Joanna how many lovers she has had and whether she currently has a boyfriend. Shaunessy concludes by persistently asking Joanna whether she has been a failure at her marriage – the longest, most stable relationship in her life outside of her relationship with her parents. Joanna is in tears. Ted is seen mouthing the word "no" at her while she tearfully answers "yes."

After Joanna's cross-examination, Ted asks Shaunessy, "Did you have to be so rough on her"? Shaunessy replies, "Do you want the kid or don't you?"

Ted begins his testimony with a passionate speech declaring that fathers can parent children as well as mothers. He affirms that women are entitled to equality of aspiration and achievements in the job marketplace, and recognizes that he probably would not have made that statement before Joanna left him. He argues that men should have equality with women in the role of parent. They, too, can provide love, affection, and nurturing to children. Ted states that he is the parent who provided Billy with stability during Joanna's absence, and warns against more emotional disruption for Billy if custody is shifted to Joanna.

During cross-examination, Joanna's attorney describes Ted's new job as "moving down the ladder of success" because of its lower pay and status. He argues that Ted pretends to be a fit parent but cannot hold a job. This prompts an outburst from Ted and a threat from Judge Atkins to hold him in contempt. Joanna's attorney then implies that Ted failed to take adequate care of Billy because of the playground incident, which Ted told Joanna about at their restaurant meeting.

Margaret testifies on Ted's behalf that he is a good and caring father and that Joanna is a good mother. On cross-examination, she admits having encouraged Joanna to leave Ted. After being excused as a witness, Margaret makes eye contact with Joanna and tells her that Ted has evolved into a good father for Billy. She tells Joanna that "if you could see them together, perhaps you wouldn't be here now." The scene makes it clear that Joanna is hurt by Margaret's testimony and sees it as a breach of their friendship and a betrayal of trust.

Ted and Joanna's courtroom combat contains the seeds of future reconciliation. Joanna apologizes to Ted in the courthouse hallway for raising the playground incident, stating that she did not know her lawyer would use it. Ted is very angry with Joanna nonetheless, and rides down in the courthouse elevator silently and angrily.

Shaunessy's advice to Ted about courts' favoring mothers in cases involving custody of young children proves prescient. Judge Atkins applies the "tender years" doctrine, which awards custody of young children to mothers unless they are unfit. He orders Billy to be placed in Joanna's custody, and grants Ted visitation time. Ted immediately states he wants to continue to fight for Billy's custody, no matter what the cost. Shaunessy tells Ted that this time "the costs will be to Billy." Should the case go to appeal, Billy will have to testify. Ted recognizes the emotional harm that Billy will suffer if he has to testify, and declines to pursue the battle further.

In the final scenes, Ted prepares Billy for the switch in custody with great sensitivity to Billy's feelings. Ted is obviously in great emotional pain, but encourages Billy to make the best of living with his mother. Joanna, however, decides not to go through with the custody change. Exactly why Joanna has this change of heart is unclear. She states when she comes to pick up Billy, "I came here to take my son home. I realize he is home."

What Are Ted and Joanna Fighting About?: The Legal Battle

From the outset, Ted and Joanna conceptualize their dispute over Billy as a "legal" problem. They consult lawyers – not a family counselor, a mental health therapist, or a mediator. They do not ask for any outside advice about what is good for Billy from anyone before facing off in court; each simply assumes that Billy would be better off in his or her custody. They perceive each other as adversaries and the contest as a zero sum game – if Ted has custody of Billy, then Joanna does not, and vice versa. While we do not see Joanna consulting with her lawyer, Shaunessy's conversations with Ted reinforce the view that the custody dispute is a battle to the death – "I'll have to play rough. And if I play rough you can bet they will too. Can you, uh, take that Mr. Kramer?"

One reason that Ted and Joanna conceptualize their disagreement as a legal battle is that American custody law, at the time *Kramer vs. Kramer* was released, offered few other options. Understanding why parents had to "play rough" requires an overview of child custody law at the beginning of the 1980s.

The law applicable to *Kramer vs. Kramer* is best understood by dividing it into substance and procedure. *Substance* is comprised of the rules that courts apply to determine outcomes of contested cases. *Procedure* is the way that courts gather information to make their determinations. The "best interests of the child" is the overarching substantive standard that Judge Atkins uses to determine whether Ted or Joanna should have custody; the tender years doctrine is a subdivision of the "best interests" test. The trial is the procedure that resulted in the gathering of the facts and arguments to make the "best interests" determination.

Essentially, in 1980, the child custody court followed what can be called a "sole custody/adversary system paradigm." Substantively, it resolved custody disputes by awarding one parent sole custody and the other visitation rights. It made that decision through adversary procedures – a trial, where witnesses are called and cross-examined and arguments made – similar to that used in all civil cases such as automobile accidents and contracts.

Substantive Law

"Custody" is a parent's legal right to control his or her child's upbringing. A lay person would call it "parenting," removing the unfortunate (and inaccurate) connotation that a parent is a child's warden. The child is deemed to be "in the custody" of parents because the child generally has no independent rights. "The basic right of a juvenile is not to liberty but to custody. He has the right to have someone take care of him, and if his parents do not afford him this custodial privilege, the law must do so."[16]

Two different functional concepts come under the single label of "custody" when referring to divorcing parents – "physical" and "legal" custody. *Physical* custody, meaning "residence" in lay terminology, is a child's primary living arrangement, and determines which parent is responsible for the child's day-to-day care. *Legal* custody, meaning "decision-making" in lay terminology, is a parent's right to make decisions for a child, such as which school a child attends, what a child's religious training will be, whether a child can enter into a contract, and what medical treatments a child will undergo.

Parents share legal and physical custody in an "intact" family. They have equal rights to make decisions for a child. Since they live in the same house, they share physical custody as well.

When parents physically separate and eventually divorce (e.g., when Joanna moves out from the apartment she shares with Ted and Billy), the legal system faces the problem of how to allocate physical and legal custody between parents. Most of the time, a court will approve an agreement that parents reach themselves. It is only when parents cannot agree that a court must decide custody for them. A child cannot live in two houses at the same time. A child must still attend school regardless of whether divorcing parents agree on which school he or she should attend.

At the time of *Kramer vs. Kramer*, courts generally used a "sole" custody framework to allocate legal and physical custody between divorcing parents. By awarding one parent sole custody, the court designates that parent as the child's primary physical custodian, entitling that parent to most of the child's physical custody. The same parent is also granted legal custody and thus all of the major decision-making rights for the child.

When a court awards sole custody to one parent, it almost always awards "visitation" rights to the other parent, which amounts to temporary physical custody of the child for a limited time. The purpose of visitation is to preserve some role for the non-custodial parent in the life of the child. As Shaunessy accurately tells Ted, a parent has to be a serious threat to the health and safety of a child before a court will cut off that parent's visitation entirely.[17] Before doing so, the court will order the visitation with a parent who presents a danger to a child to be "supervised" by a third party, a subject to be discussed in Chapter VIII.

The fundamental purpose of a sole-custody award is to designate one parent as the primary decision-maker and focus of the child's emotional life. Although contact with a child is preserved, the visiting parent often feels relegated to the sidelines. The non-custodial parent has no right to significant participation in major decisions concerning the child's future. Many non-custodial parents maintain strong relationships with their children, but the legal structure for their role makes the custodial parent a more important figure.

The Evolution and Demise of the "Tender Years" Doctrine

The substantive rules courts use to determine which parent is awarded sole custody have varied over time according to changes in morality, in child-rearing practices, and in the relative social and economic positions of mothers and fathers.[18] These rules have a history of explicit gender bias. Under early English common law, for example, Ted would have won sole custody, as the father had an absolute right to physical and legal custody of his child. In part, this rule was a logical extension of the wife's property-like relationship to her husband. It also reflected a view of the family that was closely tied to the ownership and preservation of property. Fathers had access to wealth, and since they could support their children economically, they were the logical choices for sole custody.

In the English colonies, the courts began to inquire into parental "fault" in awarding sole custody to one parent or the other. This concept was tied to the idea that divorce should be granted only upon a showing of fault. Since the courts would not award custody to a father who was morally unfit, the mother had a chance to win custody where none existed before. If Ted and Joanna had lived in colonial days, Joanna, in order to deprive Ted of custody of Billy, would have had to prove that Ted was drunk, abusive, or an adulterer to defeat the presumption that fathers should have custody. Since she could not, Ted would win custody of Billy. The morally unfit parent lost sole custody, not because of the effect of the depravity on the child, but because the parent had forfeited a legal right by his or her conduct.

Judicial definitions of fitness evolved over the years as social mores evolved. Most courts, for example, moved toward the view that a parent's adultery no longer automatically meant unfitness for custody of a child. Instead, courts looked to the functional effect of a parent's extra-marital relationships on the child (who may or may not, for example, be aware of them at the time they occur) rather than making an automatic equation between adultery and immorality.[19]

In the early twentieth century, courts increasingly began to focus on the child's emotional interests rather than on the parent's moral state. Courts' evaluation of the child's emotional interests, however, evolved in a way that replaced one gender-driven system with another. Under the tender years doctrine, mother replaced father as the presumptive sole custodial parent. The tender years doctrine awarded the custody of young children (below teenage) to the mother unless she was seriously unfit.[20] Courts justified this doctrine with statements such as: "[M]other love is a dominant trait in even the weakest of women, and as a general thing surpasses the paternal affection for the common offspring, and, moreover, a child needs a mother's care even more than a father's."[21] The maternal preference "needs no argument to support it because it arises out of the very nature and instincts of motherhood; nature has ordained it."[22]

The late nineteenth-century society and economy supported the tender years presumption.[23] Industrialization, and its demand for workers, removed men from the home and changed the economic structure of the family. Wages replaced property as the economic base of most families. Women undertook the full-time responsibility of rearing children and managing the household, while men earned the wages that provided the family's economic support. It became "natural" in the sense of being the established social pattern that mothers reared children as a full-time occupation.

The tender years doctrine also received support from early psychoanalytic preoccupation with the primacy of the mother-child relationship in the child's emotional development. "Although Freud acknowledged that infants did ... identif[y] with both parents ... he stressed that both boys and girls formed their first and most important relationships with their mother."[24] Because of Freud's influence, "the prevailing assumption in American development psychology [was] that the more secure and undiluted the infant's attachment to a single caregiver, the greater the child's ability to form close emotional relationships and to cope with psychological stress in the future."[25]

Mother usually filled the role of primary parent. During the period when the tender years doctrine dominated judicial thinking, the father in middle-class families worked full-time and the mother stayed home full-time to take care of the children. It was thus logical, and perhaps inevitable, that sole custody should be awarded to the mother, who had the time and energy to devote to the private dimensions of family life after divorce and few skills with which to earn money in the marketplace. A study of appellate court decisions in 1960 found that mothers won about 50% of the cases, whereas fathers won about 35%.[26] Other estimates around the time of *Kramer* were that mothers received custody in over 90% of cases in which it was contested.[27]

The tender years doctrine, and the philosophy of sole custody of choosing one parent, also received support from the underlying theory that motivated the early no-fault divorce movement. Until the second half of the twentieth century, only virtuous spouses could obtain divorces and "the divorce laws of every state assumed an adversary proceeding between spouses in which the plaintiff had to prove the defendant's 'fault.'"[28] Today, every state has a no-fault divorce ground that allows spouses to divorce each other without accusations of wrongdoing.[29] One scholar has described the philosophical shift to no-fault divorce as a "silent revolution" that took place without extended public debate or dramatic political controversy.[30]

The purpose of no-fault divorce laws was to eliminate marital fault as the basis for judicial divorce-related decision-making, including determinations in custody cases.[31] At first, the administrative ideal of no-fault divorce was that former spouses should make a "clean break" from each other and build new lives for themselves. The clean-break notion assumes that both members of a divorcing couple are better off if they can cut ties with one another and start life afresh. The doctrine began as an attempt to define what an ideal economic settlement should be at the time of a no-fault divorce – the spouses should be left with assets and income to lead entirely separate lives. It later became part of judicial thinking about all aspects of divorce, including custody.[32] It fits naturally with the idea of sole custody, which gives one parent all rights over the child, relegating the other to legal insignificance.

As Judge Atkins decides (in *Kramer vs. Kramer*), mechanical application of the tender years doctrine means a victory for Joanna solely because she is Billy's mother. This result was, no doubt, included in the movie for dramatic effect. In reality, the tender years doctrine was in retreat at the time that *Kramer vs. Kramer* was released, and Judge Atkins probably misapplies it.

Three developments challenged the assumptions underlying the tender years doctrine and the predominant pattern of sole custody awards to mother: the entry of women into the labor force, the drive for legal equality of the sexes, and the empirical evidence establishing the importance of the child's father in the child's life, both before and after divorce.

The entry of women into the workforce contributed substantially to the erosion of the tender years doctrine. Either out of choice or economic necessity, women entered the labor force in staggering numbers, undermining the "mother stays home while father works" assumption of the sole custody system. In 1900, only 6% of married women worked outside the home. In 2000, that percentage had soared to 61%. The percentage of working married women with children under the age of 6 years is even higher – 64%.[33] Divorced mothers are more likely to be in the labor force than married mothers – 73.7% compared with 61.1%.[34] The established work pattern simply no longer supports the theory that only the mother has the time necessary to devote to proper child rearing.

The drive for legal equality of the sexes spurred by the women's movement also undermined the tender years doctrine. The dominant modern metaphor for describing the legal organization of the family is the "partnership" model of marriage. Under the partnership model, husbands and wives are legal equals, although they might contribute in different ways and in different degrees to the total welfare of the family unit.[35]

The partnership model has been applied generally only to the economic aspect of marriage. For example, community property states reflect this theory by recognizing that all income and property received during marriage belongs to both partners equally, regardless of which partner is the actual earner.[36] A stay-at-home spouse is thus awarded a share of the business that a working spouse develops. The partnership concept cannot be limited logically and emotionally to dollars and cents. Its reach extends to the other major task of the family – raising children. If marriage is an economic partnership regardless of the role a partner plays in creating the family's economic wealth, it is also a parental partnership regardless of the role each parent actually plays in raising the children.

At the time of *Kramer vs. Kramer*, women spent far more time than men bringing up children. This is still true today, although the amount of time men devote to child-care has increased substantially in recent years.[37] Divorced men nonetheless came to question the idea that their pre-divorce involvement with the child should determine their post-divorce parenting role. They viewed the unequal division of caretaking responsibilities between parents as part of an agreed upon division of labor, and felt they should not be penalized for working outside the home for the benefit of the wife and the child.[38]

Men thus took advantage of the feminists' drive to eliminate sex discrimination to attack what they saw as gender discrimination against men in custody disputes.[39] As Herma Hill Kay writes, "The sex discrimination cases exhibited a two-way model in which female plaintiffs sought equal treatment with men in the public sphere, while male plaintiffs sought equal treatment with women in the private sphere, notably the family."[40] Most of the legal doctrines attacked in the courts on the grounds of gender discrimination put women at a disadvantage by disqualifying them irrationally from jobs or positions that they were functionally capable of performing as well as men.[41] The tender years doctrine, however, favored women irrationally on the basis of gender, as some men were as capable as women were of being as good, if not better, nurturing parents to their children after divorce. Despite the support that some feminist scholars continue to give to it,[42] the drive to eliminate gender stereotypes in law could not be confined to those that disfavor women. It called into question all gender-based discrimination, both for and against women, and thus the tender years doctrine too.[43]

A final development that undermined the tender years doctrine was the increasing empirical evidence questioning its psychoanalytic underpinnings: the primacy of the mother-child relationship and the importance of a child's intense attachment to a single caregiver for future emotional well-being. Ted's dramatic testimony that fathers can be good parents and are important nurturers in the lives of their children captured the trend of research findings. Numerous studies, to be reviewed in detail later in this chapter and in Chapter III, confirm the importance of both parents in the child's emotional life in intact families as well as in divorced families. A 1983 law review article states, "[T]he great importance of the father in the development and education of his children – sons and daughters – is one of the best documented findings within the social sciences in the last twenty years."[44]

It is sufficient to note at this point that the research findings confirm the idea that the partnership model of parenting not only symbolizes the legal equality of the sexes, but also serves the emotional needs of most children. Both parents remain important to a child's development despite the difference in the amount of time each spends with the child. Available evidence indicates that a child generally has emotional attachments to both parents, as well as to caretakers, grandparents, and other significant persons in his or her life. Except perhaps for unweaned breastfed babies, neither mother nor father is categorically *the* parent with whom a child's relationship is more necessary than with the other.

All of these changes began a revolution in child custody law, to be discussed in detail in later chapters. For our purposes, it is sufficient to note that most states abrogated the tender years presumption by statute or case law. Indeed, by 1980, New York's custody statute stated that "in all cases there shall be no prima facie right to custody of the child in either parent,"[45] strongly implying that a parent's gender should not decide a custody contest. About the time *Kramer vs. Kramer* was released, a lower New York court had declared the tender years presumption unconstitutional,[46] and several decisions, though over dissents, awarded sole custody to fathers.[47] Furthermore, even assuming the tender years doctrine was in force, as Michael Asimow points out, Judge Atkins applied it incorrectly in *Kramer*:

> Ted effectively rebutted the [tender years] presumption. In no event should the presumption be applicable to a modification of custody, as opposed to an initial determination of custody at the time of divorce. The most important point is that Ted, not Joanna, had been Billy's primary caretaker for a year and a half. After all, Joanna had abandoned Billy. Ted had formed a close emotional bond with Billy and had been an excellent and caring parent. Changing custody could only be terribly disruptive to Billy. At a minimum, Billy would suffer short-term trauma; he might well suffer long-term damage. The court was impressed with none of this. As the judge saw it, assuming that a mother of a young child is not somehow unfit, she gets custody.[48]

Mental Health Experts and the "Psychological Parent" Standard

The tender years doctrine had a great advantage for courts: Because the outcome of most custody cases was known in advance, few fathers were willing to invest the financial and emotional resources to fight what was likely to be a losing battle. Once the doctrine was eliminated, the judicial floodgates were opened for custody fights in the courtroom.

Eliminating the tender years presumption required the courts to shift from a relatively simple issue (was the mother unfit?) to a wide-ranging, multi-factored "best interests of the child" inquiry in order to predict what custody arrangements were the best for the future of a particular child.[49] As will be discussed in Chapter XIII, some state statutes that set the standards for the way courts should decide contested custody cases simply tell them to make decisions in the child's best interests, leaving it to judges to flesh out the meaning of that term.[50] Other statutes describe factors that a court should explicitly consider in a "best interests" analysis, such as the love and affection between parents and child, the "moral fitness" of the parents, or the preferences of the child if "reasonable."[51] Yet the factors remain general considerations, without rank or order, and include a catchall allowing the judge to consider "any other factor . . . relevant to a particular child custody dispute."[52] In such jurisdictions, the typical judge's "best interests" decision becomes a potentially idiosyncratic prediction of which parent is more suitable to be the primary custodian based on a comparative evaluation of his or her fitness for the task.

Around 1980, courts began to ask mental health experts to fill the indeterminacy gap in the sole custody system created by the demise of the tender years doctrine with their expertise. At the time when *Kramer vs. Kramer* was released, the most notable attempt to create a workable mental health standard to guide courts in making custody determinations was Goldstein, Freud, and Solnit's "psychological parent" test. GFS's work "helped to transform the role of mental health professionals in child custody determinations, implicitly assuming that mental health professionals are uniquely situated to provide a sound basis for determining the best child custody arrangements."[53] These distinguished law and mental health academics urged courts to create, above all, emotional stability for children caught between warring parents by making a final and decisive award of custody rights to one parent.

Working from a psychoanalytic framework, GFS defined the task for child custody courts as identifying the single parent with whom the child had primary psychological relationships. To GFS, a child's psychological parent was the one "who, on a continuing, day-to-day basis, through interaction, companionship, interplay and mutuality, fulfills the child's psychological needs for a parent, as well as the child's physical needs."[54] Stability of the child's emotional relationship with that parent was so important to GFS that they advocated granting the psychological parent the power to preclude the other parent from even visiting with the child for fear it would cause emotional conflict. While no court took the policy of stability so far, GFS's emphasis on the importance of emotional stability for the child by empowering the sole custodial parent was enormously influential.[55]

GFS's psychoanalytic argument for identifying a single more important parent also found theoretical support in the attachment theory of development psychology. "Attachment theory is a theory of close relationships. At its core is the premise that humans, because of our vulnerability and immaturity during infancy and childhood, are biologically predisposed to seek proximity to protective caregivers."[56] Research findings support the idea that stable adult attachments for the child predict a child's psychological well-being.[57] A child can become emotionally insecure if its caregiver, for example, becomes depressed and can no longer function, or if all contact with a parent with whom a child is emotionally bonded is ended.

Some early-attachment theorists argued that a young child had only one significant attachment to an adult (usually the mother) that needed protection even if relationships with other adults had to be weakened. "Like the psychoanalysts . . . many developmental psychologists . . . have long focused exclusively on mothers and children, presuming fathers to be quite peripheral and unnecessary to children's development and psychological adjustment."[58]

The problem, however, is that research has established that children have multiple emotional attachments to adults, not just a single attachment that is more important than all others. As summarized by Richard Warshak: "The notion that children have only one psychological parent has been thoroughly discredited by a large body of evidence that has demonstrated that infants normally develop close attachments to both of their parents, that this occurs at about the same time (approximately 6 months of age), and that they do best when they have the opportunity to establish and maintain such attachments."[59]

In a recent review, Joan Kelly and Michael Lamb further elaborate the nature of modern attachment theory:

In general, the ways in which mothers and fathers establish relationships with and influence their children's development is quite similar. Although much has been made of research showing that mothers and fathers have distinctive styles of interaction with their infants, the differences are actually quite small and do not appear to be formatively significant. The benefits of maintaining contact with both parents exceed any special need for relationships with male or female parents.[60]

Who can say with confidence that Ted or Joanna is *the* psychological parent to Billy? He has important relationships with both, and they with him. Furthermore, a parent's psychological importance to his or her children is not static. Even if Ted and Joanna had not divorced, their psychological salience to Billy would probably vary with his age and developmental stage, their individual willingness and ability to make an emotional commitment to him, and vice versa. Joanna certainly spent more time with Billy before she left for California, and probably was thus his "psychological parent" if one had to be chosen. Joanna's relationship with Billy changed dramatically after she had left; by the time of the trial, Ted had become Billy's "psychological parent." Billy nonetheless retained an important emotional bond with his mother, which Joanna began to repair when she began visiting again.

Many men saw the psychological parent test as simply a more sophisticated version of the tender years doctrine. The psychological parent test is gender-neutral, since either the father or the mother can take care of the child on a day-to-day basis. In operation, however, it favors mothers, who are more often the day-to-day caretakers of young children, and rewards them for a particular function they perform in the family in opposition to the spirit of the partnership model of marriage.

More importantly, the psychological parent standard assumes one parent is more important to the child than the other and that the more important parent can be identified and rewarded with sole custody. It frames the court's custody decision in a competitive context and simply expands the arena for adversarial courtroom combat to include a comparative analysis of a parent's role in the child's emotional life. It encourages parents to engage in courtroom warfare over which parent is more important to a child and who did what for the child's day-to-day care.

Expert Witnesses and Problematic Scientific Support

The only mental health professional mentioned in *Kramer vs. Kramer* is Joanna's therapist, who is never seen in the movie and whose report is nonetheless offered into evidence at trial. It is highly unlikely that in a hotly contested case, a court would receive Joanna's therapist's mental health report into evidence without requiring the writer of the report to testify in person. Furthermore, had *Kramer vs. Kramer* been a real case, Judge Atkins would have heard testimony from mental health experts, hired by one parent or the other, to help him decide Billy's custody.

At the time of *Kramer vs. Kramer*, a parent generally hired a mental health expert to testify on his or her behalf, much as a party hires an expert to testify in a medical malpractice or auto accident case. Today, testimony from mental health experts, particularly from a neutral expert appointed by the court rather than hired by one of the parents, is a staple of contested child custody trials. The standards of practice of neutral mental health evaluators have evolved substantially since 1980. As will be discussed in Chapter XIII, such neutral mental health evaluations perform a valuable function for parents and the court in presenting a perspective to the court that is based on the child's needs, one that neither parent may be capable of performing. This neutral perspective both informs judicial decision-making and encourages settlement.

At the time of *Kramer vs. Kramer*, however, the expertise of the mental health professionals involved in child custody disputes was in its formative stages. Very little systematic and validated research had been conducted at the time about the effects of divorce on children. Much of what passed for expertise was really opinion that had some theoretical basis. Lawyers for parents sought victory for their clients. Mental health professionals who testified for parents were pushed by the engine of the adversary system to reject their basic training, which emphasizes doubt and uncertainty and is open to revision based on experience and new data. The demands of partisan advocates forced them to state what should have been qualified, tentative observations with much greater clarity and certainty than the state of the supporting data warranted.

While *Kramer vs. Kramer* illustrates the general combativeness and fault-finding of the child custody trial in 1980, it does not examine how the role of mental health experts chosen by the parents sometimes exacerbated the problems of adversarial justice in the child custody context. *Rose v. Rose*, a real case, provides a graphic illustration of how badly the adversarial procedure and the sole custody system challenged the credibility of mental health experts retained by the parents at about the time *Kramer vs. Kramer* was released. That hearing was held in a courtroom in the State of Washington and is extensively excerpted in a textbook used widely to teach family law in law schools.[61]

One does not gain confidence in the role of mental health professionals in custody disputes from the *Rose* transcript. Partisan witnesses and mental health experts for each side repeat accusations of parental incompetence and infidelity and meddling by grandparents worthy of a daytime soap opera. Only one of seven expert witnesses saw both parents with the child, and even that expert did not conduct a formal mental status examination of the father. One clinical psychologist called as an expert to rebut the accusation that the mother in *Rose* was a poor parent based her testimony on her research to construct "scientific" measures of good motherhood. She compared how long "good moms" (as defined by mental health experts), "average moms," and "poor moms" interact with their infants without taking a break. She tested the mother in *Rose* and compared her with the research sample. This expert concluded:

[I]n the good moms sample, their children interacted with that mother out of a possible 50 seconds a minute, their children interacted 46.8, 47 seconds a minute. Diane [the mother in *Rose*] – [and] Jason [the infant child whose custody was contested] interacted 38 seconds a minute, and poor mom's children interacted 26.9 – make it 27 seconds a minute. And the average moms, 39 ... Diane and the average moms are absolutely together and certainly nowhere near, you know, poor parenting ... My opinion is that Diane be awarded custody.[62]

It is hard to imagine any court today taking seriously the opinion of a mental health expert on which parent should have custody when the basis of the opinion is an eleven-second differential in parent-child interaction in an experimental sample of mothers not involved in a custody dispute. The *Rose* transcript is full of opinions by mental health experts stated without adequate investigation or research.

Moreover, the *Rose* parents, their expert witnesses, and their lawyers were also in deep dispute about whether the mother or the father was the child's "psychological parent." The mother had the closest relationship in terms of time spent with the child, until she attempted suicide, one of the events that precipitated the divorce and the custody dispute. During the mother's recovery period, the father (a medical student and then a doctor) – and most significantly, the paternal grandmother – took over care of the child. Much of the transcript of the custody hearing is devoted to attempts by each parent to bolster evidence of the child's psychological attachment to him or her and to minimize and disparage the child's psychological attachment to the other. One of the authors of the "psychological parent" standard, Goldstein (a lawyer and psychoanalyst), testifies as an expert on behalf of the father, and asserts the primacy of the father's emotional bond with the child without interviewing any of the parties or the child. The only confident conclusion one can draw from the *Rose* transcript and the extensive mental health testimony is the obvious one that the child had psychological attachments to both parents and their extended families.

The *Rose* custody trial was a sad exercise in futility and revenge and an illustration of the bias that mental health professionals, paid by the parties, stating subjective impressions without sound empirical basis or clinical practices, bring to the adversarial process. Fortunately, the movie audience for *Kramer vs. Kramer* and the fictional Ted, Joanna, and Bill were spared a similar spectacle.

The Child's Involvement in the Adversary System

Kramer vs. Kramer also spares the movie audience the problem of considering the possibility of Billy's involvement in the custody trial. We never see Billy's reactions on screen as the trial unfolds. One of the main reasons that Ted chooses not to challenge Judge Atkins' decision in further proceedings is that Billy might be called to testify or be interviewed by the judge. The audience recognizes this decision as an admirable attempt to keep Billy out of the middle of Ted and Joanna's conflict.

Real children are not spared from involvement in most adversarial custody trials. A real Judge Atkins might have decided that Billy was old enough to have a voice in his own custody dispute. As will be discussed in detail in Chapter XI, the governing law is that a child's "mature" preference can play a role in the court's decision, the court can interview the child, and the older the child the more weight his or her preference receives. Everything is left to the judge's discretion.[63]

A child's custody preferences may have a solid factual base (e.g., if one parent abuses the child). On the other hand, a child's preference for a parent might be based on bribery, emotional dependency on one parent, or unjustified alienation from the other parent. Children also sometimes become parental figures to troubled, depressed parents, and feel guilt, anxiety, and anger toward the other parent. The overriding danger of including the child's preference as a datum in a child custody system that chooses between parents is that it makes the preference a tool of litigation and subjects children to pressure from their parents. Ted and Joanna admirably spare Billy these dangers. Other embroiled parents do not.

The Problem with the Sole Custody System

The underlying problem that *Kramer vs. Kramer* illustrates is that the sole custody system and adversary procedure forces parents like Ted and Joanna to behave as enemies rather than to seek compromise to benefit their child. It is in Billy's best interests that both of them play major roles in his future life. The audience senses that both parents should not spend time, money, and emotional energy, nor should they threaten Billy's well-being in a courtroom battle, in order to choose one of them as the more important parent. They are both decent people, and should have been able to work out a parenting plan for Billy without demeaning each other in polarized arguments and cross-examination. Eventually, despite their pain and anger, perhaps by listening to each other in the courtroom, they develop the capacity to see the situation through the eyes of the other and their child. They ultimately come to understand that each has something valuable as a parent to contribute to Billy.

So what is keeping them from reaching an agreement that will shield Billy from their courtroom combat? No one seems to be encouraging Ted and Joanna to do so. Shaunessy never really mentions that possibility to Ted. Ted wants to fight, and Shaunessy does not suggest settlement. The judge does not initiate settlement discussions, nor do the lawyers pursue them. Ted and Joanna communicate with each other only through courtroom testimony and apologies thereafter. The further Ted and Joanna go down the adversarial road, the less likely they will be able to parent Billy together.

Kramer vs. Kramer illustrates the truth that courtroom combat between parents does not necessarily lead to wise or just judicial custody decision-making. Billy would have been better off if Ted and Joanna had decided how he was to be parented, rather than Judge Atkins. As David Ray Papke writes, "While the two Kramers are clearly battling one another over young Billy, the former spouses do not have a monopoly on antagonistic relationships in *Kramer vs. Kramer*. Another antagonist emerges and stands in opposition to Ted, Joanna, and Billy. This antagonist is the law itself, and in the end the characters reject law, its styles, and its determinations on the way to achieving their final peace."[64]

The Legacy of *Kramer vs. Kramer*

Kramer vs. Kramer implicitly affirms two very important policies that have heavily influenced the development of the child custody court since the time the movie was released. The first is that of the importance of fathers in the lives of the children of divorce. Some feminist scholars continue to challenge the ideal of gender equality in child custody decision-making largely on the grounds that children are more central to women's lives than they are to men's, and that economic inequality between men and women remains a persistent reality of the modern American economy.[65] In contrast, *Kramer vs. Kramer* affirms the equality of fathers and mothers in the emotional life of the children of divorce and the importance of a child's having continuing relationships with both parents after divorce. Those values are the driving forces behind the joint custody revolution described in Chapter IV.

The second policy that *Kramer vs. Kramer* affirms is that parents should reach their own agreements for custody of their children – call it parental self-determination. Ted and Joanna both recognize that they should never have gone to court in the first place. They know Billy's best interests better than Judge Atkins. Joanna shows her love for Billy by sacrificing her legal victory, and Ted declines to challenge the judge's decision because it will cause Billy pain. By emphasizing Ted and Joanna's final peace through self-determination, *Kramer vs. Kramer* asserts the hopeful premise that divorcing parents can transcend their anger toward each other and agree between themselves what is in their child's best interests. The movement for alternative dispute resolution, particularly mediation, and parent education described in Chapters V and VI is the child custody court's way of encouraging more parents to take that same path.

III   Divorce, Children, and Courts

An Empirical Perspective

> You fight about money. About me and my brother. And this I come home to. This is my shelter. It ain't easy, growing up in WW3. Never knowing what love could be. You see I don't want love to destroy me. Like it has done my family. Can we work it out? Can we be a family?[66]

This chapter summarizes empirical data about divorce, children, and case-filing trends in the child custody court, with the following highlights:

1. Parental divorce has increased dramatically during the twentieth century to the point where it is a predictable event in the lives of a large percentage of children.
2. The level of conflict of divorcing parents ranges from cooperative to high. For many, the level of conflict changes over time.
3. The level of conflict between parents is one of the most important influences on how well children cope with the challenges that divorce presents to them. The lower the conflict and the better a child's relationship with both parents following divorce, the better his or her emotional, educational, and economic well-being.
4. The increasing divorce rate parallels a dramatic increase in the caseload of the child custody court.
5. Most parents who bring their disputes to the child custody court are *pro se* (not represented by lawyers) either because they cannot afford a lawyer or because they fear that lawyers will suck them into endless conflict.
6. The public is deeply dissatisfied with the child custody court and the adversarial process for resolving child custody disputes.

The Divorce Rate and Children

Each year in the United States, approximately 1.2 million marriages end in divorce. Between 1940 and 1998 (the last year for which complete data is available), the divorce rate in the United States rose from under 20% of all marriages to 50%.[67] These divorces involve more than 1 million children.[68] One in sixty children sees his or her parents divorce each year.[69] Almost half of first marriages in the United States end in divorce, and 65% of those couples have minor children.[70] "Parents with young children are the fastest growing segment of the divorcing population, presently constituting the majority of those who are divorcing in the 1990s."[71] The population of divorced children "mirrors the ethnic heterogeneity of our country: 81.9% non-Hispanic whites, 12.9% African Americans and 12.4% Hispanic Americans."[72]

Divorce is the single biggest reason that children live in single-parent families. In 2001, 69% of American children lived with two parents, down from 77% in 1980.[73] Of children living with one parent, 38% live with a divorced parent, 35% with a never-married parent, and 19% with a separated (married but living apart) parent.[74] Women head most single-parent families, though the number of men heading single-parent families is growing rapidly. Men now comprise one-sixth of the nation's 11.9 million single parents. Single-father families make up 2.1% of all American households, and single mother families 7.2%.[75]

The Strengths and Limitations of Empirical Research

Before summarizing the research results on the effects of divorce and parental conflict on children, it is important to recognize the strengths and limitations of the enterprise. Empirical research has immeasurably improved our understanding of the subject. Prior to the 1970s, the public generally believed that divorce was catastrophic for all children. Starting in the 1970s, the public's view of divorce changed, largely as a result of the influence of the feminist movement, which argued that divorce was a way for women to escape abusive relationships and that the increase in single-parent families was a manifestation of women's economic independence. Many believed at the time that "children are resilient, and the great majority of them are able to cope successfully with the transition to a single-parent household."[76] Divorce as a catastrophe for children evolved into the view that "children are better off if unhappy parents divorce."[77] As summarized later in this chapter, the extensive empirical research that has been conducted since the 1980s on the effects of divorce on children has created a more sophisticated understanding of the positives and negatives of the experience that defies such easy categorical generalizations.

As a result of extensive empirical research, we have moved beyond the simplistic view that divorce is either all bad or all good for all children. It has good and bad aspects for all children. For some, the good and bad aspects net out positively, and for others negatively. We have also learned that it is very hard to make a prediction with any high degree of confidence about how any individual child will fare as a result of his or her parent's divorce.

Empirical research has, however, identified factors – particularly the level of conflict between parents – that are likely to tip the outcome for children in either a positive or negative direction.

Well-designed empirical studies illuminating complex family relationships are expensive and difficult to initiate, implement, and interpret.[78] Few studies of the effects of divorce on children, for example, control carefully for pre-existing levels of conflict between parents.[79] Empirical research in the area of divorce and custody tends to be *relational* rather than *experimental*, making cause-and-effect judgments difficult. Correlation does not necessarily equal causation. We have no studies (and probably never will have), for example, that compare parents and children randomly assigned to joint custody and sole custody in a controlled laboratory setting. Research, at best, can simply observe that children in joint custody arrangements do better than children in sole custody arrangements; it cannot attribute the difference to the joint custody arrangement.

Furthermore, the best data on the effects of divorce on children comes from long-term longitudinal studies of aggregate populations. From these studies, we can only make judgments about what the aggregate needs, not what any particular child or parent needs. The reactions to divorce that parents and children report in those studies also are based on custody arrangements shaped years ago under different legal regimes that emphasized sole custody outcomes and used adversary procedures. As will be discussed in Chapters IV–VI, child custody courts today operate on a different philosophy that emphasizes involving both parents in the life of a child after divorce and education and mediation to resolve disputes. The longitudinal studies simply do not take these advances into account. We hope, as we follow divorcing families in the future, we will find that problems for parents and children have decreased, as the quality of the procedures that the child custody court uses to manage parental conflict improve.

The perfect empirical study that definitively answers all questions that policymakers and judges face simply does not exist, and maybe never will. Policymakers and judges should be careful consumers of empirical data and should subject studies to critical scrutiny. As Richard Warshak writes, "[N]o single study, particularly one with significant limitations, should have to take responsibility for molding parenting practices and family law policy."[80]

We need more data and research to illuminate complex family situations and public policy dilemmas. A 1998 comprehensive review by the Canadian parliament bemoans the absence of robust data for policymakers. It also asks for a comprehensive program of empirical research covering such topics as false allegations of abuse and neglect, parental alienation, the different patterns of domestic violence involved in child custody disputes, parental child abduction, the effect of continued contact with grandparents and on losing contact with a parent, the long-term well-being of children in different parenting arrangements, and the effect on the child of an amicable settlement between parents.[81]

Inevitably, public policy choices in legislation and decisions in individual cases have to be made in the face of empirical uncertainty. As Katherine Bartlett puts it, "Many questions to which answers might be sought are not, fundamentally, empirical questions but rather normative ones."[82] No study is ever likely to definitively resolve the comparative weight our society places on gender equality, risks to safety, the importance of a child's relationship with both parents and a parent's access to his or her children, and parental autonomy and self-determination. All of these values are at stake in the decisions and operation of the child custody court, and are often in conflict. In the end, all empirical research can do is frame choices for informed discussion; it does not make hard decisions between competing values. In a democracy, that task is left to the judicial and legislative process.

Divorce, Parental Conflict, and Children

Overall, the research studies, while different in nuance, generally establish a congruent and coherent picture of the effects of divorce on children. From a child's perspective, divorce is a period of difficult emotional adjustments that begins before the family is legally dissolved, and continues long after.[83] Children with divorcing parents experience greater distress even before marital disruption than their peers with parents who remain married. Families on the verge of breakup have fewer intimate parent-child relationships, less commitment to their children's education, and fewer financial resources.[84] As a review of relevant studies stated:

[T]here is general agreement [among researchers] that parental separation precipitates a crisis for most children. The vast majority of youngsters are not anticipating divorce when it occurs, even when there has been considerable conflict between their parents; and only those experiencing repeated, intense conflict and family violence are relieved. The most common crisis-engendered reactions include intense anxiety about their future well-being and care taking, sadness and acute reactive depressions, increased anger, disruptions in concentration at school, distress about the loss of contact with one parent, loyalty conflicts, and preoccupation with reconciliation.[85]

Divorce, in essence, places children at risk but does not doom them to eternal failure and anguish. The long-term effect of parental divorce and conflict on any particular child is highly individual, and depends on the child's resilience and support systems. Andrew Cherlin, another leading divorce researcher, sums up the relevant data: "[D]ivorce is bad for children, but not for all children equally. It is very bad for a small group of children, and moderately bad for many more."[86]

Divorce raises the risk of long-term social and emotional difficulties for children who experience it compared with children whose parents do not divorce. Children of divorce have higher rates of mental health problems, higher levels of drug use, and levels of lower academic achievement. For example, 41% of the children from divorced families report receiving mental health services by ages 18-22 years compared with 22% of their peers from two-parent families.[87] The negative effect of divorce for some children can persist into adulthood, with a higher rate of mental health problems and earlier death.[88] Mavis Heatherington concludes from her long-term longitudinal study over approximately three decades that 25% of children from divorced families have serious social, emotional, or psychological problems, as opposed to 10% of children from intact families. The other 75-80% of children of divorce recover and get on with their lives. The extra risk to children of divorce is nonetheless substantial. As Heatherington states, "It's larger than the association between smoking and cancer."[89]

Better lives for children of divorce are associated with a number of inter-related factors, especially reduction of parental conflict, a well-functioning custodial parent, and contact with a non-custodial parent. The problem is that these factors may conflict with each other. Some custodial parents may function better, for example, and conflict between parents minimized, if a child has no contact with a parent the custodial parent despises. On the other hand, that child will not have the benefit of a meaningful relationship with a parent whom the child never sees.

Levels of Parental Conflict

Children who are exposed to more intense conflict between parents are more likely to suffer harm resulting from their parents' divorce. The lower the level of conflict between parents, the more likely those children will emerge emotionally whole. It is, however, "uncertain what levels and types of conflict are tolerable and which are pathogenic [for children]. Both pre- and post-divorce conflict can be harmful to children . . . [M]ost experts agree that conflict localized around the time of litigation and divorce is less harmful than conflict, which remains an intrinsic and unresolved part of the parents' relationship and continues after their divorce. Similarly, conflict from which children are shielded does not appear to affect adjustment, whereas conflict that includes physical violence is more pathogenic than high conflict without violence."[90]

Divorcing couples, like married couples, create different levels of conflict. The great majority of divorcing parents reach agreement on a parenting plan with little or no outside intervention. Research suggests that a relatively small number of parents continue at a very high level of conflict over family reorganization for a number of years.[91] Constance Ahrons found that about 25% of her small samples of divorcing parents were "Angry Associates," who repeatedly fought with each other in and out of court.[92] Janet Johnston and Vivian Roseby estimate that "about one-fourth of all divorcing couples with children have considerable difficulty completing the legal divorce without extensive litigation" and about one-fifth of families relitigate custody issues after divorce.[93] A 1996 empirical study of five court systems found that 16% of divorcing families with children had been to court for another family-related matter during the previous five years.[94] Other studies estimate that 5-10% of the total population of divorcing and separating parents consists of repetitive litigants at a high level of conflict.[95]

Researchers and practitioners have begun to develop assessment tools to classify levels of conflict between divorcing parents. Garrity and Baris, for example, divide conflicted parents into five categories – minimal, mild, moderate, moderately severe, and severe.[96] "Minimal conflict" parents display the following characteristics:

- Cooperative parenting.
- Ability to separate children's needs from their own needs.
- Validation of the importance of the other parent.
- Affirmation of the competency of the other parent.
- Conflict-resolution between the adults using verbal exchange, with only occasional expressions of anger.
- Bringing negative emotions more quickly under control.

In contrast, Garrity and Baris offer this classification of parents in "moderately severe conflict":

- Do not directly endanger the child, but might be a danger to each other.
- Threaten violence.
- Slam doors, throw things.
- Verbally threaten harm or kidnapping.
- Continually relitigate custody issues.
- Attempt to form a permanent or standing coalition with the child against the other parent (alienation syndrome).

Garrity and Barris reserve the "severe" parental conflict category for divorcing couples who show evidence of physical or sexual abuse, serious drug or alcohol impairment, or diagnosable mental illness.

Much more research is necessary to separate the population of divorcing parents more precisely into different levels of conflict. Drawing on current research, one can speculate that a pie chart dividing the population into different segments would look like Figure 3.1.

One can get a sense of the difference between low and moderately severe parent conflicts by profiling parents who litigate child custody problems chronically. The parents in the New York case of *Braiman v. Braiman*[97] illustrate the problems that intense parental conflict can create for the children

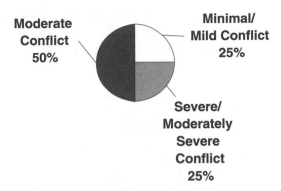

Figure 3.1 Hypothetical distribution of parental conflict levels in divorce

and the child custody court. The following facts are taken from reported judicial opinions.

The Braimans' divorce decree gave the mother sole custody of their three children. The father remarried. The mother apparently did not cooperate in the sale of the marital house, igniting a chain reaction of continuing conflict and court actions. The mother sued to set aside the separation agreement on the grounds that father and her former attorney had deceived her. The father stopped paying the mortgage, fuel bills, and child support. He employed his secretary's husband to spy on the mother. He persuaded two state troopers to enter the mother's home during the early hours of the morning because a vehicle with dealer's plates was parked in her driveway. The state troopers found a man fully clothed, asleep on the living room sofa, who later testified that he was there at the mother's request because of the mother's fear of the father's harassment.

Two years after the divorce agreement, when the mother said she would leave the state with the children, the father began a custody modification action. He alleged that since the divorce, the mother had become sexually promiscuous, a heavy drinker, and a reckless driver, and had been neglectful and physically abusive to the children. The mother denied the father's accusations. She countercharged that the father drank and gambled heavily, that he had not visited the children for four months, and that the house would have been without heat and the children without food had it not been for aid from the maternal grandfather and the mother's new husband. The mother also charged that the stepmother had a vicious temper and had hit one of the children on numerous occasions.

The evidence at trial included the testimony of physicians, psychiatrists, teachers, and neighbors. There were many contradictions, typical of high-conflict child custody cases. At a preliminary hearing, two doctors hired by the father examined the children and testified that the boys were in poor physical and emotional condition. The trial judge granted the father temporary sole custody of the boys, but kept the daughter in the mother's sole custody. At a later hearing, the children's pediatrician, neighbors, and teachers all testified that the mother took good care of the children. In spite of this testimony, the trial court awarded sole custody of all the children to the father.

The intermediate court of appeal reversed the award. That court held that the testimony of the children's regular pediatrician was more important than that of the father's medical experts, who had never seen the boys before the custody modification began. The intermediate appellate court ordered joint custody for these highly conflicted parents.

The New York Court of Appeals (the state's highest court) in effect reinstated the trial court's order of sole custody to the father while it considered his appeal from the order of the intermediate appellate court. The father retained sole custody of the children for two more years as the Court of Appeals reviewed the case. During that period, the father defied a court order and denied the mother visitation rights. The mother apparently disappeared for an undisclosed period of time while the case was being reviewed by the Court of Appeals.

After all of this, the Court of Appeals heard the father's appeal, reversed the intermediate court of appeals' order of joint custody, and remanded the case to the trial court for a new hearing. It told the trial court to appoint a Guardian Ad Litem to investigate and independently recommend a custody plan. In effect, after years of contention, the Court of Appeals told the Braimans to start fighting all over again.

Chronic-litigant parents such as the Braimans have typical attitudes and patterns of behavior. They see the world in black and white. Each is good and the other parent is evil. They are continuously angry with someone – the other parent, the judge, the custody evaluator, the law guardian for the children, his lawyer, her lawyer, and so on. They interpret court orders literally, narrowly, and try to ignore them if they benefit the other parent. They question the competence of the other parent and the quality of the environment that he or she provides for the children. They use the children as messengers and try to alienate the children from the other parent. They may make threats of abduction or allegations of child abuse or neglect. They drag everyone around them into their conflict.

Continuing conflict between parents of the kind exemplified by the Braimans creates substantial risks for the children of divorce.[98] One can only imagine how the Braimans' children reacted to the intense and continuous controversy between their parents that was the central feature of their childhood. Researchers have found that "ongoing high levels of [family] conflict, whether in intact or divorced homes, produce lower self-esteem, increased anxiety, and a loss of self control."[99] After conducting an extensive empirical study of California families experiencing divorce, Eleanor Maccoby and Robert Mnookin concluded that "as the parental alliance weakens, the behavior standards for the children decline. If parents quarrel openly in front of the children, and show contempt for each other, the atmosphere of mutual respect that underlies their joint authority and effective co-parenting is seriously weakened."[100]

The importance of the level of parental conflict in determining children's well-being after divorce is also illuminated from another direction – studies of joint custody. The term "joint custody" will be defined more precisely in the next chapter. For now, it is sufficient to loosely define it as a post-divorce parenting arrangement in which parents substantially share decision-making for their child (joint legal custody) and the child spends substantially equal time at each parent's residence (joint physical custody).

Joint custody is associated with lower levels of conflict between parents and substantial benefits for children. A recent meta-analysis (a sophisticated review comparing different research methodologies and results) of thirty-three studies concludes that "children in joint custody are better adjusted, across multiple types of measures, than children in sole (primarily maternal) custody. This difference is found with both joint legal and joint physical custody and appears robust. . . ."[101]

Highly conflicted families are less likely to have joint custody arrangements and regular visitation by the non-custodial parent. Continuing abrasive interactions make non-custodial parents more likely to withdraw from the child's life and simply "give up."[102] The lower the level of conflict between the parents, the more the child benefits from contact with the non-custodial parent.[103] Non-custodial parents are, for example, far more likely to pay child support if they have joint custody or visitation arrangements than if they do not. Over three-quarters of parents who had such arrangements received at least some support payments, compared with less than half of the parents who did not.[104]

Parallel and Cooperative Parenting

The conflict levels of divorcing parents are not frozen and static. Some highly conflicted parents, for example, can improve their interaction with each other over time. Many angry divorcing parents can engage in a period of *parallel* as opposed to *cooperative* or *joint* parenting, with a positive effect for their long-term relationships with each other. Under parallel parenting models, each parent does not include the other when interacting with the child. In essence, each parent raises the child as if he or she were a single parent during the period that the child is in residence.[105] Interaction between parents is limited to the minimum extent feasible. For some parallel parents, anger fades over time, and more cooperative patterns of interaction with each other emerge. Based on their extensive research of families in custody disputes in the

California court system, Eleanor Maccoby and Robert Mnookin concluded that:

> It appears that parents can manage to share the residential time of their children even though they are not talking to each other or trying to coordinate the child-rearing environments of the two households. Although this is not the "first best" alternative, it is far better for children than open conflict. Spousal disengagement during one period of time also leaves open the possibility that in the future parents may be able to establish cooperative co-parenting relations. Our evidence suggests that for some number of parents this sequence does occur. Cooperation is far more likely to emerge from disengagement than from conflicted co-parenting.[106]

The Quality of the Lives of Children in Single-Parent Families

Divorce is the most significant reason why children live in single-parent families. Nonetheless, placing divorced children and children of never married parents into the joint category of single-parent custodial families may create a misleading impression of the circumstances of children of divorce. There are poor divorced parents, but there are more poor never-married parents. "[N]ever married families with children come disproportionately from the lower socio-economic strata, with both fathers and mothers having low income capacity. In divorced families . . . with both parents having on average far higher education than never marrieds, as well as a stronger attachment of father to child, the poverty figures are far less dramatic."[107] The rate of payment of child-support obligations for non-custodial parents in these two groups is different – far lower for never-married parents.[108]

Children raised in single-parent families (the majority of which result from parental divorce) do less well than children raised in two-parent families on aggregate measures of emotional health, economic well-being, and educational achievement.[109] There is a strong link between poverty and single parenthood. Children who live in a household with only one parent are substantially more likely to have family incomes below the poverty line than are children who live in a household with two parents.[110]

The disadvantage of growing up in a single-parent family is not limited to economics. Less adult involvement in the children's lives also leads to less adult investment in their emotional development and education. Studies have established that father absence, in particular, correlates with greater risk of educational and cognitive deficits in children, with greater mental illness, with drug use, and with crime.[111] Sara McLanahan found, for example, that boys from families where the father is absent as a result of divorce are more likely to be unemployed, girls are more likely to bear children at an early age, and all children are more likely to underachieve at school.[112]

Children in single-parent families score lower on virtually all indicators of childhood stability and quality of life than do their counterparts living with two parents. Overall, these children tend to be pessimistic about their capacity to master life's opportunities and problems and about developing lasting relationships with others, a pessimism that reduces their aspirations for achievement and weakens their physical and mental health.[113] Children in single-parent families are, in general, far more likely to be in poor physical health, have a higher rate of suicide and mental illness, and suffer more accidents and injuries than children in two-parent families.[114] Family disruption significantly increases the risk of adolescent drug use, particularly among boys.[115]

Educational problems for divorcing children begin during the period preceding the parent's separation, and continue thereafter. A recent study measured the effects of divorce on children's emotional well-being and educational achievement in 10,000 adolescents at four points in time – three years and one year before the divorce and one year and three years after it. Compared with their peers in intact families, children of divorce fared less well on all measures at all points in time. By three years after the divorce, their emotional well-being had improved, but their success in school continued to decline. The researchers speculate that this permanent drop in academic achievement results from the children of divorce's falling behind in their educational progress and either not catching up or losing motivation even after their emotional life stabilizes.[116]

The specific data on the effects of divorce on the educational success of children is reinforced by the general data on the educational achievement of children in single-parent families. "Children living with both their biological parents were about half as likely to have repeated a grade in school compared with children in all other types of families."[117] A comprehensive statistical analysis of the differences in educational achievement between children in single-parent families and their two-parent peers concluded that "[i]n general, the longer the time spent in a single-parent family, the greater the reduction in educational attainment . . . Controlling for income does not reduce the magnitude of the effect noticeably."[118] A review by the Educational Testing Service shows that although the ratio of two-parent families to single-parent families varies widely from state to state, it is closely correlated with variations in academic achievement.[119]

Children of single-parent families do less well in school than their two-parent peers because adults invest less in their development. A large number of them have little effective relationship, including financial support, with the parent (usually the father) living outside of the home.[120] Findings from a recent study indicate that "when fathers talk to their children on a consistent basis about school activities and events, they may be playing a critical role in lessening the negative impact that factors such as parental illiteracy, English as a second language and cultural discontinuity between home and school settings have on student achievement."[121]

The Child Custody Court's Docket

Family law court is where they shoot the survivors.[122]

Not surprisingly, the increase in divorces involving children parallels an increase in child custody court filings. According to the National Center for State Courts, "[D]omestic relations cases [which include, but are not limited exclusively to, child custody disputes] are the largest and fastest-growing segment of state court civil caseloads. In 1995, 25 percent of total civil filings, over 4.9 million, were domestic relations cases. The total number of domestic relations cases increased 4.1 percent since 1994 and 70 percent since 1984."[123]

Figure 3.2, court filings in the State of Florida, illustrates these trends. The graph compares the number of filings in the family division (where not all cases involve child custody) with filings in the criminal, civil, and probate divisions over a number of years. For family division filings, the trend is upward, while for the other filings in other classes of cases, it is either stable or in decline. The gap between filings in the different divisions is also growing.

Disputes about children resulting from divorce and separation are the largest category of family-related filings in the New York State court system.[124] It is important to note that the increase in custody cases also includes disputes between parents who were never married as well as custody disputes arising from divorce. Even though the divorce rate has stabilized in recent years, the number of custody disputes reaching court has grown, largely because of the increase in custody disputes between unmarried parents.[125]

No end to the increase in the caseloads of the child custody court is in sight. Figure 3.3 shows the projected caseloads of the New York State Family Court, which hears many of the child custody cases in the state.

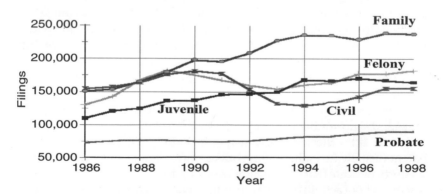

Source: Summary Reporting System (SRS)
Office of the Courts Administrator, 08 Oct99

Figure 3.2 Trends in state court filings by subject matter in Florida

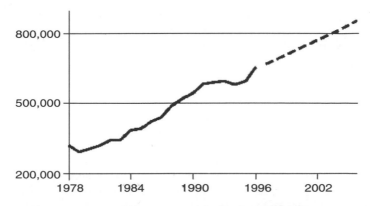

Source: New York State Office of Court Administration

Figure 3.3 Projected caseload of New York State Family Court

The Oregon Future of the Courts Committee attributes the growth in family disputes brought to court to trends in American society that include increasing social disintegration tied to poverty, violence, and crime, and a general increase in alienation and mistrust.[126] Others might offer different explanations. Whatever the cause, there is certainly no prospect for a rapid turnaround in the upward trend of court filings.

Parents thus face an increasingly long wait for a judge to finally decide their custody disputes. It is unlikely that increases in state court budgets will keep pace with the increases in custody court caseloads, particularly in urban areas. The average caseload of a New York Family Court judge (which hears modifications of divorcing parents' child custody agreements and disputes between unmarried parents and other family matters) is 2,500. In Brooklyn, New York, family court cases in 1997 "received slightly over four minutes before a judge on the first appearance and a little more than eleven minutes on subsequent appearances."[127] The Oregon Future of the Courts Committee found that the total state court civil caseload increased at roughly four times the rate of the estimated increase in Oregon's population over the last decade. If no new judges are added, and caseloads increase as projected, the Committee projects that by the year 2020, the time it will take for a case to reach trial after it was first filed in court will increase from an average of 7 months in 1995 to 113 months (9.5 years). If these trends continue for the next decade (something no one can predict with any degree of assurance), the Committee estimates that the Oregon state courts will need an increase of more than 300% in the number of judges and an increase of 225% in the number of court employees just to keep the ratio of judges and employees to current caseloads constant.[128]

It is hard to imagine any state being willing to pay that kind of price to keep the backlog of the child custody court to a tolerable minimum.

Increased personnel and resources for the judicial system can help relieve crisis conditions, but they are unlikely to be enough to resolve the number of new cases with reasonable dispatch or to respond adequately and humanely to the conflict and dysfunction that divorcing parents and children bring to court.

Pro Se Parents

Caseload increases are only part of the problem that the child custody court faces. The cases are also becoming more difficult to manage. One particularly important reason is the increasing percentage of *pro se* (not represented by lawyers) child custody litigants.

Divorcing parents do not have a constitutional right to counsel at state expense in a child custody dispute.[129] Eligibility for legal services is generally limited to those with annual incomes below federal poverty guidelines (approximately $12,000–$14,000 for a family of four),[130] and there are not enough legal services lawyers to meet the demands of the burgeoning caseloads. Recent studies show that the American legal aid system (which is far less generous than that of other democracies) meets about 20% of the legal needs of the poor.[131]

Those parents not eligible for government-funded legal services have to retain a lawyer privately. Lawyers' fees can be substantial in protracted custody disputes. Though there are no comprehensive studies of the cost of private counsel in child custody disputes, many parents report informally that during high-conflict custody disputes, they spend the equivalent of the cost of tuition at a four-year private college on legal fees.

Parents who are represented by lawyers in the child custody court are, in fact, the exception rather than the rule. The child custody court's docket contains a majority of *pro se* parent litigants. Overall, 80% of all family law cases involve at least one *pro se* litigant at some point during the case.[132] An ABA study of Maricopa County (Phoenix), Arizona, in 1990 found that neither party had a lawyer in 52% of the divorce cases filed there. In 88% of the cases, one party had no lawyer, or defaulted.[133] A Florida study replicates these findings.[134] Figure 3.4, prepared by the Family Division of the Circuit Court of Baltimore, Maryland, illustrates that the growth in the number of *pro se* litigants in recent years in child custody court has been nothing short of phenomenal.

Pro se parents come from various income and educational levels. Many with modest incomes conclude that legal services are too expensive, and opt to represent themselves. The 1990 ABA study revealed that those with annual incomes of less than $50,000 were much more likely to proceed *pro se*, and that nearly one-third of the *pro se* litigants could not afford a lawyer.

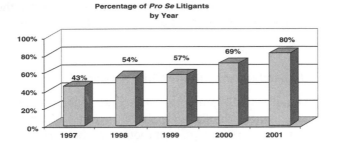

Source: Office of the Associate Administrator, Family, Circuit Court for Baltimore, Maryland

Figure 3.4 Growth of *pro se* litigants in Family Division of Circuit Court for Baltimore, Maryland

The increase in *pro se* representation is the Catch-22 of the adversary system for parents in a child custody dispute. Divorcing parents must resort to a complicated court system to settle their differences. Yet the system does not provide them with the lawyers they need to navigate it, treating representation as a privilege for the wealthy or as charity for a small number of the very poor.

The increase in *pro se* representation poses special challenges for the child custody court. At their best, lawyers can guide parents through a mystifyingly complex system at a time of great emotional turmoil, identify problem-solving strategies to help their children, encourage them to participate in education and mediation, and prepare and present their cases in court with full knowledge of the formal rules of procedure. *Pro se* parents do not get the benefit of this help. As a result, they suffer serious disadvantages in the legal system. Substantial numbers of *pro se* parents have difficulty finding out where to file court papers, understanding and completing forms and obtaining evidence to support their position in court. Parents with representation are more likely to be awarded physical custody than parents without representation. Where both parents are represented, they received joint legal custody 92% of the time, as compared with 50% of the families where neither parent was represented.[135]

From the court's perspective, processing of *pro se* cases is more difficult, more time-consuming, and less efficient than if parents are represented by lawyers. The self-represented often do not know how to behave in court or what is expected of them. They frequently express themselves through outbursts of intense emotion, unmediated by the influence of counsel. Many do not understand underlying legal principles such as joint custody or the standards for supervised visitation. *Pro se* litigants sometimes place the judge in the untenable position of having to explain the law to them without appearing to take sides in the dispute. These litigants sometimes take unreasonable positions in court and make unreasonable settlement demands because they do not have the influence of counsel. They often feel like outsiders in the judicial process, and have less respect for a system they feel does not address their needs.

Public Dissatisfaction with the Child Custody Court

A growing number of *pro se* litigants can afford representation but do not want it. They do not believe that lawyers serve their best interests or their children's. Parents who choose to represent themselves have a constitutional right to do so.[136] "[M]ore than 20 percent of the *pro se* litigants studied said they could afford a lawyer. Self-help litigants are younger than those represented by lawyers and are reasonably well-educated, with most having some college education."[137] As the Oregon Task Force on Family Law (a legislatively authorized interdisciplinary reform group) reported to Oregon's governor and state legislature after statewide public hearings on the divorce system: "Many *pro se* litigants can afford lawyers. They do not seek the legal representation they need because they fear that to consult a lawyer would be to 'shake hands with the tar baby.'"[138]

In fairness to parents, it must be recognized that they make their evaluations of the performance of the child custody court, their lawyers, and associated professionals at a time of stress and disappointment. Divorce lawyers and clients sometimes speak different languages; clients emphasize "guilt, fault and responsibility" while lawyers try to focus on more practical legal concerns and issues in a no-fault world.[139] The result is inevitable miscommunication and misunderstanding. It also must be recognized that there is little fully reliable empirical data about the actual behavior of divorce lawyers and their role in the resolution of child custody disputes.[140]

Nonetheless, surveys, public hearings, and other data strongly suggest strong public dissatisfaction with the child custody courts and the adversary process. Many parents feel that after the litigation process starts, it quickly spirals out of control. They also feel that lawyers, judges, and custody evaluators often make decisions for them without even listening to them.

Some divorce lawyers may convey a message to clients that magnifies distrust of the court system. Observations of divorce lawyer-client interviews indicate that some divorce lawyers tell their clients that courts do not reach rational results, that their clients are its victims, and that their only hope is for the lawyer to manipulate the system through insider knowledge on his client's behalf.[141] It is not at all clear how many divorce lawyers give this kind of advice.[142] Those who do give it certainly do not boost public or client confidence in the quality of child custody courts. Parents in distress and conflict want to know that they are participating in a rational process whose personnel are motivated by concern for them and their children.

A national commission recently reported survey results in which 50–70% of parents characterized the legal system as "impersonal, intimidating, and intrusive."[143] A report of a committee of distinguished New York lawyers and judges who heard public testimony from numerous divorce litigants, judges, and lawyers about their experiences confirms that "[l]itigants describe the courts as being unsympathetic, unresponsive, impotent and overwhelmed by delay, and claim that the main concern of lawyers is not to serve their clients' best interests but their own."[144]

A recent empirical study of a sample of divorcing parents and their children in Connecticut on their attitudes toward their lawyers also confirms these findings. It reports "an overall consensus that the attorneys' roles and responsibilities in the divorce process are not translating into actual practice. The parents and children did not feel they had adequate representation through guidance, information, attention or quality of service." Parents in the survey felt that the process took control of their lives, and was too long, too costly, and too inefficient. "Many of the parents did recognize that they were already feeling angry and hostile, but 71 percent of them maintained the legal process pushed those feelings to a further extreme."[145]

Divorce lawyers are at the receiving end of more ethics complaints than lawyers in other fields of practice. Although most lawyers are exonerated, the number of complaints against them is another reflection of public dissatisfaction with the adversary process.[146] Even those who defend divorce lawyers honestly admit that "lawyers sometimes loose their objectivity and identify too much with their clients' desire to punish and blame their spouses."[147]

The Oregon Task Force on Family Law summed up public dissatisfaction after extensive public hearings on that state's divorce system:

The divorce process in Oregon, as elsewhere, was broken and needed fixing. Lawyers, mediators, judges, counselors and citizens in Oregon agreed that the family court system was too confrontational to meet the human needs of most families undergoing divorce. The process was adversarial where it needn't have been: All cases were prepared as if going to court, when only a small percentage actually did. The judicial system made the parties adversaries, although they had many common interests.

The Task Force found that the family court system was collapsing under the weight of too many cases. Too often, children were treated like property while parents clogged the courts with bitter fights over money, assets, and support. The combative atmosphere made it more difficult for divorcing couples to reach a settlement and to develop a cooperative relationship even after a divorce agreement had been worked out on paper.[148]

Overall, the child custody court functions in an extraordinarily complex environment. The number of cases it hears is staggering, and fraught with deep emotional significance for parents and children. Many of the parent-litigants who come before it do not have lawyers. The families before it range from the highly functional to the deeply dysfunctional, and have diverse needs for conflict-resolution and mental health and social services. In most cases, a child's need for relationships with both parents after divorce is not well served by the adversary procedure that is the mainstay of the judicial process. The court's resources are diminishing at a time when its task has become more complex.

IV Parents Are Forever I

Joint Custody and Parenting Plans

Parents are forever, even if marriages are not.[149]

This chapter discusses joint custody and the recent growth of court orders requiring parents to plan for their child's future by submitting parenting plans to the court. Chapters V and VI discuss alternative ways of settling parenting disputes, especially mediation, and court-mandated education programs. Taken together, the developments discussed in these three chapters create an alternative paradigm to the sole custody/adversary system in which courts choose a more important parent through a trial.

Joint Custody

Joint custody symbolizes both the gender and emotional equality of the parents for the child. The court begins from the premise that both parents care deeply about their child, that there is no reason to prefer one or the other as the custodial parent, and that the child benefits from having a relationship with both of them. Neither parent is deemed to be more "fit" or the superior decision-maker for the child. Joint legal custody means that parents share decision-making equally. Joint physical custody generally means that the child shares the parents' residences approximately equally. Neither parent is designated the custodial parent or the visiting parent.[150]

Until the late 1970s and early 1980s, courts did not distinguish between joint legal and joint physical custody, and were hostile to the concept of joint custody in any form for essentially the same reasons Goldstein, Freud, and Solnit advanced in support of their "psychological parent" theory. Courts believed that ordering joint custody for conflicted parents created emotional instability and turmoil for the child that could be eliminated only by choosing one over the other. In 1934, the Maryland Court of Appeals denounced joint custody as an arrangement "to be avoided, whenever possible, as an evil fruitful in the destruction of discipline, in the creation of distrust, and in the production of mental distress in the child."[151] As late as 1979, the Iowa Supreme Court declared:

This court historically has opposed [joint] custody, "except under the most unusual circumstances." Reasons cited for opposition include that [joint] custody is destructive of discipline, that it tends to induce a feeling of not belonging to either parent, and that in some instances it permits one parent to sow seeds of discontent concerning the other, which can result in a spirit of dissatisfaction in the children and their rebellion against authority. Courts in many states have shared this reluctance to divide custody, declaring that divided custody is to be avoided as not in the best interests of the children and that it will be sanctioned only under exceptional circumstances.[152]

Courts typically manifested their hostility to joint custody by allowing one parent to veto it without investigating the underlying reasons for the veto. Each spouse could veto a joint custody arrangement because of a sincere belief in the superiority of his or her own parenting abilities. A veto could also be based upon feelings of anger or hatred toward the other spouse, or it could be employed in a strategic attempt to seek more financial concessions in divorce settlement negotiations. The court – and the opposing parent – might even believe the child would benefit from joint custody. The court, nonetheless, would not probe for the basis for the opposition, assuming instead that the opposition signaled that the parents were in such serious conflict that joint custody was impossible.

The substantive standard that courts apply in deciding contested child custody cases comes from two basic sources – state statutes and judicial precedent. The elected representatives of the people in the state legislature enact statutes that courts are bound to apply unless the statute is unconstitutional. All states have statutes that establish the standard that courts should follow in making awards in child custody cases. In the 1970s, most of those statutes delegated courts a great deal of discretion by providing that the courts should award custody based on the child's "best interests," without further defining that term. Judicial interpretation filled in the gaps left by the legislature. Whether the best interests test should be replaced with an alternative standard is discussed at length in Chapter XIII.

For our purposes, it is sufficient to note that courts began to change their views of joint custody in the late 1970s and the early 1980s by beginning to award joint custody even over the opposition of one or both parents. Change came in two forms: (1) Under the influence of fathers' groups, a state legislature enacted a revised child custody statute that authorized a court to award joint custody in contested cases; (2) A court reinterpreted its state's current statute to the same effect,[153] and the legislature later amended the statute to incorporate the court's rulings.

Why would a court order joint custody when the parents did not agree on it? Designating one of them as the custodial parent, and relegating the other to visitation, creates a risk that the visiting parent will gradually opt-out as an important figure in the child's life. Parents' ability to cooperate with each other, the court might reason, should not be assessed in what one court has called "the 'emotional heat' of the divorce."[154] The court might reason that parents do not need to be friends in order to co-parent effectively; they need to tolerate each other's legal rights. While parents may be in conflict now, their conflict levels may change over time with education, mediation, therapy, and the reorganization of their lives after a period of instability. Indeed, as discussed in Chapter III, many divorcing parents begin with a period of "parallel" parenting as opposed to cooperative parenting, and find that their anger level subsides over time.

The change in substantive legal doctrine to incorporate joint custody heralded a "small revolution . . . in child custody law."[155] The number of state custody statutes that mention joint custody has increased from a mere three in 1978 to an overwhelming majority in 1998.[156] A 2002 survey finds that 42 states authorize courts to award joint custody in some form.[157] "[A] small number of states have some type of preference for joint custody arrangements, while a slightly smaller number explicitly disfavor such arrangements."[158] Some state statutes create a presumption of joint legal (but not equal physical) custody that can be rebutted by a showing of intractable parental conflict. Most states allow a court to award joint custody if it is in the best interests of the child, without any preference for or against such arrangements.

The unifying theme of these legal developments is that they all support the notion that both parents should have a continuing relationship and an involvement with the child after divorce. All constitute a radical break with the sole custody system. A parent can no longer arbitrarily veto joint custody. Courts no longer assume that parents are hopelessly conflicted simply because one or both says so, and that "stability" requires the court to choose between them. Instead, the court works at reducing and evaluating the parents' levels of conflict, and carefully determines what degree of joint parenting is possible.

The movement toward encouraging both parents to have a continuing relationship with the child after divorce, reflected in custody statutes and court decisions, does not mean that the child custody court automatically presumes that joint physical and legal custody is always in the child's best interests. Other principles of child custody decision-making, such as continuity of care-giving and the need to protect safety, continue to compete with the strength of the principle supporting the need for a child to have relationships with both parents in any particular case.

Mandated presumptions of equal joint physical custody, in particular, have come under attack from some mental health professionals and feminists who argue that very few parents actually share physical custody, with the burden of child care falling primarily on mothers.[159] Many statutes, for example, make clear that a court may award joint custody without requiring equal residential time for each parent.[160] This subject will be discussed in detail in Chapter XIII.

Other professionals are concerned that mandated joint custody is inappropriate for high-conflict families, particularly those involving domestic violence, because it creates opportunities for batterers to further manipulate their victims. As a result, many states have created exceptions to joint custody presumptions if a parent can prove that he or she is a victim of domestic violence. California, for example, has a statutory presumption "that an award of sole or joint physical or legal custody of a child to a person who has perpetrated domestic violence is detrimental to the best interest of the child."[161] This subject will be discussed in greater detail in Chapter VIII.

Actual joint custody agreements and court orders can encompass a variety of parenting arrangements, emphasizing the flexibility of seemingly rigid legal terminology in the hands of creative judges and lawyers, and its adaptability to real family life. The unifying factor in all of these joint custody agreements and orders is that the labels promote a greater degree of equality between the parents in the post-divorce life of the child than the terms "sole custody" and "visitation." Joint custody can be true, equally shared decision-making and residence. Sometimes, however, joint legal custody agreements designate one parent as the sole decision-maker for the child on some matters (e.g., medical decisions when one parent is a doctor) and provide for joint decision-making on others. Joint physical custody, furthermore, does not always have to mean exactly fifty-fifty division of a child's residence. Court orders and agreements can label a parenting arrangement as joint custody if it consists of joint legal custody and a residence arrangement for the child with time divided between parents in a manner akin to a traditional visitation plan. Sometimes, parents with such arrangements are called "joint custodians," and one parent is designed the "primary residential parent."

Parenting Plans

Some states have moved beyond the concept of "custody" altogether and instead encourage parents to agree to, and courts to award, "parenting plans." A parenting plan is a written description of the division of parental decision-making, parenting time, and residential arrangements. It replaces term such as "physical custody" and "legal custody" with more neutral language such as "custodial responsibility," "parenting time," "residence," and "decision-making responsibility." A parenting plan includes provisions describing how major decisions for the child will be made, provisions for resolving disputes if they arise, and where a child lives over an extended period of time (e.g., one-year) on a day-to-day basis.

The term "custody" makes parents think in the language of criminal law and property. It projects a negative image of the role of the visiting parent in the lives of children after divorce, thus encouraging parental competition and combat. The core idea of the parenting plan, in contrast, is to help parents plan for their mutual involvement in the future life of their child by encouraging them to think in terms of actual parenting tasks rather than legal labels. Development of a parenting plan also encourages parents to recognize the complexity of modern life in their thinking about roles and responsibilities. In many families, both parents work, and complex arrangements are necessary to get a child to after-school activities, medical appointments, and religious observances.

Almost half the states specifically provide for parenting plans – some requiring them in every case, some requiring them when joint custody is ordered, and some requiring them at judicial discretion.[162] Professor Linda Elrod recently noted that many states "require parents to draft parenting plans, either filing a joint plan or for each to submit a plan when seeking custody."[163] The State of Washington, for example, requires by statute that parents submit parenting plans for all divorce cases involving children.[164] The Washington statute does not use the term "custody," substituting instead "decision-making" and "residential time." In Colorado, the legislature has changed the traditional child custody proceeding to "a proceeding for the allocation of parental responsibilities."[165] A national commission recently recommended that all states adopt the parenting plan idea.[166] The concept has also received the support of the American Law Institute, an influential organization of judges, practicing lawyers, and law professors founded in 1923 "to promote the clarification and simplification of the law and its better adaptation to social needs, to secure the better administration of justice, and to encourage and carry on scholarly and scientific work."[167] The parenting plan concept is a central feature of the ALI's recent proposals for change in the child custody decision-making process,[168] and will be discussed in Chapter XIII.

V Parents Are Forever II

Alternative Dispute Resolution and Mediation

The Alternative Dispute Resolution (ADR) Movement and Child Custody Disputes

The joint custody revolution described in the last chapter proceeded in parallel with a revolution in the role of the child custody court and its procedures. Conflicted parents ordered to parent together by joint custody had to have some procedural forum to resolve their disputes that did not require adversary warfare. Courts thus began to diversify the processes available to divorcing parents for resolving their disputes to include "alternative" methods of dispute resolution, "a reference to the use of these processes in place of litigation."[169]

In every movement, there is a defining event that shapes and frames what is to come. For the alternative dispute resolution movement, that event was the Pound Conference [convened by the American Bar Association], held in April 1976, in which more than 200 judges, scholars, and leaders of the bar gathered to examine concerns about the efficiency and fairness of the court systems and dissatisfaction with the administration of justice. At this conference, then Chief Justice Warren Burger called for exploration of informal dispute resolution processes.[170]

Professor Frank Sander, Reporter for the Pound Conference's follow-up task force, projected a powerful vision of the court as not simply "a courthouse but a dispute resolution center where the grievant, with the aid of a screening clerk, would be directed to the process (or sequence of processes) most appropriate to a particular type of case."[171] The Pound Conference emphasized ADR processes – particularly mediation – as better for litigants who had continuing relationships after the trial was over because it emphasized their common interests rather than those that divided them.

Custody disputes were a natural fit with the movement for ADR for several reasons. First, the no-fault divorce movement and the movement for joint custody eroded the long-held practice of using fault and adversarial procedure as the best mechanism for making decisions about post-divorce parent-child relationships. The focus of custody law became the child's emotional well-being, not moral judgments about parental conduct. If children need continuing relationships with both parents in order to manage their conflict for the benefit of the child, then parents in turn need an alternative procedural forum to the courtroom.

Second, courts had too many custody cases to handle. During the 1970s and 1980s and beyond, huge numbers of child custody disputes were filed in the nation's courthouses. They could not all be tried. Courts needed new ways to handle this growing influx of cases without becoming overwhelmed.

Finally, growing public discontent with the adversary system for resolving divorce disputes encouraged several pioneers to systematically conceptualize "mediation" as a credible alternative to "adversarial." Most prominently, John Haynes[172] and O.J. Coogler began the task of creating a theory and practice of divorce mediation during this period of ferment in thinking about the role courts and law play in divorce. Coogler's 1978 book, *Structured Mediation in Divorce Settlement*, in which he quotes Mahatma Gandhi, captured the spirit that motivated the growth of mediation:

I am indebted to my former wife and the two attorneys who represented us in our divorce for making me aware of the critical need for a more rational, move civilized way of arranging a parting of the ways. Her life, my life and our children's lives were unnecessarily embittered by that experience. In my frustration and anger, I kept thinking of something Mahatma Gandhi wrote over half a century ago:

I have learnt through bitter experience that one supreme lesson, to conserve my anger, and as heat conserved is transmuted into energy, even so our anger can be transmuted into a power which can move the world.

This system of structured mediation is, therefore, my anger transmuted into what I hope is a power to move toward a more humane world for those who find themselves following in my footsteps.[173]

The Continuum of ADR

Since the Pound Conference, many different processes that are labeled "alternatives to litigation" have evolved. All ADR processes share the common characteristic of resolving a child custody dispute without a judge's order after an adversary trial. Nonetheless, ADR processes such as mediation, education, expert evaluation, and arbitration are different from each other. It is important to distinguish between different ADR processes, as they serve different kinds of parents in different levels of conflict and involve different value choices. The processes available "provide multiple opportunities, both before and after divorce, for parents to settle custody and access disputes and to exit the legal system at the earliest time possible. The interventions range from the most widely available, most benign, and least expensive, such as divorce education programs, to the most coercive, intrusive, expensive, and least used forms of dispute resolution, such as trial and [arbitration] programs."[174]

Court-affiliated education (discussed in detail in Chapter VI) is not a dispute resolution process at all. Education programs provide parents with information and therapeutic and legal perspectives on how to help their children adjust to divorce. They do not provide a forum for parents to negotiate a resolution of their custody dispute. Indeed, parents generally attend education courses individually, and have no interaction during them.

Negotiation is a process through which parents or their representatives (usually lawyers) seek a resolution of their dispute through direct discussions. There are different philosophies of the goals of negotiation, summarized in the phrases "problem-solving or interest-based" in contrast to "adversarial or positional" negotiations. These different ways of thinking about the goals of negotiation were popularized by Roger Fisher and William Ury of the Harvard Negotiation Project in *Getting to Yes*, first published in 1981,[175] and the categories and the principles of problem-solving negotiations have been a major influence in the development of all ADR processes.

Positional negotiators view negotiations as an exchange of offers and counter-offers for a limited resource (e.g, time spent with a child or the right to make key decisions). They approach negotiations with a "win/lose" mindset – a gain for them is a loss for the other side, and vice versa. The goal of negotiations is to win as much of the limited resources for the negotiators' side as possible.

In contrast, problem-solving negotiators operate from four basic principles: (1) separate the people from the problem, (2) focus on interests, not positions, (3) invent options for mutual gain, and (4) insist on objective criteria to resolve disputes. Problem-solving negotiators ask, for example, why the parents want to make a decision about the child's medical care unilaterally rather than jointly, and seek to understand the needs that underlie the positions that parents take and then reconcile them. A parent might want to make a decision on medical care unilaterally for fear that consultation with the other parent will take too long, or that the other parent will be unreasonable in withholding consent. Problem-solving negotiators might suggest clauses in an agreement that sets procedures for consultation and for sharing information and fixed time limits for the process. If differences remain, problem-solving negotiators will seek objective criteria to resolve them, such as suggesting that a pediatrician in whom both parents have confidence could make the decision.

Mediation, perhaps the most widespread ADR process, is essentially a dispute-resolution process in which problem-solving negotiations are facilitated by a neutral third party. Mediators stimulate parents' consideration of their own interests, and seek to inspire creative solutions to impasses.

The mediator's goal is to generate an agreement that satisfies the parties' diverse needs and interests, defined in largely psychological and economic terms. Mediators, however, do not universally agree on the theory and practice of their craft. Differences between them can be usefully categorized on a continuum between "facilitative" and "evaluative." "One end of this continuum contains strategies and techniques that facilitate the parties' negotiation; at the other end lie strategies and techniques intended to evaluate matters that are important to the mediation."[176]

A primarily facilitative mediator uses techniques to help parents better communicate. He or she asks probing questions to encourage parents to articulate why they want custody and what role they see for the other parent in the child's life. The facilitative mediator asks parents to complete parenting plans to exchange concrete proposals for what days each wants a child to live with that parent and how differences can be resolved.

A primarily evaluative mediator seeks to get the parents to understand the strengths and weaknesses of their positions and interests. An evaluative mediator might predict what will happen in court if the parents do not settle, will evaluate proposed solutions, and will offer his or her own suggestions for settlement and solutions to impasses. The differences between evaluative and facilitative mediators are often a matter of degree, rather than of kind; many mediators combine facilitative and evaluative techniques, as they deem appropriate.

Another school, transformative mediation, views conflict as a crisis in human interaction that results in hostile and aggressive communication patterns between parties that in turn causes further deterioration in each party's perception of self and the other party.[177] The goal of the transformative mediator is to change the quality of the parties' interaction, not to solve the problems that divide them. Success in mediation is not measured by agreements reached, but rather by party shifts toward greater self-confidence, responsiveness to the other party, and constructive interaction.

Expert evaluation (sometimes called a *forensic evaluation* or a *neutral mental health evaluation* and discussed in detail in Chapter XII) is the process used when a mental health professional expert (e.g., a psychiatrist, psychologist, or social worker), acting under the authority of the court, conducts an investigation and provides the court with a report and recommendations to help it fashion a parenting plan. The judge is free to accept, reject, or modify the evaluator's recommendations.

An expert evaluation is designed to be an aid to better informed judicial decision-making. It is often also thought of as an ADR process because many parents settle their custody disagreements after reviewing the evaluator's report and recommendations. Some do settle because the parents believe that the evaluator's recommendations are in the child's best interests. Others settle because they recognize that the expert's report and recommendations will be highly influential with the judge and they feel that they do not have the resources to challenge it effectively.

Arbitration is the procedure by which parents, by mutual agreement, voluntarily delegate the power to decide on a parenting plan to a third party. Parents can choose a psychologist, a lawyer, a religious figure, or anyone else to arbitrate. The courts will generally enforce the arbitrator's decisions.

Voluntary arbitration is widely used in commercial disputes between businesses. Businesses agree to arbitration to resolve their disputes because they can choose an expert to decide the matter (e.g., a scientist rather than a judge can serve as an arbitrator to resolve a complex patent dispute). Businesses also choose arbitration over litigation because the rules of arbitration are less formal than those of a trial, and arbitration is generally confidential. Overall, businesses arbitrate disputes because of faster resolution and decreased cost compared with litigation. The decisions of an arbitrator are presumptively final and subject only to very limited judicial review in the courts before enforcement. An arbitrator's factual or legal mistake is generally not sufficient grounds for a court to overturn an arbitration award; for that, fraud, corruption, or misconduct or finding of truly serious error is required.[178]

Arbitration has many of the same advantages for child custody disputes as it has for commercial disputes: the opportunity to choose an expert decision-maker, informality of rules, confidentiality, reduced expense, and increased speed. Many courts, however, believe they have a special responsibility to protect the best interests of the child, and give no deference to a privately selected arbitrator's decision in a child custody dispute. Arbitrators' awards in child custody cases are thus in some states subject to more-searching judicial review than awards in commercial cases.[179] In those states, discontented parents have a greater incentive to contest an arbitrator's award by appeals to the courts. The advantage of finality that arbitration offers is substantially reduced.

While the various ADR processes are all different, it is possible to join them in creative combinations. Neutral evaluation can, for example, be combined with mediation by agreement of the parties. Parents in mediation may agree that the best way to resolve their parenting dispute is to engage an outside expert to evaluate their family situation and to make recommendations for a parenting plan. Sometimes, divorcing couples in disagreement about how to divide an asset will engage a neutral financial consultant to determine the value of property in dispute. Special mastering/parent coordination combines education and mediation with arbitration in custody disputes. It is aimed at high-conflict families as an alternative to their continuous litigation in courtrooms. It will be discussed in more detail in Chapter VIII.

ADR Processes Compared and Contrasted

Figure 5.1 summarizes the relationship between negotiation, mediation, expert evaluation, arbitration, and trial on a continuum of three critical

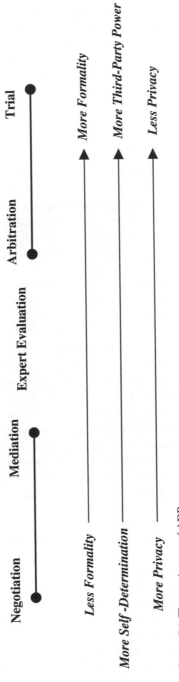

Figure 5.1 The continuum of ADR

dimensions: formality of rules, self-determination (parents deciding versus delegation of power to a third party to decide), and privacy.

On the left side of the continuum are the dispute resolution processes in which parents have the greatest ability to make their own agreements, procedures are informal, and what is said generally remains private. On the right side of the continuum are the processes in which a third party has power to order custody arrangements even over parental objections, the rules of procedure are more formal and more adversarial, and the decision-making process and results are more open to the public.

Negotiations take place in private. No one tells parents in a negotiation where to stand, who should speak first, or what sort of information parents can consider.

Mediation is more structured than negotiation, as the mediator sets the format and the agenda for the sessions in consultation with the parents. Compared with arbitration or trial, mediation is highly informal. Mediators do not enforce rules of evidence to determine what information parents can consider. The mediator has no power to order a parenting plan over the objections of either parent. Parents can choose either to accept or reject any offer or counter-offer made during mediation just as they can if the mediator were not present. Mediation sessions, as will be discussed, are generally confidential.

In contrast, on the right side of the continuum are dispute resolution processes in which parents delegate their power to make decisions to a third party. Here, the rules are more formal and adversarial because of the demands of due process of law. The process and the results also become increasingly open to the public. A custody trial often takes place in a public courtroom and, in some circumstances, can be observed by the press. The judge dictates the terms of a parenting plan, and may order something that neither parent wants. The parents must obey the judge's decision under threat of sanction, such as citation for contempt, if they do not. The parents are adversaries, and the rules of procedure and evidence for trials are highly formal and well established by history, tradition, and governing statutes.

Compared with a trial, the procedures of arbitration are less formal and the proceeding is private. Arbitrators have broader scope to disregard formal rules of evidence than a judge has. Arbitrators' decisions are subject to significantly less scrutiny by appellate courts than the decisions of a judge or jury. Nonetheless, there are rules of procedure in arbitration that are more formal than the rules for neutral evaluation or mediation. The arbitrator must make decisions based on evidence presented to him or her by the parties, even though what may be presented is broader than what would be admissible in court (for example, an arbitrator can rely on evidence presented in writing in an affidavit, while a judge must hear the same evidence in live testimony).

Fundamentally, arbitration is an adversarial process, and the arbitrator, like a judge, has the power to decide on a custody arrangement that contains provisions that one or both parents may not want. Each parent makes arguments in an attempt to persuade the arbitrator to adopt his or her point of view, and can object to evidence that is presented. Most important, the arbitrator dictates custody, and a disappointed parent has to accept the arbitrator's decision because the courts will enforce it. An arbitrator is thus unlike a mediator. The mediator has no power to make decisions for parents, only to facilitate their decision-making process.

Expert evaluation has some of the characteristics of arbitration. Both the expert evaluator and the arbitrator are not bound by formal rules of evidence of the courtroom. As will be discussed in Chapter XII, there are as yet no uniform standards of practice for the way an expert evaluation should be conducted, though progress is being made in that direction. Many expert evaluators nonetheless follow certain recognized standards of practice in conducting their investigations. These standards of practice guide evaluators in interviewing parents and children, sometimes conducting psychological testing and contacting third parties such as teachers or physicians ("collateral sources") for relevant information. Unlike the fact-gathering process of the arbitrator, however, fact-gathering by an evaluator occurs without a formal adversarial presentation of conflicting information and points of view from the parents, as would occur at an arbitration hearing.

The expert evaluator also cannot order a parenting plan over the objections of a parent. The expert evaluator writes a report to the court, with recommendations that are likely to influence the judge's decision. The court still has to make an independent decision to accept or reject the expert's report and recommendations. The expert evaluator has to be available to testify in court, and the parents can cross-examine the expert about the basis of his or her recommendations.

Mediation

Mediation is the most widely used ADR method in child custody courts today. Because it is both an important and unfamiliar process, it is worth providing a detailed look at its structure and regulation.[180] It is important to recognize that widespread use of mediation in child custody disputes is a relatively recent development, and there is significant diversity in mediation practices from state to state and from child custody court to child custody court.

Efforts have recently been made at the national level for more uniformity in the standards of practice of mediation. The American Bar Association, the Association of Family and Conciliation Courts, the Association for Conflict Resolution, and other mediation organizations adopted uniform *Model Standards of Practice for Family and Divorce Mediation* (*Model Standards*), a statement of good practices directed to mediators.[181] The National Commission on Uniform State Laws and the American Bar Association have developed a *Uniform Mediation Act (UMA)*, and encourage all state legislatures to adopt it.[182] More information on both the *Model Standards* and the *UMA* is presented in the discussion that follows.

Mandated Mediation

Before 1980, parents could agree voluntarily to mediate their custody dispute, but courts did not force them to do so. Early experience with voluntary mediation in child custody cases established that both parents rarely agreed to mediate. One or the other parent rejected mediation even when courts offered them the option.[183] This result is consistent with the general finding that high percentages of people in all types of disputes – not just child custody – who are offered the opportunity to mediate, decline it.[184] As will be seen in the next Chapter, the same finding holds for court-affiliated education – when parents are offered the opportunity to voluntarily participate in education programs, they overwhelmingly decline it.

Parents who are compelled to participate in mediation and parent-education programs nonetheless report they have a positive experience and believe that mediation and education programs should be mandated for divorcing parents. The most plausible explanation for this paradox is that parents refused to participate because they were unfamiliar with mediation or because they did not view mediation as a viable alternative in an overwhelming adversarial legal system and culture. Mediation also forces parents to talk to each other during a time of great pain and anger in their lives, a task that many parents may not want to undertake voluntarily.

Beginning in about 1980, legislatures and courts created programs that allowed courts to compel parents to attend mediation. First enacted in California,[185] these programs have various names: public (as opposed to private), court-affiliated, court-compelled, or court-mandated mediation. All allow the court to require the parents to attend mediation sessions even if one or both do not want to. As will be discussed in Chapter VIII, almost all of the mandatory mediation programs create exceptions or special procedures for categories of parents for whom mediation is especially risky, notably parents who are victims of domestic violence or parents who are alleged to have abused or neglected a child.

A recent national survey of state statutes and court rules (written regulations issued by the court system on its own authority to govern practices in cases before it) found that custody mediation is mandatory in thirteen states, with an exception for cases involving allegations of domestic violence in all of them. Another thirteen states have no statutes or court rules on the subject. Most of the remaining twenty-four states give judges discretion to order parents to enter into mediation.[186]

Why should a child custody court mandate that parents mediate their disputes? The *Model Standards* identify three reasons that families benefit from mediation:

> Experience has established that . . . mediation is a valuable option for many families because it can:
> • increase the self-determination of participants and their ability to communicate;
> • promote the best interests of children; and
> • reduce the economic and emotional costs associated with the resolution of family disputes.[187]

Mediation serves vitally important social goals by promoting voluntary settlement of custody disputes by parents. Above all, it reduces parental conflict, and thus creates a much greater likelihood that children will be able to cope with the transitions required of them by divorce without serious emotional, educational, and economic problems. Voluntary settlements reduce the emotional and economic transaction costs of custody dispute resolution. The reduced stress on parents resulting from a voluntary settlement increases their capacity to be effective care-givers, employees, and citizens. A voluntary settlement also limits state intrusion into parental autonomy with judicial decrees, and allows parents to shape their parenting plans to reflect their own values.

Without mandatory mediation, only the children of a tiny minority consisting of the most cooperative parents will benefit from the voluntary settlements and conflict reduction that mediation promotes. Mandatory mediation, in effect, gives all participating parents a viable opportunity to opt out of the adversary system for resolving child custody disputes, a process many parents intensely dislike. It gives them the opportunity to have a voice in the settlement of their dispute, a voice that is not likely to be heard in court, where dialogue is regulated by the rules and procedures of the legal process and restricted by the court's limited time and its need to gather reliable information for a decision. As a result, parents are more likely to adhere to agreements reached through mediation and feel more respect for the process and the society from which the agreement resulted. A child should be entitled to these benefits whether his or her parents initially want them or not.

Mandatory participation in mediation is a limited intrusion on the parent's autonomy. It is important to understand that mandatory mediation does not mean that parents have to agree to anything. It means only that they both have to appear for a mediation session. In most court-based mandatory mediation programs, the court is not informed about what parents say during the mediation sessions. Rather, it is informed only whether the parents attend the mediation session and whether, in the mediator's opinion, future sessions would be useful. In a few court mediation programs, however, mediators make recommendations to the court on custody arrangements if the mediation does not result in an agreement, making the process akin to a neutral evaluation.[188]

Training and Qualifications of Mediators

Mediators come from a variety of professional backgrounds such as law, mental health, and dispute resolution. The *Model Standards* identify qualities that all mediators of custody disputes from any profession of origin should possess: training in mediation; a working knowledge of family law; knowledge of the emotional issues facing children and families undergoing divorce, domestic violence, child abuse, and neglect; and an ability to understand the effect of culture and diversity on family reorganization.[189]

Mediation is neither therapy nor the practice of law. Unlike therapy, mediation is task-oriented and time-limited. Mediators use some of the same techniques found in therapy textbooks. Mediation may also produce therapeutic byproducts such as a better relationship between parents and children. But mediation is not therapy. Parents are not patients, but are instead participants. The mediator seeks to facilitate agreement on a parenting plan, not long-term behavioral change.

Even though some mediators are lawyers, mediators do not represent either parent nor provide legal advice to them. A parent is a participant in mediation, not a client in a lawyer-client relationship. Certainly, legally related information may be discussed during mediation sessions (e.g., custody standards or typical parenting plans ordered by courts), but the mediator does not advise parents on how that information applies to them individually. Their own lawyers perform that task.

Regulation of Mediation

State laws vary in the way they regulate the practice of mediation. As previously mentioned, many states have passed legislation that sets standards and practices for mediation programs and mediators. In some states, courts have passed rules on their own authority regulating mediation practices in disputes filed in the courts. Regulatory mechanisms include licensing, certification, accreditation, registration, and requiring mediators to subscribe to a code of ethics.

Private Practice, Court Employees, and Mediator Panels

Some mediators work in private practice and mediate disputes not yet filed in court. Parents sign an agreement to work with private mediators, and are responsible for the mediator's fees. Other mediators are full-time employees of the child custody court and only mediate disputes among parents who have filed a case with the court. The state or local government that funds the courts pays for the costs of the mediation services.

Some child custody courts mandate mediation and refer parents to a panel of private mediators for which the court sets the criteria for membership. Parents pay for services from panel members at a set hourly rate, and panel members are typically required to mediate a number of cases on a sliding scale of fees for parents who cannot afford high hourly rates.

Scope of Issues Mediated

The scope of what is discussed in mediation is often limited by statute or regulation. Most states limit mandated mediation to child custody or parenting disputes. Some include child-support issues as a subject of mandatory mediation. No state mandates mediation of all of the issues in a divorce, including spousal support and property division, though many parents undertake mediation of all issues voluntarily with mediators in private practice.

Confidentiality of Mediation

Confidentiality of communication in mediation is vitally important to ensure that parents can speak freely without the fear of having what they say used against them in later court proceedings. Many state legislatures have supported this policy by enacting mediation privilege statutes.[190] A mediation privilege statute is a relatively narrow and technical enactment that prohibits a mediator or a participant from disclosing communications made during mediation in future court proceedings. It does not necessarily prohibit disclosure of communications made in mediation outside of legal proceedings, such as to the newspapers or other interested parties. Since state statutes vary in comprehensiveness and scope, it is extremely important that mediators and participants be aware of the scope of the protection for confidentiality for their communications in the particular state in which they are mediating. The *UMA* attempts to create a uniform approach to mediation confidentiality throughout the nation by proposing that all states enact a law that makes most communications in mediation not subject to discovery or admissible in most legal proceedings.

The *UMA*, however, recognizes exceptions to the privilege against admissibility or discovery of mediation communications in the case of threats of bodily injury and communications containing evidence of child abuse and neglect. The drafters of the *UMA* note that state mediation confidentiality statutes frequently recognize a similar exception.[191]

Other sources requiring confidentiality in mediation are provisions in private contracts between participants and the mediator and ethical standards for mediation practice. The *Model Standards* require mediators to preserve the confidentiality of all information acquired during the mediation process. This ethical obligation is broader than simply not testifying in court.[192] Rather, it requires that the mediator not make statements about the mediation to the media or any third party unless the participants to the mediation consent. Like the *UMA*, the *Model Standards* make an exception to the mediator's confidentiality obligations by requiring a mediator to report a participant's threat of suicide or violence against any person to the threatened person and to the appropriate authorities if the mediator believes such threats are likely to be acted upon and the disclosure is otherwise permitted by law.[193]

The Role of Lawyers for Parents in Mediation

The *Model Standards* ensure that participants are informed of their right to consult a lawyer and to have the lawyers participate in mediation if the participants so desire. The standards require the mediator to "recommend that the participants obtain independent legal representation before concluding an agreement,"[194] and "[i]f the participants so desire, the mediator should allow attorneys, counsel or advocates for the participants to be present at the mediation sessions."[195]

Evaluation of Mediation

Research supports the conclusion that mediation achieves the goals of promoting parental self-determination, reducing the emotional and economic costs of resolving custody disputes, and improving parent-child relationships. "There is considerable evidence of user satisfaction with mediation and some evidence that the agreements reached through mediation are both less costly to the conflicting parties and more robust than traditional adjudication."[196] "If there is any consistent finding in the mediation research, it is that the participants like the process and view it as fair, regardless of whether a settlement was reached."[197] "In California, about 20–30% of the total population of separating families file to resolve their disputes over the care and custody of their children in court and are thus mandated to mediate. Mediation attains full resolution in one-half, and partial resolution in two-thirds, of these disputes."[198] Researchers have commented: "This solidly researched 'success rate' of mediation supports the philosophy that most couples have the capacity to re-order their lives in a private, confidential setting, according to their personal preferences, with the relatively limited help of a mediator who focuses on specific issues."[199]

"Mediating couples report liking the focus on the children, the chance to air grievances, the opportunity to discuss real issues, and having the discussion kept on track ... Research shows that both men and women are more satisfied with mediation than with the adversarial process. Seventy-seven percent of mediating couples are pleased with the mediation process, but only 40% of litigating couples are satisfied with court procedure. In fact,

50% to 70% of those litigating express active dissatisfaction with the legal system."[200]

Studies report that mediation parents reach a resolution of their disputes more quickly than litigation parents, taking less than half the time and at lower cost to produce a parenting plan.[201] Even mediation parents who fail to reach agreement are more likely to settle prior to trial than litigation parents. Mediation is thus a benefit to them because the issues in dispute have been narrowed and a climate for later agreement created.

Studies report that mediated agreements result in higher rates of children's involvement with both parents following divorce. A recent 12-year follow-up of 71 divorcing families randomly assigned in the late 1980s to either a mediation group or a litigation control group shows important long-term benefits of 5 hours of mediation 12 years later. Parents in the study were randomly assigned to mediation or litigation groups. "[I]t was not the case that the cooperative families chose mediation and the families involved in conflict chose litigation."[202] Random assignment to mediation or litigation allowed the researchers to attribute the statistically significant differences between the groups to the dispute resolution process the parents participated in, not to outside factors such as attitudes toward each other or to socio-economic status. The researchers found that non-residential parents who mediated their dispute were far more likely to see their children every week than non-residential parents who litigated their dispute. The non-residential parents who litigated generally followed the national trend by dropping out of their children's lives; the non-residential parents who mediated tended to be much more involved with their children, through both in-person and telephone contact. Residential parents who mediated reported that non-residential parents who mediated were more involved with discipline, school, and church activities and in problem-solving than non-residential parents in the litigation control group.

Mediated agreements tend to be more specific and detailed than those negotiated by attorneys alone, and certainly are more specific than those drafted by *pro se* parents. Some studies show that mediated agreements are more likely to include joint custody provisions, whereas sole custody awards are more likely in courts.[203]

Mediation also results in higher rates of compliance with parenting plans and child support agreements compared with agreements reached by negotiations in the shadow of the adversarial process.[204] This finding is consistent with the data discussed in Chapter III showing that reduced parental conflict and higher rates of parent-child contact following divorce significantly increase the chances that child support obligations will be paid.

Mediation reduces the intensity of the adversarial divorce process because it "reshapes the norms and expectations of communities of practice [that govern the behavior of divorce lawyers] by bringing mediators' goals and perspectives directly into the interaction among divorce lawyers."[205]

Once mediation is incorporated into divorce practice, lawyers tend to embrace it either because they want to or because they have to in order to maintain the economic viability of their practices. Studies have shown that as lawyers become more familiar with mediation, they become supportive of the process.[206] In a recent survey of the Florida bar (a state with a long history of requiring mediation of child custody disputes), for example, 91% of the members of the Family Law Section described the effect of mediation on family court as positive, whereas 8% viewed it as both positive and negative, and only 1% saw it as negative.[207]

Mediation positively influences the way lawyers represent clients. Before the mediation era in California, approximately 10% of child custody dispute filings went to trial. Today, only about 1.5% are tried. Respected researchers have attributed the difference in the number of contested cases in California to the introduction of mediation and associated court-affiliated programs for parental-conflict management.[208] In a comparative study of divorce practice in Maine and New Hampshire, researchers found a significant drop in pre-trial motions filed in Maine cases that coincided with the introduction of mandatory mediation in custody disputes. Mediation is not mandatory in New Hampshire, and no similar decrease occurred in New Hampshire divorce cases. "With a changed institutional framework for divorce [resulting from the introduction of mandatory custody mediation], Maine lawyers came to rely less on adversarial legal procedures for representing their clients' interests."[209]

These research results must be interpreted with the same caveats and conditions that reliance on all empirical research to shape the policies and practices of the child custody court requires, as discussed in detail in Chapter III. Mediation is relatively new. There are different ways to conduct it, and there are serious methodological difficulties in designing definitive studies.[210] Furthermore, the conditions under which mediation occurs influences parents' perceptions positively or negatively. Mediation is more likely to result in a settlement and positive changes in parental behavior "when the couple spends more time with an experienced mediator who focuses on enhancing communication."[211] Most mediation participants in court-based programs agree that mediation gives them an opportunity to air their concerns in detail, and that is one of the main reasons they are satisfied with mediation by comparison with litigation. Many parents, however, feel that mediation in court-based programs is rushed and mechanical, a "not surprising perception given that in some counties mediation is limited to only one session."[212]

Mediation is not a panacea for all parental conflict nor permanently beneficial to all parents. It is not intensive individual or family therapy but a focused dispute resolution process. It is a brief intervention at a time of crisis that cannot be expected to change personalities and long-standing patterns of behavior. It encourages planning for responsible post-divorce parenting.

For highly conflicted parents, the main problem is not how they resolved their dispute initially but the fact that the underlying causes of their conflict have not been addressed. They need a more intensive, more therapeutically oriented process, including mediation, than the traditional public mediation program allows for.[213]

Mediation seems to deter re-litigation in the short term. Over time, however, chronically litigious parents return to court regardless of whether they initially resolved their dispute through mediation or through litigation. As Kenneth Kressel and Dean Pruitt have succinctly expressed it: "Intensely conflicted disputes involving parties of widely disparate power, with low motivation to settle, fighting about matters of principle, suffering from discord or ambivalence within their own camps, and negotiating over scarce resources are likely to defeat even the most adroit mediators."[214]

Gender and Mediation

Some have suggested that mediation is not in the best interests of women because women have fewer economic resources and are more likely to make compromises for the sake of their children than men, and thus are easy targets for unscrupulous manipulation during mediation.[215] Federal legislation in the last decade has required states to adopt child support guidelines based on parental income. The guidelines have, in turn, created greater clarity and certainty about parents' financial obligations to children after divorce, reducing the potential for manipulation in negotiation.[216] The number of mothers who received the child support they were owed increased dramatically in the strong economy of the 1990s.[217]

Financial disparities between mothers and fathers after divorce nonetheless continue to exist. Mediation, however, increases the likelihood that child support will be paid. As discussed in Chapter III, one of the best predictors of regularity in payment of child support is decreased parental conflict, as reflected in an agreement between the parents, and increased contact between the parent obligated to pay child support and the child. Both of these conditions are promoted by mediation.

There is no empirical evidence to support the argument that mediation forces women to give away custody rights or that men, as a group, engage in strategic bargaining that forces women to trade financial resources for custody rights. After sophisticated analysis of over 1,100 California divorce cases, the major empirical study on this subject found "no persuasive evidence that those mothers who experienced more legal conflict had to give up [child] support to win the custody they wanted."[218]

The unequal "balance of power" argument, furthermore, assumes that "power" over a divorce settlement correlates with economic wealth. There are other possible dimensions to negotiating power; "Weakness" may not be defined solely by financial disparities between parents. A parent may be emotionally weaker because the other parent began a divorce over his or her objections or because he or she is not living with a child and thus has less contact with the child.

Empirical evidence strongly supports the idea that men and women both perceive mediation as fair and valuable. A recent study of mandated mediation in Georgia, for example, replicates the finding of other empirical studies that "found few differences between men and women in their perceptions of domestic mediation."[219] It concludes that mediation programs seem to be doing a "fairly good job of satisfying both male and female litigants in domestic disputes."[220] The Georgia study confirms the findings of other studies that establish approximately equal satisfaction between the genders with mediation as a dispute resolution process.[221] Furthermore, women report that mediation is helpful to them in "standing up" to their spouses, and rated themselves more capable and knowledgeable as a result of participation in mediation.[222]

Although women are about as satisfied with mediation as are men, they do tend to be less enthusiastic and confident about the process. A higher percentage of women than men express feelings of intimidation about mediation. It is important, however, to note in assessing these gender differences that a higher percentage of women than men also feel more intimidated by the litigation process.[223] In essence, some women feel more intimidated than their male partners no matter what process is used to resolve their dispute.

The Place of Mediation in the Child Custody Court

The most important conclusion to draw from the child custody court's experience with mandatory mediation to date is that mediation should play a central role in the court's current and future operations. Empirical research supports the theory that mediation reduces parental conflict and offers families self-determination, dignity, and a voice that is not heard in most child custody courtrooms. It also offers parents lower emotional and economic transaction costs for resolving their disputes compared with the courtroom. Courts support mediation. Parents like it, and they and their children benefit from it. Lawyers increasingly recognize the importance of mediation, and support it.

A judgment that mediation benefits parents and children is not a blanket endorsement of mediation or a blanket condemnation of litigation. Rather, it is a call for making mediation available to all parents, for a diversified child-custody dispute resolution system that carefully directs parents to a process that best serves their needs and a court system that constantly engages in research and development.

The great majority of the children of divorce are better off if their parents resolve their disputes privately by voluntary agreement on a parenting plan facilitated by mediation. A judge should nonetheless resolve some child custody disputes. Mediated agreements are confidential. In rare cases, child custody disputes raise important undecided questions of law (e.g., whether a batterer should be eligible for joint custody) that courts must resolve in a published opinion in order to provide guidance to parents and the public. Disputes involving family violence may not be appropriate for mediation, and judicial orders may be required to protect victims against violence. Litigation is required to compel unwilling parents to mediate. Courts must make emergency custody decisions to prevent abductions. Litigation is also required as a backstop for parents who cannot resolve their dispute by voluntary agreement and to ensure that agreements and laws are enforced. Children cannot be left in limbo if their parents cannot agree despite every rational intervention to encourage them to do so.

VI Parents Are Forever III

Court-Affiliated Educational Programs

It is a sea of confusion, anger and fear out there. And most of us don't know how to swim. . . . A divorcing parent's statement about the P.E.A.C.E. (Parent Education and Custody Effectiveness) Program.[224]

During the 1990s, court-affiliated education programs for parents joined mediation as a major conflict-management and prevention tool of the child custody court. Virtually no courts had such programs in 1978, the year one of the first court-affiliated educational programs was founded, in Kansas. By 1998, 20 years later, a national survey reported that 1,516, or nearly half the counties in the United States, had court-affiliated educational programs for parents, a 180% increase since 1994.[225] By 2001, 35 states had enacted legislation or court rules that establishes and regulates parent education programs and allows judges to order parents to attend them.[226]

Many courts also offer, or require, educational programs for children as well as for parents. Children's educational programs are not as plentiful as those for parents, but are growing quickly. A 2001 national survey identified 152 counties that offer educational programs for children.[227] Courts most frequently mention plans for children's educational programs as a future innovation.[228]

This chapter describes the aims and operations of court-affiliated educational programs and the data that assesses their effectiveness.

What Are the Aims of Court-Affiliated Educational Programs?

Court-affiliated educational programs are a public health tool to help families understand how to manage divorce-related conflict and family reorganization. A standard textbook defines public health as "the organization and application of public resources to prevent dependency which would otherwise result from disease or injury," and states that "prevention is the purpose of public health."[229] The primary goals of court-affiliated educational programs are (1) to reduce the risks to children created by divorce-related parental conflict, and (2) to improve the quality of parenting children receive during family reorganization.[230]

Public education is a fundamental tool of preventive public health. A basic strategy to promote public health is to identify high-risk groups and tailor prevention efforts toward them. Over the years, the medical community has increasingly and effectively incorporated preventive education programs into strategies for reducing the spread of diseases such as skin cancer, heart disease, drug abuse, low birth weight, rubella, and infectious diseases.[231] Education that combines information and training in emotional and social skills also shows promise in helping prevent the incidence of more behaviorally oriented public health problems such as teen pregnancy and suicide.[232] Recent public health strategies "have successfully altered the behavior of individuals in the contexts of drunken driving, driving without a seat belt, and cigarette smoking" by altering "the 'rational actor's' appreciation of the 'actual costs' associated with a behavior and thus their cost-benefit analysis regarding the behavior in question."[233]

Court-affiliated educational programs have the same aim as other public health programs – to reduce risk to children. Parents in a continuing state of high conflict create risks of emotional, economic, and educational damage to their children. The goal of court-affiliated educational programs is to make parents more rational actors in the divorce system by helping them understand the actual costs of conflict to their children, and providing the parents with alternative models of behavior. These programs encourage parents to move from high conflict to cooperative parenting or, at a minimum, to parallel parenting – with safety. The goal of children's programs is to reduce the risk of emotional damage to children by normalizing their divorce experience and assuring them that they are not alone in their feelings. Parents' and children's educational programs both provide referrals to more-intensive programs of therapy or social services, if needed. We hope that court-affiliated programs will gradually have the same effect in reducing the risks of parental conflict to the children of divorce that public health programs have had in reducing the risks of drunken driving and cigarette smoking.

Primary, Secondary, and Tertiary Prevention Programs

Public health theory postulates that education can take place at "any point along the spectrum from the prevention of disease or injury to the prevention of impairment, disability or dependency."[234] It distinguishes between different types of prevention depending on the stage of a disease the patient is experiencing:

- *Primary prevention* programs seek to prevent the disease or injury itself (e.g., immunization programs or school education programs that seek to reduce smoking).

- *Secondary prevention* programs seek to block the progression of an injury or disease from impairment to disability (e.g., education about the importance of early detection of high blood pressure can reduce the probability of a heart attack or stroke through changes in diet and exercise patterns).
- *Tertiary prevention* programs seek to block or retard the progression of a disability to a state of dependency (e.g., education about the importance of prompt medical care and rehabilitation can limit the damage that a stroke or heart attack can cause).

These stages of prevention are helpful in classifying court-affiliated educational programs for divorcing parents and children. Assume that a child custody court wants to organize an education program to reduce the effect of parental conflict on children of divorce. In the court's view, a parent's filing a custody dispute in court is analogous to the manifestation of a major symptom of a disease.

- *Primary prevention programs* are those available to parents and children before an action is filed in court.

Primary prevention programs can include marriage and divorce education programs, support groups for parents and children in community centers, and family life education in schools. Courts, however, are generally not in the business of organizing primary prevention programs because the parents and children who attend have not yet filed a formal complaint with the court. As a result of the influx of *pro se* parents, courts have begun to provide helpful information to all persons, whether or not they have actually filed a case on the court's docket.

- *Secondary prevention programs*, in contrast, are organized under the auspices of the child custody court and are mandated for parents who file custody disputes in the court and sometimes for their children.

These programs are more in the nature of universal prevention rather than being aimed at parents who exhibit symptoms of serious conflict and dysfunction. Whatever their level of conflict, and dysfunction, divorcing parents and children attend and participate soon after an action is filed in court. The teachers and program organizers are court employees or independent contractors of whom the court approves. The court approves the curriculum and mandates attendance at its approved programs. These programs are thus called "court-affiliated," "court-sponsored," or "court-mandated."

- *Tertiary prevention programs* are aimed at high-conflict families.

Tertiary programs combine education with other forms of intervention such as mediation and therapy. They take up far more time and resources than secondary programs and have the explicit aim of changing parental behavior. They are aimed at a small number of high-conflict parents. The court mandates parent participation in tertiary prevention programs as an alternative to punishment for violation of a court order because jail, fines, and changes of custody do more harm than good for the children and do not address the complex causes that underlie repetitive litigation. For example, research into visitation problems has shown that parents are often unclear or confused about the visitation schedule and have long-standing relationship issues or fears about safety, problems whose resolution requires mediation, education, and therapy rather than jail terms for offenders.[235]

Figure 6.1 summarizes the different types of conflict-prevention programs available to parents in various stages of custody litigation.

The following examples of primary, secondary, and tertiary parental education programs provide a more concrete understanding of the aims and operations of these programs.

Court-Affiliated Primary Prevention Programs

Maricopa County (Phoenix), Arizona: Resources for Pro Se Litigants

Maricopa County is a national leader in providing self-help information to *pro se* divorce litigants that is aimed at making their court experience more friendly. One aspect of the program is self-service centers located at the court, shopping centers, libraries, and other off-site settings that *pro se* litigants can visit to obtain information. The court has also created a website with valuable information for *pro se* litigants about the nature of the court and the legal process of divorce.[236]

In Maricopa County, the following resources are available to all parents:

- Court staff facilitators to help *pro se* litigants.
- Telephone audiotapes explaining court procedures and offering tips on self-representation.
- Automated information kiosks with court forms and schedules.
- A seminar program called "Litigants Without Lawyers."
- Website information including forms and a step-by-step explanation of what the *pro se* litigant can expect when he or she files forms at the court.

One example of the kind of information that can be found on the Maricopa County website is a booklet describing recommended model parenting plans for children of different ages.[237] An interdisciplinary committee of judges, lawyers, and mental health professionals prepared the booklet to give parents an idea of the types of plans the courts consider to be in the best interests of children. The parenting plan booklet does not recommend a single type of parenting plan for children at all ages. Rather, it offers several

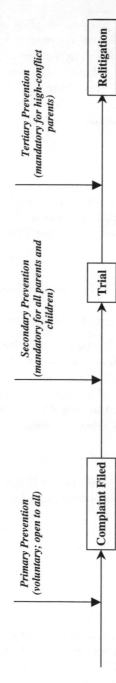

Figure 6.1 The continuum of court-affiliated educational programs

developmentally appropriate plans for children of different ages, with different options for dividing time depending on variables such as the children's ages and the parents' work schedules. It includes sample language for court orders that parents can themselves draft to submit to the court and calendars for parents to illustrate the various options that are available to them.

Court-Affiliated Secondary Prevention Programs

In many child custody courts, once a parent files a complaint for custody, both parents and their children will be ordered to attend an education program.

P.E.A.C.E. (Parent Education and Custody Effectiveness),
New York-Education for Parents

P.E.A.C.E. is an example of the kind of program that parents are required to attend. It operates throughout New York State and provides information to parents on three topics: the legal process for determining custody and child support, the effects of divorce and separation on adults, and the effects of divorce and separation on children and how parents can help children cope with this difficult transition.

Local organizing committees recruit volunteer presenters from the legal and mental health communities. Representatives of the statewide P.E.A.C.E. program train the volunteers before their first presentations. Local programs have significant flexibility, and the P.E.A.C.E. curriculum can be presented in a variety of formats. In most communities, the three topics are presented in three two-hour sessions that are generally held in the local courthouse and include both a large group lecture and a small group discussion.

At the first session, a judge explains the process and standards the court uses in deciding custody cases, emphasizing that the court supplants parents' decisions only if the parents do not reach an agreement themselves. A family-law practitioner also makes a presentation at the first session about what clients can expect of their lawyers.

Trained mental health experts lead the sessions on the effects of divorce on parents and children. They combine a lecture with small group discussions led by trained facilitators. At the end of the program, parents are provided with a list of non-profit organizations that can assist the entire family during the stressful period of divorce, and with booklets designed to help parents aid their children in coping with divorce.

P.E.A.C.E.'s mental health curriculum is typical of similar educational programs around the country. The most important topic in these programs is children's reactions to divorce and parents' reactions to children. Programs also pay attention to parental adjustment, parenting issues, and co-parenting. Generally, court-mandated educational programs emphasize that parents should solve problems rather than finding fault with each other, and emphasize the benefits of parental cooperation versus the costs of parental conflict.[238] Other programs, like P.E.A.C.E., also offer information on the legal process.

Kid's Turn, Northern California: Education for Children

Kid's Turn focuses on children ages 4 to 14. Parents are charged a sliding-scale fee for participation. Professionals with backgrounds in education or psychology teach the course. The Kid's Turn curriculum is presented in six, 90-minute educational workshops spread over a 6-week period. The workshops teach the children skills that help them cope with the changes in their family that occur when their parents divorce or separate. The workshops incorporate age-appropriate games and activities to help children learn:

- to identify and communicate their feelings about their parents' separation or divorce.
- ways to talk about these changes with other children and adults at home and at school.
- basic concepts of the legal process of divorce and child custody decision-making.
- problem-solving methods for dealing with conflict-laden situations that children of divorce frequently encounter.

Parent groups are generally informed about what topics the children discuss each week so that the parents are prepared for more open discussion at home.[239] Kid's Turn also provides information to parents to enable them to help their children adjust to family reorganization and to implement what they learn in the classroom.

Court-Affiliated Tertiary Prevention for High-Conflict Families

Tertiary programs are designed to teach chronically litigious parents how to manage their conflicts without resorting to litigation and to help the children cope with parental conflict. They are more intensive and therapeutically oriented than secondary prevention programs.

Parenting Without Conflict: Los Angeles County, California

Los Angeles County Family Court Services has developed a tertiary program, Parenting Without Conflict (formerly called Pre-Contempt/Contemnors), designed to deal with the problems of parents who have high levels of conflict, who chronically violate custody and visitation orders, and who seek frequent court intervention. The court mandates attendance, and both parents attend classes together, except where joint attendance is inconsistent with safety because of restraining orders, domestic violence, mental illness, or substance abuse. The program does not include children in the educational process.

Parenting Without Conflict was created because contempt proceedings and jail time did not provide appropriate remedies when custodial parents denied non-custodial parents access to their children. Instead of sending the offending parents to jail, the court requires them to participate in the intensive educational program. Parenting Without Conflicts' goal is to provide parents with information about the effects of their behavior on their children, and its legal consequences. It also seeks to improve parents' communication and conflict-resolution skills. The program consists of six two and a half-hour sessions of lectures, skill development, small group discussions, parental interaction, and practice sessions.[240]

As the program creators note: "The program model is designed similarly to diversion programs created to address driving under the influence and drug abuse defendants."[241] "Many [parents] come unwillingly and resentfully, others with more grace and interest. Some are ordered back a second time or required to write a class paper on what they learned. The size of the group varies widely, depending on the number of referrals (twenty-five to seventy-five at any one time)."[242]

Evaluation of Court-Affiliated Educational Programs

There is no single study that summarizes all the available evaluation data or compares and contrasts different kinds of programs or different stages of intervention. In addition, evaluating educational intervention programs presents substantial methodological challenges[243] – controlled studies are rare.[244] Most programs are evaluated by parent-satisfaction surveys. These provide valuable data about parents' impressions and reactions, but do not measure the long-term effect of the program on the behavior of parents and children.

Despite these limitations, there is promising evidence in the research so far that court-affiliated prevention programs do make a difference in parents' attitudes, and perhaps their behavior. "The good news is that these studies indicate a high level of immediate consumer satisfaction; the bad news is that there have been only a few studies which have examined the more enduring consequences of such training."[245]

Positive Parental Reactions to Secondary Programs

Parents who are compelled to attend education programs report overwhelmingly that they learn important new information, skills, and attitudes that will help their children adjust to divorce and separation.[246] Parent-satisfaction research on court-affiliated secondary prevention programs indicates that parents believe they learn responsible conflict-management attitudes and skills. Parents who attend have more-positive attitudes about their children. They also report a willingness to consider a greater degree of cooperation with the other parent and even greater willingness to accept helping services. Mediators report that parents who attend education programs are better able to focus on their children's needs and to communicate.[247] In some studies, the re-litigation and conflict rates for parents who attend court-affiliated programs appear to be lower than the rates for parents who do not.[248] Finally, the judges who refer parents to court-mandated educational programs overwhelmingly believe that parents benefit from the referral.[249]

Evaluation of Children's Programs

A recent carefully controlled six-year follow-up study of a preventive intervention program is the first to document the effectiveness of programs designed to prevent mental health problems in adolescent children of divorce.[250] Participating children ages 9–12 were recruited from families identified randomly by a computerized search of court divorce decrees and by other methods. Some parents and children were placed in one of two approximately eleven-session prevention-education programs: one for mothers alone and a second for mothers and children. Others were assigned to a control group. At the six-year follow-up, adolescents in both programs showed reduced rates of diagnosis of mental illness; marijuana, alcohol, and drug use; and number of sexual partners. Although the sample in the study consisted largely of well-educated and upper-middle-class parents and children, the results are a positive sign that children's programs can have significant prevention benefits.

Continuing program evaluation of Kids Turn participants over a five-year period found that children and divorcing parents greatly value their experience. Participants report improved parent-child and child-parent communication. Children report a reduction in feelings of discouragement, guilt, sadness, fear, hurt, confusion, loneliness, worry, and being pulled apart, and an increase in feelings of excitement, happiness, and calm. Children also report the benefit of interaction with other children and value the group's ability to make them feel less alone or unique. A substantial number of parents report that their children displayed less anger, sadness, and irritability after the children completed the program. Overall, parents and children overwhelmingly found the experience beneficial in some way.[251]

Tertiary Preventive Programs

Research on tertiary prevention programs that combine education and therapy in some form to address chronic family conflict is even less developed than research on secondary programs. Few such tertiary programs exist, and careful researchers have studied even fewer. Janet Johnston has undertaken a preliminary evaluation of the Pre-Contempt/Contemnors Group Education Program in Los Angeles County (the predecessor of Parents Without Conflict) and a group mediation program for high-conflict litigants in Alameda County, California. The Pre-Contempt/Contemnors program, as previously described, is largely an education and parental skill-building program. The Alameda Program, in contrast, is a far more intensive and expensive therapeutic counseling model in which the group is the main agent of change. Johnston reports that parents were highly satisfied with both models. Both models led to an increase in parental cooperation for both women and men, decreased physical violence, fewer disagreements over children, and an increased understanding of the children's needs. The Alameda group counseling model led to decreased re-litigation rates, whereas the Los Angeles education model did not.[252]

Research on Emotional Flooding

Another tentative confirmation of the value of court-affiliated educational programs comes from psychobiology. Research on the role of education in the management of human emotions seems to show that the roots of the emotional turmoil associated with divorce have a biological basis in the complex neurochemical reactions of the human nervous system. Conflict between parents generates intense emotional reactions and hormonal flows. Psychologists refer to the effects of continuing conflict between parents associated with divorce as an emotional "flooding." Husbands and wives are often so overwhelmed by their partner's negativity and their own reactions to it that they are swamped by dreadful, out-of-control feelings. People who are emotionally flooded cannot hear without distortion nor respond with clearheadedness; they find it hard to organize their thinking, and they fall back on primitive reactions.[253]

Anger, for example, is an emotion often associated with divorce, and can be triggered by arguments and insults between spouses in a deteriorating relationship. The physiological changes associated with anger increase a human being's capacity for vigorous responsive action. Anger increases the heart rate and the amount of adrenaline flowing through the body. It also increases the blood flow to the hands, making it easier to hold a weapon or to slash out.[254]

Psychological research shows that interventions that challenge the thoughts that trigger anger can control that emotion when it is at moderate levels. Effectively timed intervention can provide angry parents with information to challenge the flooding that can overwhelm them. The earlier in the anger cycle the mitigating information is introduced, the more likely it is to reduce anger-provoked responses.[255] Intervention through provision of mitigating information is nowhere near as effective if the hormones generated by anger come to dominate a person's emotional life. This finding strongly suggests that parents should attend education programs as soon as possible after a complaint is filed with the court.

The Role of Education in the Modern Child Custody Court

Educational programs send an appropriate social message to divorcing parents – the community has resources to help you cope with the transitions that divorce requires, but in the end you are still responsible for parenting your children. Both parents and children believe the programs to be of great value. By attending, parents and children increase their understanding of the challenges of family reorganization and conflict and acquire skills to deal with both. Parents who attend seem to improve their behavior, communication, and attitudes. Their children who attend feel less isolated and less powerless. Parents who attend educational programs seem to have greater respect for the legal system because they have more information about how it operates. Overall, experience and evidence indicate that court-affiliated educational programs should be mandatory and be made a central feature of the experience of parents and children in the child custody court.

VII Contrasting Child Custody Court Paradigms

New York and California

A useful way of summarizing the evolution of the child custody court from the sole custody/adversary system to the parenting plan/self-determination model is to compare and contrast New York and California. California has been the leader in implementing the new model, with other states such as Florida, Oregon, Connecticut, and New Jersey not far behind. New York, in contrast, continues to support a more adversarial child custody dispute resolution system.

California was one of the first states to eliminate fault divorce. It is a "pure" no-fault system in which one spouse simply has to allege that the marriage is "irretrievably broken" to obtain a divorce. Fault grounds such as adultery and cruel and inhuman treatment have been eliminated from the divorce law. In practice, this standard means that one parent can get a divorce unilaterally.[256]

In contrast, New York law requires *both* parents to agree to a no-fault divorce. *Both* parents must agree to live "separate and apart" for a year. They must also settle their property, support arrangements, and custody rights in a formal written agreement and comply with the terms of that agreement for one year after it is signed. In effect, each parent can veto the other's divorce by simply not agreeing to it for any reason. If both parents do not agree, the parent who wants the divorce must sue the other for it, and plead and prove fault – adultery or cruel and inhuman treatment.[257]

The fault grounds for divorce in New York are not directly related to child custody decision-making. Adultery, which would qualify as grounds for divorce, for example, does not automatically justify depriving a parent of custody. The court must find that the adulterous conduct has an adverse effect on the child.[258] Nonetheless, the fault divorce system in New York encourages parents who do not reach an agreement to divorce to vent their anger at each other in court pleadings by detailing each other's wrongdoing, which does not encourage parental cooperation for the benefit of their children.

All child custody disputes are heard in a single trial court in California – the superior court. In contrast, New York child custody courts are fragmented as a result of a complex and bewildering organizational structure for the state's trial courts. It is entirely possible for cases involving the same family to be simultaneously proceeding in uncoordinated fashion in different courts.[259] The supreme court (New York's closest equivalent to California's superior court) is the trial court that approves divorces and decides custody claims that arise before the parents are divorced. The family court hears the custody cases of unmarried parents and many post-divorce custody modification requests.[260] Both courts have authority to grant protective orders. This fragmentation makes creating uniform policy and practices for child custody cases especially difficult.

The child custody law of both states is also very different. California's substantive child custody law has a detailed definition of joint physical and joint legal custody.[261] It presumes that it is in the best interest of the child for parents to agree on joint custody. It allows a court to order joint custody on the application of one parent, even if the other does not agree.[262] It explicitly requires child custody courts that make sole custody orders to consider "among other factors, which parent is more likely to allow the child frequent and continuing contact with the noncustodial parent."[263]

As previously discussed, California was the first state to authorize courts to require parents to go to mediation in child custody disputes. The use of mediation has become so extensive in California that it is the primary process for child custody dispute resolution. California also has specific court rules that require parents to attend educational programs. One California court rule stipulates that "[a]fter filing for dissolution or legal separation, those parties with children will be required to attend an educational program designed to inform parents of the effects of divorce or long-term separation on their children. This program is mandatory and must be attended within four months of filing."[264] Family Court Services of the San Francisco Superior Court advises parents that it coordinates Kids Turn, the educational program for children in Bay Area families who are undergoing separation or divorce and described in Chapter VI.[265]

New York's basic child custody statute requires only that the child custody court make orders in the best interests of the child. It does not identify the factors that the court should consider in making a "best interests" determination, other than domestic violence.[266] It makes no mention of the power of the court to award joint custody. Case law in New York holds that "[j]oint custody is primarily encouraged as a *voluntary* alternative for relatively stable, amicable parents behaving in a mature civilized fashion."[267] Most courts and lawyers interpret that statement as allowing a parent who is opposed to joint custody to veto an award of it by the court.[268] New York's statutes do not authorize a judge to order parents into mediation or education programs.

The actual operation of New York's child custody system is more complex than its statutes and court rules indicate. New York case law, particularly in the context of extreme cases in which a parent abducts a child or falsely accuses the other of abuse, suggests parental cooperation should be a factor in child custody determinations.[269] Some New York courts have awarded joint custody even when one parent objects. This variability exists because of the great discretion given to judges in the statute setting out the criteria for making child custody awards. Mediation and parent education programs do exist in different localities, and are affiliated with different courts. Some New York judges strongly suggest that parents attend those programs, and the parents often understand these suggestions as informal orders. New York has also created innovative problem-solving courts that coordinate the treatment of victims of domestic violence and child abuse.[270]

The Paradigms Applied: Harry, Wendy, and Cindy in the Custody Courts of New York and California

Consider how differently Harry, Wendy, and Cindy,[271] a fictitious family, would be treated in the courts of New York and California.

Harry and Wendy began dating 15 years ago while in college. Harry went on to get his master's degree in education, while Wendy went to medical school. After Harry finished his master's degree and obtained a teaching position as an elementary school teacher in a local public school, the couple married. Wendy then continued her medical training, and eventually joined a small pediatric practice. A year later, Wendy gave birth to a baby girl named Cindy.

Cindy was perfectly healthy except for a chronic asthmatic condition that required her to be closely monitored and treated with medication. Harry and Wendy both agreed that they would continue working after Cindy was born, so they hired an *au pair* to help take care of Cindy while they were both at work. Harry was usually the first one home. He would take care of Cindy and prepare dinner for the family. Wendy's practice demanded a great deal of time, but on most nights she managed to get home in time for dinner and also to put Cindy to bed. On weekends, the couple shared responsibility for the household chores and spent quality time with Cindy. Wendy also spent a great deal of time monitoring Cindy's asthma.

Around the time of Cindy's second birthday, the couple lost their live-in help and had difficulty finding suitable care for Cindy. At the same time, Wendy's practice began to thrive, and her income was nearly triple that of Harry's. They decided together that it was in everyone's best interest to have Harry stay home with Cindy while Wendy continued to practice medicine and provide financially for the family.

After quitting his job, Harry took Cindy to early childhood development classes and took on a larger share of the household chores. Wendy stayed as involved with Cindy as her busy practice permitted. She was particularly active in supervising Cindy's medical care.

Two years later, Harry and Wendy enrolled Cindy in a nursery school that Harry had found. Harry took Cindy to school every day, and it was there that he met Missy, Cindy's teacher. By the middle of the school year, Harry and Missy had begun an affair. Wendy's best friend had a son in the class, and she told Wendy that she suspected that Harry and Missy were having an affair. Wendy talked to Harry about her friend's allegation, and Harry confessed to his relationship with Missy. He also said that he was in love with Missy and was not willing to give up his relationship with her. Wendy was angry and hurt by her husband's betrayal and contacted a lawyer about a divorce.

During the negotiations for the divorce, Harry was adamant that Wendy pay him lifetime maintenance, child support, and at least half of the value of her medical practice. He also wanted to continue living in the house with Cindy, wanted Wendy to move out, and wanted Wendy to continue paying all the bills for the home after the divorce was final. Harry and Wendy and their lawyers argued for months over marital assets and a parenting arrangement. Harry was confident that the court would find him to be the "primary care-giver," and completely fit. Wendy, on the other hand, was worried because she had heard that courts favor the primary care-giver and "psychological parent," when one could be identified. She now regretted the decision she had made to continue working and to provide for the family financially. Wendy worried constantly about Cindy's health and wanted to remain an integral part of Cindy's life. She desperately wanted to remain an active parent in order to participate in decisions about Cindy's education, and she wanted to be able to provide medical care to Cindy in the event of an emergency.

Meanwhile, Cindy's asthma seemed to be getting worse, and her teachers reported significant deterioration in her ability to concentrate and her relationship with her peers at school. Cindy seemed to sense that her parents were angry at each other, and withdrew from them. She spent a great deal of time alone in her room. Her parents could not agree on whom her therapist should be.

Wendy approached Harry with a proposal for a joint legal custody arrangement, whereby each parent would have an equal voice in Cindy's child-rearing. Harry told Wendy that he thought it would be best if they did not have joint legal custody because it would be difficult and awkward to co-parent with Wendy in light of all their current disagreements. Harry also felt it would be unnecessary because Wendy would be allowed to visit Cindy every other weekend. He felt that during those times, Wendy would be able to make some decisions regarding Cindy, albeit minor decisions (i.e., what to eat, what to wear, where to go, etc.). While Harry recognized Wendy's expertise as a pediatrician, he felt that he could find another pediatric practice that could take care of Cindy equally well. In the end, Harry offered to agree to joint legal custody if Wendy would agree to his financial terms. Harry felt this was an adequate quid pro quo. Wendy thought Harry was being totally unreasonable, so she asked her attorney to take their dispute to court.

The following is the likely progress of Wendy and Harry's divorce and parenting dispute in the courts of New York:

- The divorce, custody, and financial issues are inextricably intertwined, and conflict is thus prolonged. Since Wendy and Harry have not agreed to live separately and apart and have not settled their parenting and financial disputes in a separation agreement, that ground for divorce is not available to them. Since Harry is the one who wants the divorce, he must sue Wendy for divorce. Since Harry is the one who committed adultery, he does not have a fault ground on which to do so. Wendy can, however, sue Harry for divorce on adultery grounds if she so chooses. She has no incentive to do this at the moment as she does not want to remarry and has greater financial resources than Harry does to wait out the conflict.
- Harry must thus try to persuade Wendy to agree to the divorce by making financial and parenting concessions that may not be in Cindy's best interests.
- Wendy must decide, in turn, if she is prepared to trade custody rights to get Harry to lower his economic demands.
- Local court practices will determine whether Wendy and Harry are required to attend a parent education program or to mediate their dispute before their case is tried. Education is more likely to be mandated than mediation. Harry and Wendy will not be required to attend mediation or education programs in many areas of the state.
- The custody trial, and the process leading up to it, will inflame the conflict between Wendy and Harry still further. One can imagine some of the allegations Harry will make: Wendy puts her career before family, Wendy has no time to care for Cindy, Wendy has little psychological connection to Cindy since Harry is the one who takes the time to raise Cindy, Wendy is seeking custody of Cindy merely to avoid her financial responsibilities. Among Wendy's allegations: Harry is a cheating lecher, Harry used his child-care time to have an adulterous affair with Missy, Harry has not taken the time to concern himself with Cindy's chronic asthma condition, Harry does not really want custody of Cindy; rather, he has tried to use custody of Cindy a tool to force Wendy to pay above and beyond what would have been a fair and reasonable financial settlement.
- Joint custody will likely not be available as an option for the court to consider since Harry opposes it. As Harry is Cindy's primary caretaker and psychological parent, he is likely to be awarded sole

custody, with Wendy relegated to visitation rights. Much will rest on judicial discretion.

In contrast, in California:

- Harry will be able to obtain a divorce from Wendy on the grounds of irreconcilable differences, leaving their financial and parenting issues to be decided separately.
- Harry, Wendy, and Cindy will be ordered to attend a court-affiliated educational program that emphasizes both the importance of keeping Cindy out of their conflict and the importance of her having a relationship with both parents after divorce.
- Harry and Wendy will be required to mediate their parenting dispute before the court tries the case.
- A custody trial in California is as likely to be filled with ugly allegations as a custody trial in New York. The difference is that the trial is much less likely to occur in California because of mandated mediation and education programs.
- The court will be able to order Wendy and Harry to have joint custody of Cindy even though Harry opposes it. Harry will thus have far less leverage trading joint custody for financial concessions from Wendy.

The difference between the child custody courts of California and New York is thus profound. California has made a systematic attempt to develop policies and practices that encourage parents to manage their conflicts over their children responsibly, reach an agreement voluntarily, separate financial issues and grounds for divorce from parenting issues, and keep both involved in the post-divorce life of their child. New York has not.

The anger and sense of betrayal that parents in custody disputes feel are the same in both places. There is certainly no guarantee that Harry and Wendy will reach a voluntary agreement to parent Cindy because of mandated education or mediation, or that the judge will make a wiser decision if their custody dispute is litigated in the courts of California rather than in the courts of New York. Nonetheless, if Cindy had a say in the matter, she would likely prefer that her parents' custody dispute over her be litigated in San Francisco rather than in New York City.

VIII Family Violence

> [A]buse by a family member inflicted on those who are weaker and
> less able to defend themselves – almost invariably a child or a
> woman – is a violation of the most basic human right, the most basic
> condition of civilized society: the right to live in physical security, free
> from the fear that brute force will determine the conditions of one's
> daily life.[272]

The term "family violence" is used here to include both parent-to-parent violence (*domestic violence*) and violence by a parent against a child (*child abuse*).
These problems differ in frequency, effects, and risks. Nonetheless, research
has established a significant connection between domestic violence and child
abuse in families, though estimates of the exact correlation vary widely.[273]
Domestic violence and child abuse allegations in child custody disputes raise
similar problems; when either is alleged, child custody courts must verify the
charges, devise parenting plans that maximize safety, attempt to preserve a
relationship between a violent parent and a child, and coordinate resolution
of the dispute with the criminal justice system and child protective services.
It is therefore valuable to consider them together while remembering that
they are also distinct.

Allegations of family violence raise the already high stakes in a custody
proceeding. The child custody court often has to determine the truth of extremely serious charges against a parent with less than perfect information
and with less than perfect certainty. Evidentiary standards by which courts
assess claims of child abuse or domestic violence in a child custody dispute
vary widely from state to state – from "credible evidence" to "independent
corroboration" to the equivalent of a criminal conviction.[274] Family members are sometimes reluctant or unable to testify. Child sexual abuse, for
example, is difficult to detect because the acts often do not leave definitive
physical signs, occur in secret, and the child is the only witness. As the Vermont Supreme Court stated in ruling in a child custody case in which the
proof of allegations of sexual abuse of a child was less than conclusive: "[I]t

85

may be comforting... to pretend to judicial omnipotence or infallibility, or else simply to ignore ambiguity and doubt. To do either, however, is to deny reality and, indeed, the very humanity of judicial institutions."[275]

Evaluating evidence is not the only challenge the child custody court faces. The court must also decide what effect violence will have on parent-child relationships. Family violence is never admirable, and must always be condemned, but, as we will see, it occurs in degrees and in different contexts. Children often have important emotional and economic ties to violent parents, including one that abused them. As Janet Johnston, one of the nation's leading clinicians and researchers in high conflict divorcing families observed: "All violence is unacceptable . . . however . . . not all violence is the same... [violent] families need to be considered on an individual basis...."[276] The child custody court must inevitably balance the need to protect vulnerable family members from future violence with the need of children to have continuing contact with a dangerous parent. Calculated risks are inevitable in making these determinations.

These incredibly difficult determinations must also be made in a manner that protects the important parental rights of the allegedly violent parent, to respect due process of law, and for practical reasons. A violent parent is more likely to comply with a court order imposing restraints on his or her relationship with the child if the court makes an effort to ensure that the offender perceives the process that resulted in the order as fair. "Researchers evaluating why people obey the law have found that the manner in which an official directive is reached has an independent, and often more powerful, effect than does the outcome of the directive itself. The likelihood of a person's compliance with the dictates of police and probation officers, or with court orders issued in civil or criminal cases, is at least as firmly rooted in his perception of fair process as in his satisfaction with the ultimate result.... [P]rocedural justice research indicates that the use of fair procedures – allowing a person to state their views, ensuring that their perspective is taken seriously, and demonstrating that officials maintain an open mind about this person and their case – enhances a person's sense that authorities are moral and legitimate. This perception facilitates a person's sense of self-worth and, in turn, his degree of compliance..."[277]

This chapter provides examples from actual cases and research data to provide an overview of the challenges that family violence presents to the child custody court. It discusses how the conflict-management services of the child custody court – mediation and education – can help protect members of violent families while engaging them in a measure of self-determination. It then describes supervised visitation, the main tool the child custody court uses to balance the goals of safety and the need for a continuing relationship between a violent parent and the child. Finally, the chapter describes the emerging service of "special mastering" and how it can help families in which violence and high conflict are present.

Chapter IX continues the discussion of violent and high-conflict families by describing Differentiated Case Management (DCM). DCM is a philosophy of judicial administration that asks the child custody court to triage disputes according to the risks they present and to develop service plans for children and parents tailored to the need for intervention.

Child Abuse: Illustrative Case

Mullin v. Phelps[278]: An eight-year marriage produced two boys who were aged six years and one year at the time of the divorce. The Vermont trial court ordered joint custody, with primary physical custody to the father based on the parents' agreement to that plan, despite the custody evaluator's concern about the high level of conflict between the parents. The father moved to modify the court order to grant him sole custody. The mother charged the father with physical abuse, which a mental health evaluation found unsubstantiated. The trial court awarded the father sole custody of both boys.

Two months later, the mother alleged for the first time that the father sexually abused the boys. According to the mother, during visits in the spring and summer, the then five-year-old younger child made three separate requests that she put a stop to the "bug game." Allegedly, this "game" consisted of the father's inserting his finger in the younger child's rectum or placing his penis in the child's mouth. The then ten-year-old older child told the mother that the father had sexually assaulted him five years before, and that the younger child had been similarly assaulted during the previous summer.

A comprehensive investigation by child protective services found no evidence of abuse. One child protection investigator expressed concern that the mother's allegations coincided with the end of the boys' visitation periods with her, a pattern typical of her numerous modification motions. The trial court continued the father's sole custody award unmodified.

About a week later, the father sought permission from the court to relocate to a Western state for a job opportunity. The mother, in response, again alleged sexual abuse, and sought to modify custody. Another court ordered expert evaluation, in which the older child again described incidents of sexual abuse by the father. Again, however, the evaluator rejected the allegations. "The examining psychologist ... concluded that [the older boy's] report of abuse was not credible because it was inconsistent and provided no contextual detail, that the father posed no risk of harm to the safety and welfare of the children, and that the boy's anxious and depressive behavior patterns were the result of the protracted and contentious custody battle, not sexual abuse." The trial court allowed the father to relocate, and required him to provide counseling for the older boy to address the problems created by the reports of abuse.

The mother continued to allege sexual abuse in repeated motions for modification. In a later evaluation, "[the same psychologist] again found the allegations of sexual abuse incredible, and advised that the need for continuity in [the older son's] life weighed in favor of his returning to Utah, despite tensions between the father and son. [The psychologist] also recommended intensive family therapy involving the older son, his father, and his stepmother." At some point, when speaking to the psychologist, the older boy retracted his claim that the father had sexually abused him.

Because of another modification motion by the mother, the younger boy was eventually referred to a prestigious regional medical center for a physical examination, which revealed a slight cleft in his anal opening that could have resulted from old trauma. A psychologist at the medical center recommended a full psychological evaluation of the family and a psychosexual examination of the father – which the trial court ordered.

This time, the evaluation team found the claims of abuse to be credible "despite their similarity to [the older boy's] previous unsubstantiated and retracted claims." The evaluation team concluded that the past evaluations were "unreliable due to the [previous psychologist's] lack of expertise in assessing child victims of sexual abuse." The evaluation team discounted the older child's claims that the mother had coached him and his brother regarding the abuse and had staged incidents to make it appear the boys feared their father. It recommended an immediate shift of custody to the mother and that the father be barred from contact with the boys until he admitted he was an abuser and completed a treatment program.

The evaluation team did not consider the report of the out-of-state psychologist who had conducted the court-ordered psychosexual evaluation of the father. That psychologist concluded that it was "highly unlikely" that the father had sexually abused his children.

The father continued to deny he was an abuser. The trial court concluded that it was more probable than not that he was. The court then transferred custody to the mother, although the father had been the children's primary custodian for six years.

With a dissent, the appellate court affirmed both the trial court's finding that the father was an abuser and the transfer of custody of the boys to the mother. The numerous previous mental health and judicial findings dismissing the allegations of abuse were not controlling, since, based on the evaluation team's report, the trial court had enough evidence to conclude that abuse of the younger son had occurred at least once. A single substantiated allegation of sexual abuse was sufficient to transfer custody.

The appellate court modified the portion of the trial court's order that, as recommended by the evaluation team, conditioned the father's contact with the children on the father's admission of abuse. It remanded the case to the trial court and strongly suggested it order supervised visitation between the boys and the father. Recognizing the risks on all sides, the appellate court concluded:

Thus, the proper course in a case such as this will be found in a resolution that seeks to accommodate the rights and interests of all concerned, not one that may be appropriate if the court managed to get the facts right, but unfathomably destructive if it was mistaken. Limited, supervised visitation, for example, might not provide complete psychological protection for these children if, indeed, their father was guilty of the conduct alleged. In our view, however, that risk is preferable to an unwarranted death sentence on the relationship between this man and his children.

Domestic Violence: Illustrative Case

Borchgrevink v. Borchgrevink[279]: At the time of the custody trial, three children of a marriage were nine, six, and three years old. Following the parents' separation, at the mother's request, the Alaska trial court entered an interim restraining order that gave each parent custody of the children on alternating weeks pending trial.

The testimony of the mother's friends and family established the fact that the father, "commencing early in the marriage and up to the time of separation engaged in a systematic course of conduct...through coercion and threats and most significantly, physical abuse" to intimidate the mother. His controlling behavior included prohibiting the mother from developing relationships outside the home, visiting her brother, and engaging in outside activities without the father's permission. The father's verbal abuse escalated to physical abuse, such as punching her in the face, vehicular assault, kicking, and slapping. On one occasion, the father dragged the mother by the hair through the trailer park where the family resided.

The father did not dispute the allegation that he physically abused the mother, but did disagree about the extent of the abuse. The father testified that the mother verbally abused him. Both the mother and the father agreed that the father's physical violence ended after they separated.

The father was most likely to be abusive when drinking; the children would hide whenever they could when he was angry. Nonetheless, the children, especially the two older boys, witnessed much of the violence and verbal abuse. Both the mother and the father disparaged each other in front of the children.

The trial court found that the violence witnessed by the children "has resulted in the older [boy's] identification with [father] who is perceived as the 'power' parent. For this reason, expressions of preference by the two boys (even aside from the issue of their tender age)...are of little assistance to the [trial] Court in determining legal and physical custody." The children failed to respect the mother's authority at times; the older boy had become more disrespectful of her.

Both parents attended parenting-skills courses, and the father attended an anger-management course. The trial court described the father as "minimizing" the nature and extent of his involvement in domestic violence and its effects on the children. It described the mother as needing to learn to keep her children out of disputes between the parents.

The trial court found the mother to be unemployed and without the resources to support the children or to pay for therapy. The father had a steady job with decent pay. The trial court also found that although the mother was a poor housekeeper, neither the mother's nor the father's residence presented a risk to the children.

Both parents and the trial court believed that continuation of the week-on/week-off physical custody schedule that had been awarded pending trial was not in the children's best interests. The trial court thus awarded primary physical and legal custody to the mother, with liberal visitation rights to the father. It also adopted the recommendations of the custody evaluator that the children receive counseling and that the parents attend parenting classes.

With a dissent, the appellate court affirmed the trial court's order. It rejected the father's argument that the trial court had placed too much emphasis on his acts of domestic violence in shaping the custody award.

Family Violence in the Child Custody Court: An Overview

We do not know with great certainty how many victims of child abuse or domestic violence are involved in custody proceedings. Estimates vary because of different definitions of family violence and inconsistent reporting techniques. Nonetheless, even the lowest estimates indicate that a high level of some violence occurs between parents as their marriages end and they bring their disputes to court.

Domestic Violence

The term "domestic violence," used loosely, can include very different types of behavior. Social scientists tend to define it as a pattern of coercive behavior aimed at the control and intimidation of an intimate partner. These researchers emphasize the overall pattern and context of the violent partner's acts, which can include financial restraints, restrictions on relationships with others, verbal abuse, and acts of physical violence. Social scientists thus can include in the definition of domestic violence acts that are not physically threatening (e.g., verbal statements by a batterer, such as "I don't want you to go out with your sister" or "what do you need a credit card for?") that are designed to discourage a victim of domestic violence from financial or emotional independence. Legal definitions of domestic violence, in contrast, focus on the specific acts of physical or sexual violence committed by the violent partner.[280]

Researchers have developed a number of ways to describe the variety and complexity of different forms of domestic violence.[281] One useful way is the distinction articulated by the interdisciplinary team of psychologist Geri Fuhrmann, social worker Joseph McGill, and law professor Mary O'Connell between "conflict-instigated violence" – physical violence used as a tool of conflict resolution – and the more-threatening "control-instigated violence" that occurs when an aggressor's goal is to dominate his or her partner and is part of a larger and planned pattern designed to break the victim's will.[282] Depending on past behavior, a wife's impulsively throwing a lamp at her husband when she learns of his affair with another woman might fall into the first category. A long-time batterer's slap across a spouse's face designed to remind her of previously inflicted violence and to intimidate her when she states she wants to get a job or go out with friends might fall into the second category.

Divorce is often associated with violence between parents, violence that is hard to uniformly characterize as either conflict- or control-instigated without a detailed examination of the family history. "Incidents of violence (for example, hitting, throwing objects) are quite common at the time a marriage breaks up, and husbands and wives are almost equally likely to engage in violent acts, though women are much more likely to get hurt. Furthermore, allegations of physical abuse are common during divorce negotiations and verifying their frequency or severity is often difficult."[283] The danger that one parent will commit an act of violence against the other parent increases both six months before and six months after the physical separation of parents.[284]

Some estimates state that somewhere between 50% and 80% of parenting disputes referred to court-based mediation programs involve allegations of violence.[285] Another study estimates that 23% of divorcing parents have a history of violence.[286] A study of parents referred to mediation in Portland, Oregon, divided violence into three categories: intimidation (threats, stalking, telephone harassment), physical abuse (e.g., slapping, grabbing, punching) and severe abuse (beating or choking). The most common type of violence alleged was intimidation, reported by 74% of the women and 64% of the men. Physical abuse was reported by 68% of the women and 55% of the men. An alarming 38% of the women and 20% of the men reported severe abuse – the kind of control-instigated violence exemplified by *Borchgrevink*.[287]

In both *Mullin* and *Borchgrevink*, the father was the perpetrator of violence. Research indicates that fathers perpetrate a higher level of violence than mothers, both against their partners and their children. Violence directed toward women is one of the most frequently reported crimes in the United States. While the exact number of incidents is uncertain because of differing definitions of domestic violence, male partners seriously physically abuse about 2 million women every year.[288]

A number of men suffer abuse each year at the hands of their female partners. The physical violence inflicted by women tends to result in less serious injury than that inflicted by men. Janet Johnston and Linda Campbell found men to be the victims of female-initiated violence in 10–15% of their sample of 140 domestic violence cases.[289] Canadian data shows that in 1996, 11% of the victims of domestic violence were male, whereas 89% were female.[290] Survey data from 1994 suggest that women now account for a quarter to a third of all domestic violence arrests, up from less than a tenth a decade ago.[291]

We still have a great deal to learn about the nature and kinds of domestic violence. Some domestic violence is a less-than-admirable response to less-than-admirable behavior by the other parent, and not part of a pattern of attempted control. Recent research suggests that the number of women who hit first or hit back against an intimate partner is greater than initially assumed, and is approximately equal to the number of men who do so, suggesting that programs for the prevention of violence cannot focus on men alone, and be effective. It is nonetheless important to emphasize that whatever the comparative rates of violent acts by gender, researchers generally agree that women suffer more-serious physical injury from intimate violence than men do.[292] An actual case illustrates these findings:

Brown v. Brown[293]: A one-year marriage resulted in a daughter, a divorce, and a custody dispute in an Oklahoma trial court. The neutral mental health evaluator reported that both parents had a good relationship with the child. He recommended custody to the father because of the mother's "tendency towards dissembling and denial, and a high degree of evasiveness in response to questions." Two male witnesses testified that the mother sexually propositioned them.

Evidence at trial established the father's record of violent and aggressive behavior. He once shoved the mother against a doorway and broke the windows in another man's car because he believed, with some justification, that the mother had been carrying on an extramarital affair with the man. During another incident, the father became very upset at the mother's lack of fidelity, and threatened her with violence. The father readily admitted that his temper had then gotten the best of him on those occasions (and a few others). While not condoning the father's behavior, the appellate court found that it did not qualify as "ongoing domestic abuse." It affirmed the trial court's award of custody to the father.

Effects of Family Violence on Children

"[I]t is estimated that 3.3 million children witness domestic violence each year,"[294] though this figure does not tell us how many of their parents are involved in child custody disputes. A New York appellate court recently summarized the effects of children's witnessing violence between parents succinctly: "[T]here is overwhelming authority that a child living in a home where there has been abuse between the adults becomes a secondary victim and is likely to suffer psychological injury. Moreover, that child learns a dangerous and morally depraved lesson that abusive behavior is not only acceptable, but may even be rewarded."[295] There is strong data that suggests children are powerfully affected by being exposed to violence even if they themselves are not actual victims.[296] Children who witness domestic violence are, for example, ten times more likely than those who do not to become either aggressors or victims of domestic violence when they become adults.[297] They also suffer emotional damage – hopelessness and helplessness, anxiety, and an increase in somatic complaints.[298]

Substance Abuse, Mental Illness, and Violence

Violence in divorcing families may be influenced by mental illness and substance abuse, an interrelationship exemplified by the father in *Borchgrevink*, who tended to become violent while drinking. While we cannot pinpoint the relationship with precision, research suggests that substance abuse is an important factor in many high-conflict families, and is related to family violence. One-quarter of the 160 parents in a study of high-conflict families had substance-abuse problems.[299] Drug and alcohol use and abuse seem to be associated with particularly violent forms of battering of partners.[300] Substance abuse also seems to reduce the ability of some parents to care for children.[301]

Child Abuse

Child maltreatment (a generic term for serious harm caused by adults to children) consists of two general categories – abuse and neglect. "Abuse" is used to describe what happens when an adult physically violates a child, whereas "neglect" is used when a responsible adult fails to provide adequate care and supervision for a child. In 2000, "[a]pproximately 879,000 children were found to be victims of child maltreatment. Maltreatment categories typically include neglect, medical neglect, physical abuse, sexual abuse, and psychological maltreatment. Almost two-thirds of child victims (63%) suffer neglect (including medical neglect); 19 percent are physically abused; 10 percent are sexually abused; and 8 percent are psychologically maltreated."[302]

The number of confirmed findings of child abuse or neglect is significantly less than the number reported to child protection agencies. In 2000, child protection agencies received reports of approximately 5 million abused or neglected children. The discrepancy between the number of confirmed findings of child maltreatment by those agencies and the number of reports of maltreatment is explained by the fact that a report to a child protection agency begins a process of assessment; it does not mean that the agency can prove to a court's satisfaction that the child was abused or neglected.[303]

Parents are the principal perpetrators of child maltreatment. Mothers and fathers tend to commit different types of child abuse and neglect. Mothers are significantly less likely than fathers to physically abuse their children. The role of mothers in physical abuse tends to be limited to tolerating and sometimes facilitating abuse by male partners. Mothers, however, are more likely to neglect children than fathers. Mothers tend to be the children's primary care-takers and thus are the parents primarily held accountable for any omissions and or failures in care-taking. Females are thus more often guilty of child neglect than men (87% to 43%). In contrast, men more often than women physically abuse children (67% to 40%) and are far more likely to commit sexual abuse.[304]

Child abuse has devastating consequences for children – acts of abuse are likely to continue after first being committed, victims are likely to be repeatedly abused, and the longer the abusive behavior continues, the more severe the damage to the child.[305]

There are many different kinds of child abuse, and thus the practice has many different negative effects on children, too many to summarize here. Perhaps the most critical fact is that violence begets violence – child abuse, like domestic violence, replicates itself across generations.[306] Children who are abused are much more likely to be abusers themselves when they grow up than children who are not abused. Intervention to treat both the abuser and the abused is critical to break the intergenerational cycle.

Child Sexual Abuse

The discussion in this Chapter focuses on allegations of child abuse – especially child sexual abuse – in divorce-related custody disputes. Child sexual abuse, as the *Mullin* case demonstrates, raises especially difficult issues in the child custody court. Every year, about 500,000 children are sexually abused.[307] Child sexual abuse is thus a small proportion of the overall problem of abuse and neglect but an emotionally powerful one because of the seriousness of the charge and the harm that results.

The *Mullin* case is somewhat atypical because it involves sexual abuse of boys after a father remarries. While boys certainly suffer sexual abuse, "child sexual abuse most commonly involves adult males victimizing young girls."[308] Child-abuse victimization rates are generally similar for male and female victims (11.2 and 12.8 per 1,000 children, respectively), except for victims of sexual abuse, where the rate of abuse is about double for girls.[309] About 1 or 2 of every 20 boys will be sexually abused during childhood, whereas about 4 out of every 20 girls will be abused.[310] Most sex abusers of children are not strangers but fathers and men in long-term relationships with their mothers, and the risk of abuse, particularly of girls, significantly increases following divorce.[311]

How Family Violence Allegations Affect a Child Custody Dispute: An Overview

Allegations of violence dramatically change the nature of a child custody dispute. In effect, they transform a largely private dispute between parents into a proceeding with criminal and child-protection overtones. The focus of the proceeding becomes the determination of whether the parent committed the alleged violent act, and what to do about it. If proven, serious family violence becomes the predominant factor in shaping the court's decision. The court will generally restrict the relationship between the violent parent and the child. Family violence allegations poison the atmosphere between parents, a factor that, combined with safety concerns, makes it even more difficult for the court to facilitate a settlement of a custody dispute. Such cases tend to stay on the court's docket, whereas others are more likely to be settled earlier.

The child custody court faces significant coordination problems when an allegation of family violence is made in a dispute before it, as those same allegations can be the basis of a criminal prosecution or a child protection proceeding. A father who has a sexual relationship with a minor child, for example, commits a serious crime for which he may be prosecuted. Allegations of child abuse and neglect can also trigger an investigation by a state's child protective services (CPS). CPS can initiate a child protection proceeding against the offending parent to terminate that parent's custody rights if it believes the violence allegations are true. To conserve scarce resources, prosecutors and CPS often count on the child custody court to determine the truth and make appropriate orders.[312]

Much progress has been made in recent years in clarifying the relationship between violence and child custody awards in the direction of providing more protection for victims. In 1990, the United States Congress unanimously adopted a resolution urging states to revise their child custody statutes to create a presumption that batterers [parents who use violence as part of a pattern of control and intimidation of their partners] should not be awarded custody.[313] In 1994, the National Council of Juvenile and Family Court Judges created a *Model Code on Domestic and Family Violence* that contains a rebuttable presumption that abusive parents should not be awarded sole or joint custody.[314] Many states responded by enacting statutes that required child custody courts to take a proven allegation of child abuse[315] or domestic violence[316] into account in a child custody determination. A 1997 law review comment finds that "there are custody statutes which address domestic violence in forty-four states and the District of Columbia."[317] Even without specific statutory authorization, child custody courts have the power to take the risk of future child abuse into account in a custody determination and to order parents to take concrete steps to protect children against it.[318]

"True" and "False" Allegations

Accusations of being an abuser or a batterer made in a child custody dispute are extremely serious. As one state supreme court has noted, "a parent's reputation, access to the custody of her children and even liberty may be lost over a false accusation."[319] There are documented instances in which children have made allegations of child abuse that later turned out to be false.[320] The focus on false claims that follows must be placed in context. The problem of family violence is very serious, and a focus on false claims should not be taken to minimize it. "We must always temper the incidence of true disclosures with the possibility of false ones."[321]

Child custody disputes create a particularly troublesome setting for accusations of family violence. Divorce is often a time for disclosure of violence that was previously hidden from public view. Parents may leave the marriage to protect the child and themselves against further violence. On the one hand, parents must be encouraged to bring allegations of violence to the attention of authorities who have the power to provide protection to the vulnerable. On the other hand, parents in a custody dispute are often very angry at each other, misinterpret each others' behavior, and have an incentive to disclose previously unreported child abuse to the court, as the court is more likely to award the non-violent parent greater rights. This constellation of factors leads to some false or exaggerated allegations of violence or abuse.

An additional short case study further illustrates the problem of potential miscommunication and misinterpretation of parental behavior by angry parents.

Lenderman v. Lenderman[322]: The mother accused the father of getting into the bathtub naked with their four-year-old daughter every night. She also alleged that the father played on the living room floor with the daughter every night and that: "[h]e has kissed her face and kissed her stomach as if she were a grown woman. And he would absolutely get up [from] the floor with an erection." The father, in turn, accused the mother of threatening to kill the daughter, stating that she said she wished the child had died at birth. He further accused the mother of jerking the daughter around, hollering at her, and throwing a portable typewriter at her and at him. The Arkansas appellate court remanded the case to the trial court for further fact finding.

In *Lenderman*, the father takes a bath with his daughter and rolls her around on the floor. These acts may simply indicate bad parental judgment that can be influenced with education and therapy or they may be part of a more sinister pattern of behavior. There is apparently no physical evidence that confirms the mother's allegations of sexual abuse. The father has made serious counter-accusations against the mother of family violence. Not surprisingly, the appellate court sends the matter back to the trial court for more fact-finding.

Different definitions of "false" allegations cloud the question of whether false allegations of child abuse are more common in child custody disputes than allegations made against parents who are not involved in custody disputes. False allegations should not be confused with "unsubstantiated" or "unfounded" allegations as determined by a child protection agency. When a child protection agency finds an allegation to be unsubstantiated, it means only that the agency is of the opinion that there is not enough evidence to continue investigation and file an action in court. A child custody court is not bound by that finding, as it is possible that with further investigation and evaluation, some unsubstantiated allegations might eventually be validated. False allegations, furthermore, can encompass a variety of different kinds of behavior ranging from deliberate, malicious false reports to misinterpretation of events and intentional or unintentional coaching of children.

Rates of reported child sexual abuse seem to be about six times higher in families involved in child custody disputes than in the general population.[323] There is significant debate about whether the rate of false allegations (however defined) is especially high. Some argue that the elevated rates of reporting reflect higher rates of abuse in divorced families; others suggest that the higher rates of reporting reflect higher rates of emotional distress and anxiety associated with child custody disputes. Nicholas Bala summarizes the available Canadian data that exposes the difficulties that child custody courts face when they assess the truth of allegations of family violence:

Some studies suggest that allegations of physical or sexual abuse are made in only 1%–2% of *litigated* cases, though in some locales at some points in time as many as 8%–10% of *litigated* cases may raise child abuse allegations. In the divorce context, the rate of unfounded or unproven allegations of child abuse seems much higher than the rate of unproven allegations of domestic violence. Research suggests that in the context of parental separation, as many as 25%–75% of allegations of child abuse are unproven in family law proceedings. However, unfounded allegations of child abuse are mainly due to poor communication and misunderstanding rather than deliberate manipulation or a desire for revenge. Especially if the children are young, suggestive questioning by a parent with a negative attitude towards the statements that may be interpreted as indicative of abuse. Parents who have a poor relationship with each other may misinterpret innocent acts as abusive.[324]

A 1998 study of abuse allegations in child custody disputes in the Australian Family Court (Project Magellan) sheds further light on the problem.[325] The Australian research team carefully tracked 200 custody and visitation cases in which child abuse of all kinds was alleged. The study was done in two cities – Canberra, a small city (and Australia's national capital), and Melbourne, Australia's second largest city.

The resulting data did not support a blanket conclusion that allegations of child abuse made for the first time in a custody dispute should be treated as presumptively false. Rather, it supported the idea that each should be taken seriously and evaluated on the merits. The researchers studied a subset of 30 cases and found that 9% of allegations were false, the same rate of false allegations as those reported to the Australian CPS in traditional child protection cases. They also noted that a different study of 50 custody and access cases conducted the previous year produced similar findings.[326] These results are also similar to the results in some other studies conducted in the United States.[327] Other researchers conclude that the rate of false allegations is much higher, ranging from 35% to 50%.[328]

Despite the findings, statistics about how many allegations of violence are true, how many are false, and which gender makes the allegations and why are irrelevant to the child custody court's responsibility in any individual case. A society dedicated to due process cannot rely on statistics to predetermine the result when such important interests as parent-child relationships, safety, and reputation are at stake. All allegations of child sexual abuse must be taken seriously and investigated according to the best techniques available, without preconceptions as to their validity. The child custody court must recognize the possibility that in any particular case, the allegations may be true or false, and must apply rules allocating the burden of persuasion fairly. It must also recognize that there are many different possible reasons as to why false allegations may be made, and treat them accordingly.

Evaluating whether a child's allegations of sexual abuse are true is a particularly complex and demanding task that sometimes leads to inconclusive results. As seen in *Mullin*, it can be extremely difficult to validate sex abuse allegations with a high degree of confidence.[329] "[T]here are no diagnostic behavioral indicators of sexual abuse that occur in all or even most abused children but that are simultaneously absent in all nonabused children."[330] Different mental health professionals can attempt to validate allegations of sexual abuse of a young child and come to different conclusions.[331]

In *Mullin*, there was some physical evidence to support the abuse allegation, but it was not definitive. The other indications of sexual abuse in the case were also not conclusive. *Mullin* illustrates the fact that some children delay disclosure of child abuse for a substantial period of time after the abuse occurs.[332] The timing of the mother's abuse complaints came after the children's visitation with her ended, raising a concern that she was making the complaints because of emotional loss or to seek legal advantage. On the other hand, extended visitation periods provided the mother with time for significant face-to-face contact with the children when she could learn from them in detail about what happened at their father's house. One child recanted his allegations of abuse and stated that the mother influenced him to make them. These factors do not definitively rule out abuse, but cast doubt on the certainty of the conclusion. Doubt is reinforced by the fact that a series of mental health evaluations concluded that the abuse did not occur. A later, perhaps more sophisticated, evaluation came to a different conclusion. That evaluation, however, did not take into account a mental health evaluation of the father that seemed to exonerate him.

It is hard to review the *Mullin* case and conclude confidently that the father did or did not commit the abuse. One can only pity the family because it endured the ongoing turmoil of repeated evaluations that did reach a definitive conclusion.

Dealing with "False" Allegations

The child custody court must also be careful not to punish parents who make false allegations of child abuse indiscriminately. Social policy favors bringing allegations of abuse to the attention of authorities. Abuse allegations in a child custody dispute can reveal secrets that were once hidden. While the exact number is disputed, a significant percentage of allegations of violence made for the first time during a child custody dispute are later verified. Indeed, as *Mullin* illustrates, some allegations of violence are validated even after they are repeatedly dismissed. Some parents may leave their spouses because they can no longer tolerate the abuse of their children. Rather than being a cause of a child abuse allegation, the custody dispute results from the fact that the child was actually abused.

There is no doubt that false allegations cause great harm – reputations are ruined and parent-child relationships are seriously harmed. Courts must make distinctions about the motivation for a false allegation in determining the reasonableness of the complaining parent's conduct.

Most false allegations of abuse seem to be mistakes made in the heat of emotional distress and misunderstanding and miscommunication. Those who make false allegations of this kind should be open to information and analysis that refutes the charges they made, and be happy if the abuse is proved to be false, as their children will not have suffered. A few false allegations are deliberate lies based on suggestions made to susceptible children by malicious parents who will go to any lengths to win a custody victory and are not open to contrary information and conclusions. There is a significant moral difference between these two categories of offenders, and the punishment should be structured accordingly.[333]

In all other kinds of civil cases, courts routinely assess the motivation behind litigant conduct. They punish "frivolous" conduct with various levels of sanctions appropriate to the misconduct depending on the litigant's state of mind.[334] They can also do it in the context of false allegations of family violence in custody disputes. False allegations based on misunderstanding or miscommunication, in which the accusing parent has a reasonable, albeit misguided, belief in the truth should be remedied with therapy, education, and perhaps payment of the legal fees of the falsely accused parent. Deliberate, false allegations, in contrast, must be seriously punished when discovered. In Minnesota, for example, it is a crime for a parent to deliberately falsely accuse the other parent of abuse.[335] Perjury prosecutions may be appropriate. In the most egregious cases, parents who make deliberately false accusations of child abuse may lose their parenting rights because they show a "lessened ability and willingness to cooperate and work with the other parent in their shared responsibilities for the child," in the language of Maine's custody statute.[336]

Violence-Sensitive Mandated Education and Mediation

Whether parents who allege violence should be included in court-mandated mediation is a subject of intense debate. This issue intersects with a larger philosophical debate over the approach the child custody court should take to violent parents. Two distinct points of view can be identified. In one, domestic violence is a crime, and the child custody court's prime responsibility is to punish the offender and protect the victim. In this view, the court should separate the offender from his or her children and the other parent to reduce the risk of future violence. Above all, abusers should be held accountable for their behavior and prevented from further opportunities to control the victim. Victims of domestic violence are seen as too incapacitated to negotiate directly with the aggressor on an equal footing. Mediation thus has no place in child custody disputes involving violence because it allows the criminal to negotiate his or her punishment with the incapacitated victim. Violent parents' promises of rehabilitation are simply further attempts to manipulate and control.

An alternative view of domestic violence in child custody disputes also stresses safety, but includes therapy and rehabilitation. It assesses domestic violence in the context of a particular family. In this view, violence is always deplorable, but is not always part of a pattern by a batterer to control and manipulate a victim. Sometimes it is instigated by conflict or as a response to provocation. The future danger that the violent parent presents must be assessed in the proper context. Future safety is the primary goal of court intervention, but children, and often the other parent, may still need and want a relationship with the offender in the future. At least some victims of domestic violence are deeply ambivalent about their abusive partners. They continue to love them, are afraid of them, and do not want the offender locked up but want their behavior to change.[337] Victims of domestic violence are not presumptively incapacitated but are the best judges of what is good for them and their children. Under this view, mediation with safety precautions helps victims of violence exercise a measure of self-determination, as well as develop realistic plans for safety in future relationships with the batterer. With support and assurances of safety, they are capable of making decisions for themselves about what kind of relationship they should have with the aggressor.

The American Law Institute (ALI) recently completed work on its *Principles of the Law of Family Dissolution* and addressed the question as to whether domestic violence should preclude court-affiliated education and mediation. As previously discussed, the ALI is an influential organization of judges, practicing lawyers, and law professors.

The *ALI Principles* strongly and appropriately encourage courts to be sensitive to domestic violence risks in formulating parenting plans. Courts are required to develop a screening process to identify cases in which there is "credible evidence" that domestic violence has occurred, and to conduct evidentiary hearings to evaluate them.[338] When domestic violence is proved, "the court should impose limits that are reasonably calculated to protect the child or child's parent from harm."[339]

Education Programs

The *ALI Principles* cautiously allow courts to require parents to attend court-affiliated educational programs, including those that provide parents information about "mediation or other non-judicial procedures designated to help them achieve an agreement."[340]

No one should be deluded into believing that a 4- to 6-hour educational intervention or mediation can change the underlying dynamics and causes of family violence. Courts and society are increasingly aware of the limitations of treatment programs in modifying the behavior of batterers.[341] Such violent parents need far more intensive intervention beyond what an educational program aimed at the entire universe of divorcing parents can provide. Educational programs can, however, promote recognition and understanding of the problems of family violence and refer parents to appropriate programs and resources. A P.E.A.C.E. Program evaluator provides one example: "One woman labeled her husband an abuser during her group session. The husband, in a separate group, presented some of his insights into the couple's interactions. Later he admitted having heard the views 'from the other side' of similar situations which he found helpful and insightful. At the end of the evening he inquired about getting therapy for himself."[342] Hopefully, he did.

Mandated court-affiliated parent education programs are already becoming increasingly sensitive to domestic violence.[343] Many education programs, for example, exclude domestic violence victims if they make a confidential request for exclusion. Many programs schedule an abusive parent on a different night from the victim. They also provide security for all participants.[344]

Court-affiliated parent education programs are also modifying their message about post-divorce parenting relationships from "parents should cooperate for the benefit of the children" to "parents should cooperate if it is safe for parents and children to do so."[345] Many programs emphasize the notion that parallel parenting is more appropriate than cooperative parenting if parents engage in conflict-instigated violence. Finally, court-affiliated educational programs are developing specialized curriculums for high-conflict and violent families. Programs for children can also provide at least minimal counseling for those children who witness violence, and can teach them peaceful conflict-resolution techniques.[346]

Mediation

Reflecting concerns about the risks of coercion and intimidation in mediation exemplified by custody disputes involving domestic violence, the *ALI Principles* reject mandatory mediation for all parents.[347] Parents mediate under the *ALI Principles* only if both want to. The ALI recognizes that its "voluntary" position is inconsistent with the mediation statutes in many states that either mandate mediation for all custody disputes or authorize the court to use its discretion to order unwilling parents to mediate.[348]

Although the ALI's position that participation in mediation should be voluntary for all parents is superficially attractive, it undermines the welfare of children and parents. As discussed in previous chapters, only very few parents at the lowest level of conflict and with the highest regard for the welfare of their children voluntarily attend parent education and mediation. Without mandatory attendance, most parents and children do not get the benefits that mediation provides.

The ALI mentions, but does not emphasize, parents' overwhelming satisfaction with mandated parent education and mediation and their distaste for the adversary process. Parents who are compelled to attend both parent education and mediation find the experience to be of significant value, even if they did not want to participate initially. Virtually all parents who attend court-affiliated education programs – the overwhelming majority of whom would not attend without a court order – believe that they learned something important about themselves and their children. Parents, in essence, have overwhelmingly approved mandatory education and mediation after being exposed to it. Their only regret is that they were not required to attend earlier in the divorce process.

The ALI does not mandate mediation for all parents because mandated mediation will compel some victims of domestic violence to meet their abusers face-to-face. In such a situation, there is a danger that a true batterer can coerce the victim into a settlement that threatens the safety of the victim and the children. There is no doubt that batterers can be quite cunning or are in denial about their behavior. There is also no doubt that many domestic violence victims fear the batterer and fear losing their children, a weakness that batterers can exploit in traditional mediation. Some batterers contest custody in order to further intimidate and control their victims.

Since mediation encourages face-to-face communication between parents, batterers can use it as a tool to manipulate their victims further.

Nonetheless, a policy that exempts all who allege they are victims of violence from mandated mediation excludes from mediation too many parents who could benefit from it, and rewards false or exaggerated allegations of violence. Incidents of violence are quite common at the time a marriage dissolves. They often involve both parents, not just one. All violence between partners, while deplorable, does not constitute a pattern of domestic violence that should disqualify parents from mediation. There is not a "one size fits all families" solution to the question as to whether victims of domestic violence should mediate parenting issues with the batterer, assuming that risks to their safety of coerced settlements can be minimized.

No one can, in good conscience, advocate forcing an unprotected battered woman who is a victim of a calculated pattern of control and intimidation to mediate with a batterer. Indeed, most states that mandate mediation create an exception of this type for victims of domestic violence.[349] Recognition that a battered woman whose will has been broken should not be forced to mediate does not mean that all victims of different levels of violence should be precluded from the choice of mediating with safety and special precautions.[350]

Absolutely barring victims of domestic violence from mediation does not recognize their capacity for self-determination. Many victims of domestic violence will not choose to opt out, and will benefit if they mediate. Research suggests that victims of domestic violence want to mediate if they feel the process is safe.[351] They report as much satisfaction, if not more, with the mediation process as women who do not experience domestic abuse. Many domestic violence victims want to remain with their partners if the abuse stops; others who divorce their abusive spouse also want to mediate post-divorce parenting relationships. Mediation can help both groups devise a detailed parenting plan that includes safety precautions and is based on the principle of parallel, not cooperative, parenting. Furthermore, nothing precludes a victim of domestic violence who mediates from filing criminal charges against the batterer.

There is no evidence that most domestic violence victims feel coerced into settlement through mediation. Indeed, they do not expect the violence to continue (a potentially problematic assessment for some whose risks victims should be informed about) and object to being barred from mediation. Victims believe that mediation will give them a safe forum in which to deal with visitation and support issues. Empirical studies of custody mediation in Ohio and Maine report that victims of domestic violence favor mediation over attorney-negotiated settlements. "More women [who are victims of domestic violence] reported feeling pressure to settle *outside* mediation than in mediation. . . . Clearly, not all women feel a need to cut off all contact with [an abusive] former spouse. Adherence to such assumptions places all abused women into a single group and ignores evidence suggesting there is much variability among abused women as a class."[352]

Some victims of domestic violence want to mediate and are generally not well protected by the adversary process. For many victims, the realistic choice is between some protection from coerced choice in mediation, or no protection at all. The ALI notes, but does not emphasize, the research findings in which participants have more favorable reactions to mediation than litigation.[353] While it is a theoretical possibility, litigation is often not a feasible option for many domestic violence victims. They do not have the money to pay counsel and must join the increasingly large ranks of *pro se* litigants.

Mediation may also have benefits for victims of domestic violence. Trained mediators may be better able to identify domestic violence victims and help them develop safety plans than litigants in a custody dispute who are not represented by counsel. The adversary process may also encourage batterers to deny their conduct, while education and mediation may encourage them to make commitments to future treatment, particularly if the batterers feel their perspective is heard in mediation even though their violent behavior is condemned. There is some evidence that "voluntary, multi-session mediation is more effective in preventing future violence than either coerced mediation or lawyer negotiations."[354] Parenting plans devised in mediation and with the benefit of education tend to be more specific than court orders. The more specific the plans are, the more the provisions can be tailored to address risks of violence, particularly when children are exchanged between parents for visits.[355]

The ALI's position is "due in large part to the sense of many involved in the project that the quality of mediation nationwide was not yet at the level to justify a broad, mandatory approach."[356] It does not take into account the fact that mediation programs are integrating violence-sensitivity in their curriculums and operational protocols to recognize the need for differential treatment of high conflict and violent families.[357] The *Model Standards of Practice for Family and Divorce Mediation* include the following basic principle:

Some cases are not suitable for mediation because of safety, control or intimidation issues. A mediator should make a reasonable effort to screen for the existence of domestic abuse prior to entering into an agreement to mediate. The mediator should continue to assess for domestic abuse throughout the mediation process.[358]

The *Model Standards* require mediators to be trained in domestic violence and child abuse if the mediator participates in family disputes that involve such behavior. They also require mediators to consider taking concrete steps to structure the mediation process to ensure a safe environment for victims and children when those mediator find that violence appears to be present. These steps include: considering separate sessions for victim and batterer, even if the batterer does not agree to them; suggesting the need for an advocate to a victim; referring the victim and the family to community resources;

developing a safety plan; and, if necessary, terminating the mediation.[359] The *Model Standards* thus incorporate state laws such as California's that require the mediator to meet separately with parents where one of them has formally accused the other of domestic violence.[360] Finally, if either of the parents discloses child abuse, or credibly threatens the other with violence, the *Model Standards* suspend the mediator's general obligation of confidentiality.[361] The ALI, too, endorses these principles.[362]

In summary, the potential participation of victims of domestic violence should not exclude court mandates for parent education and mediation. A screening process should be developed through which a parent who is a victim of domestic violence is able to opt out of mandated services. The decision to opt out should be made after the advantages and disadvantages of participation are explained to the victim and the victim is provided with a confidential setting in which to express any fears. Mediation should proceed if requested by the victim and if conducted by specially trained mediators. Mediation programs should assume a continuing obligation to both screen participants for family violence and take appropriate safety measures if previously undetected violence is discovered. Through these measures and polices, parents and children in violent families can benefit from a safe environment in which they can plan their future relationships.

Supervised Visitation

Even after the violence allegation is sustained, the child custody court must continue to balance competing values and risks as it develops a parenting plan that protects victims while allowing a violent parent to maintain some kind of relationship with the child. Violent parents must get the message that their conduct is unacceptable, and steps must be taken to minimize the continuing risks they present to the other parent and the children. Children exposed to violence must understand that, as adults, they should not replicate the patterns of violent behavior they witnessed as children.

On the other hand, all violent parents cannot and should not be prevented absolutely from seeing their children. If they were, a large number of children would not have contact with one parent or the other, often on the basis of allegations that are not conclusively proven. A court cannot ignore the significant emotional bond that often exists between violent parents and children. Psychologists agree that visitation is generally beneficial to both children and parents. "Even where a parent has been abusive, contact in a safe setting allows a child to come to terms with an abusive parent and may serve to avoid destructive repetitions later in life."[363]

In *Mullin*, for example, the father was the primary custodian of the children for 6 years before the court finally determined he abused his children. In *Brown*, the court found that both parents had a good relationship with the children despite the violence in their relationship. More troubling, in

Borchgrevink, the children perceived the father as the "power parent," a perception that had to be addressed in their program of therapy and recovery, a goal that would be hard to achieve if the father were barred from participating in the program.

Supervised visitation is the child custody court's most effective tool to ensure that the violent parent has safe but meaningful interaction with his or her children. It is particularly useful for parents and children during the period in which the court assesses and resolves allegations of violence. Child abuse, neglect, domestic violence, threats or past acts of abduction, mental illness, persistent violation of a custody order, alcohol or drug addiction, and interference by one parent with the visitation of the other may compel a court to order a parent to visit with the child under the watch of a "neutral." In Arizona, for example, the court must order supervised visitation if it finds that regular visitation with a violent parent would endanger a child's physical health, emotional development, or overall best interests.[364]

Supervised visitation allows the court to compromise between terminating a violent parent's relationship with the child altogether and not restricting it at all. The level of supervision that a court can order for a parent's visitation with a child can vary considerably – from nothing beyond supervised transfers of a child from one parent to the other, to visitation in the presence of a relative or friend, to visitation in the presence of a professional supervisor, to visitation combined with education or therapy. Maricopa County (Phoenix, Arizona), for example, offers a minimally supervised program that helps parents without legal representation who have problems gaining access to their children. Termed "Expedited Visitation Services" (EVS), the program seeks to establish a regular and predictable "visitation habit" while ensuring that families comply with a court order.[365] EVS schedules conferences between parents in an attempt to resolve visitation problems, monitors visitation-compliance through telephone calls with each parent, and sets up visitation exchanges at neutral locations. In Massachusetts, an interdisciplinary group of judges, lawyers, and mental health professionals has developed an assessment scale for judges to help them determine the appropriate form of supervision for a particular family.[366] Some states require as a condition of visitation that an abuser admit abuse or obtain the consent of the children.[367]

Parents subject to supervised visitation – particularly those who deny their responsibility for violence – obviously chaff under the restrictions that supervised visitation places on their relationship with their children. Conversely, victimized parents and children sometimes do not want any contact with the violent parent, and are dissatisfied with a supervised visitation order. Supervised visitation cannot please everybody, and does involve some level of risk to safety, but it is usually better than any of the other alternatives available to the child custody court.

Supervised visitation has evolved from a service used primarily in child protection matters to one that serves divorcing parents and children in custody disputes as well. It comes in two general forms. In one, the parents select an individual to supervise visitation, often a relative or a friend. In the other, supervised visitation is provided in a program organized by a court-affiliated agency.

Supervised visitation programs have significant advantages over supervised visitation supervisors chosen by parents. Family members may be unwilling to serve. Even if they are, often parents cannot agree on who should supervise. A family member supervisor may also have difficulty maintaining objectivity when challenged by one parent or the other.

In contrast, a professionally organized supervised visitation program provides the parents with a neutral and safe setting for visitation. It provides the family with objective supervisors who care only for the health and welfare of the child. There is much less risk that the supervisor, unlike an individual selected by the parents, will be vulnerable to a parent's demands or threats. Moreover, organized programs reduce the risk of a violent eruption by providing security and staggering each parent's arrival and departure time. Supervised visitation centers can arrange the timing for drop-offs and pick-ups of children so that only one parent is present, thus minimizing the possibility of threats or conflict on those occasions.

A typical visit in a professionally supervised visitation program takes place in a cheerfully decorated room filled with toys and games. Supervisors remain in close proximity and observe the parent-child interaction. Supervisors are generally passive and do not interfere unless the child is in distress or a program rule is violated. Parents are prohibited from whispering to the child, making negative comments about the other parent or the child's extended family, or forcing any physical contact onto the child.

Following each visit, the supervisor records a detailed entry into the child's file describing the parent-child interaction. Should either parent petition for modification of visitation, these records and the testimony of visitation supervisors can be extremely valuable evidence. Courts frequently call on visitation supervisors to testify.

Research indicates that supervised visitation can play a major role in constructively managing high-conflict families. A recent study of Heritage House, a supervised visitation center in St. Louis, Missouri, for example, shows that during six months of program participation, the frequency and consistency of the non-custodial parent's access to children increased dramatically and conflict between the parents decreased.[368]

Supervised visitation programs face serious challenges. Often, they must respond to the needs of deeply wounded children. "The children who use supervised visitation services are highly vulnerable and frightened and often depleted in coping resources. The adults in their lives have not kept them safe, and to expect these children to trust an unfamiliar supervisor to provide safety may be unrealistic."[369]

Child custody courts face particularly difficult decisions about when to end supervised visitation. There are obvious risks if supervised visitation is terminated too early or if it goes on too long. Supervised visitation is generally thought of as a temporary solution to a risky situation.[370] The children need very careful monitoring and evaluation before being returned to more routine visitation. If fearful and depressed children want visitation to continue, long-term supervised visitation should be considered as an alternative to suspending visitation entirely. A comprehensive study of supervised visitation programs found that once the program ended, about half the parents reported continuing conflicts over visitation and about one-third reported no improvement or resolution.[371]

Limitations on resources prevent greater use of supervised visitation, and restrict its availability for long-term service to conflicted parents and traumatized children. A survey conducted by the Association of the Bar of the City of New York of family court judges in New York City found that the judges polled observed a need for supervision in 106 new cases in a single week, more than enough to overwhelm existing programs.[372]

Supervised visitation programs thus need to be expanded and new programs created. Funding for supervised visitation is hard to obtain because many believe that high-conflict families bring their troubles upon themselves and do not deserve help from public resources.[373] Some states have nonetheless recognized that children's needs for supervised visitation should outweigh perceptions of parental conduct by passing legislation to provide funding for supervised visitation centers.[374]

Special Masters and Parenting Coordinators

A new type of professional is emerging to help highly conflicted families – a combination educator, mediator, and limited-purpose arbitrator in parenting disputes. These professionals operate under different names, either "special master" or "parenting coordinator." Many have mediation or mental health backgrounds.

In September 2000, the Family Law Section of the American Bar Association and the Johnson Foundation sponsored an interdisciplinary conference (the Wingspread Conference) on high-conflict custody cases that designed an action plan for reforming the legal system for the benefit of children. One of the conference's recommendations was that courts appoint "[p]arent monitors, coordinators, or masters who are professionals trained to manage chronic, recurring disputes, such as visitation conflicts, and to help parents adhere to court orders" to protect the children of such parents.[375] Generically, all of these designations will be referred to here as "special master."

The concept of a special master to assist the court by supervising the activities of parties has been extensively developed in non-family law areas. The *Federal Rules of Civil Procedure* allow judges in civil cases to appoint a master in complex situations that require a high level of expertise to find the facts in order to render a decision or provide detailed supervision of a judicial decree.[376] Delegating such tasks to a master benefits judges, leaving them free to manage their calendars and cases more efficiently. Special masters have, for example, been used in a wide variety of disputes such as school desegregation cases and the dispute between New York and New Jersey over ownership of Ellis Island.[377]

Some child custody courts have appointed special masters for high-conflict families, including those whose history includes violence. Child custody court professionals are beginning to integrate the concept of masters into their case planning and management.[378] Typically, courts have appointed trained private family lawyers, mediators, or mental health professionals to perform the role of special master embodied in a written stipulation of the parents filed with the court.

A few states have enacted statutes that authorize courts to appoint special masters in high-conflict child custody disputes. In Oklahoma's statute, for example:

1. Parenting coordinator means a [qualified] neutral third party to hear and decide issues of dispute authorized in an order by the court appointing the parenting coordinator in any action for divorce, paternity, or guardianship where minor children are involved; and

2. 'High-conflict case' means any action for divorce, paternity, or guardianship where minor children are involved and the parties demonstrate a pattern of ongoing:
   a. litigation,
   b. anger and distrust,
   c. verbal abuse,
   d. physical aggression or threats of physical aggression,
   e. difficulty in communicating about and cooperating in the care of their children, or
   f. conditions that in the discretion of the court warrant the appointment of a parenting coordinator.[379]

The special master functions much like a trustee in a bankruptcy case. A bankruptcy trustee supervises the daily operations and plans of a financially troubled business with the goal of restoring it to viability. Similarly, by supervising the parents, the special master hopes to help them develop a viable working relationship (usually parallel parenting) for the benefit of their children. The special master helps parents develop conflict management skills through intensive education, mediation, and therapy.

A judge in an overcrowded child custody court cannot regulate the day-to-day details of the life of a child of highly conflicted parents. The court cannot be expected to listen to disagreements such as whether the father sends the children home with their dirty laundry or whether the mother tells the children that father's new wife used to be an exotic dancer. The special master can.

For their daily disputes, parents communicate with the special master much more than the court. The special master can monitor whether the parents are complying with the requirements of supervised visitation or other court orders. The special master meets with parents and children regularly, documents the family's progress, and, at least initially, reviews the custody arrangements and child care issues almost on a daily basis. The special master can provide intensive education and mediation as the situation merits. Meetings between the special master and the parents are usually informal, and can include both parents, each parent individually and the children, or both parents and children separately and together. If education and mediation do not result in an agreement on a particular matter, the special master acts as decision-maker whose rulings are subject to minimal judicial review.

A special master is thus an arbitrator, albeit an arbitrator who also acts as an educator and a mediator. The power and legitimacy of a special master generally comes from the fact that parents appoint the master by voluntary agreement and define the master's powers in a written stipulation filed with the court. "The parties' consent prevents this broad delegation of judicial authority from being unlawful."[380]

The areas in which a special master can make decisions for the parents are limited. Usually, for example, the stipulation prohibits the master from making changes to an existing custody determination, making relocation orders, or substantially altering existing visitation schedules. The special master, for example, cannot change legal custody from one parent to the other or allow a parent to relocate. The court still decides larger issues such as these. The special master decides details such as car-pool schedules and after-school recreation plans for children and holiday scheduling. The special master may have to manage a child's medical care when parents cannot agree. The special master is paid to listen to matters like these, to encourage compromise, and to make decisions for the parents, if necessary.

The authority of a private person who assumes such great power over the lives of parents and children must be legitimate, and the special master must be accountable to the court for his or her actions and decisions. On the other hand, if the special master's authority is unduly undermined by judicial intervention, high-conflict parents are likely to perpetuate their conflict-ridden ways. They will endlessly appeal to the judge from the special master's decisions.

A voluntarily appointed special master generally files a report with the court with his or her recommendations on a disputed matter, which the parents can challenge. Pending judicial review of the master's decision, the master's recommendation remains in effect. Courts generally uphold the decisions of the voluntarily appointed special master unless they perceive abuse of discretion, bias, or serious wrongdoing. In other words, as discussed in Chapter V, courts treat the decisions of a voluntarily appointed special master with about the same deference that they treat the decisions of an arbitrator in commercial matters.

An *involuntarily* appointed special master has very limited authority because a court delegating binding decisions to a private person without parental consent infringes on "the constitutional right of every citizen and every litigant to return to courtroom litigation."[381] If parents do not consent to the appointment of a special master, the court can still refer the dispute to a special master for fact-finding and recommendations over their objections. However, the involuntary special master can only make advisory findings that the court must review in greater depth at a contested hearing and make an independent decision about whether to adopt the findings.

Some states take a more restrictive view of the power of arbitrators in child custody disputes, even those appointed with the voluntary agreement of both parents. New York courts, for example, have held that courts should not give deference to arbitrators' decisions in child custody disputes as they do in contract disputes or securities cases because of the transcendent judicial responsibility to make decisions in the best interests of children.[382] Some other states view agreements to arbitrate child custody disputes more favorably than New York does, giving them the same wide latitude they give arbitration in other areas.[383]

In order to use the special-master concept widely, restrictive arbitration law relating to child custody has to be reexamined. Courts must develop more confidence in the decisions of a special master, justified by the special masters' expertise and training in family law, child development, and the mental health problems of children and divorce.

Financing is a significant problem in the widespread use of special masters in high-conflict child custody cases. Qualified professionals cannot be asked to do this demanding work free. Fees for private providers range nationally from $75 to $275 per hour. It thus may be difficult for parents to pay for a special master in addition to the other professional fees for lawyers, mediators, and mental health professionals that are required in a contested custody case. There are no state subsidies for the costs of special masters. Indeed, the Oklahoma statute quoted earlier (note 379) states (1) that the court will not appoint a special master unless it finds that the parents have the means to pay for one, and (2) that the State of Oklahoma assumes no financial responsibility for the fees. The option of appointing a special master in a high-conflict case will thus likely be limited to upper-middle-class parents who can afford to pay the cost from their own private resources.

Despite its cost, the special-master concept is likely to be attractive to a limited number of very-high-conflict parents and to the child custody court. The child custody court is seriously overcrowded; the waiting times for detailed attention to parenting issues from a judge are long, and conflict, frustration, and expense mount during delays. Parents often do not feel that a harassed and overworked judge has the time and energy to listen to their story. They may be willing to pay for faster and perhaps more-expert attention from a special master.

Even though the concept benefits other parents by taking cases that need extensive attention out of the child custody court, the idea that a privately paid special master is available only to wealthy parents raises serious equity concerns. Should parental wealth be the criterion that produces faster and perhaps better child custody decision-making? Purchasing the services of a privately paid special master is arguably another way that wealthier parents buy their way out of what they perceive to be inadequate public services, much as they now purchase private education when the public system is perceived as inadequate.

Given the problems and conditions in many child custody courts, it is hard to begrudge parents an option to purchase private justice, much as it is hard to begrudge them the right to buy out of inadequate public schools. The child custody court is, ultimately, however, a public institution created to protect the best interests of all children – rich and poor. If wealthier parents can opt out of the court's deficiencies and delays by purchasing a private special master, a politically powerful constituency that might otherwise advocate for the improvement and development of the child custody court will have no incentive to do so. If a special master – or a lawyer or education, mediation, neutral mental health evaluation, or any other service – serves the best interests of children, it should be available to all families regardless of parental income.

IX   Differentiated Case Management

Severely dysfunctional, conflict-ridden families need more-careful screening, more intensive services, and closer judicial supervision than low-conflict divorcing parents and children. Differentiated Case Management (DCM), a philosophy of judicial administration, is a valuable way of capturing this idea in shorthand. DCM starts from the "premise that cases are not all alike and the amount and type of court intervention will vary from case to case. Under this model . . . a case is assessed at its filing stage for its level of complexity and management needs and placed on an appropriate 'track.' Firm deadlines and time frames are established according to the case classification."[384] Many courts use DCM in business cases, classifying them as expedited, standard, or complex.[385]

This chapter discusses DCM for child custody disputes. To illustrate how the concept works in practice, the chapter will apply DCM to a hypothetical family, the Wilsons, created from a composite of actual cases. It will then provide some evaluation data for DCM programs in child custody courts.[386]

The Wilson Family

Susan Wilson is a dentist and Michael Wilson is a police captain. They have been married for 19 years. They have two children: Justin, 10 years old, and Christina, 8. Michael's tension-filled job creates great stress in his relationship with those close to him, particularly with Susan. He often yells at Susan and the children. Michael gambles regularly (though he claims he is not a gambling addict) and occasionally drinks to excess. He and Susan have not been close sexually for many months.

Tension in the house has been palpable since Michael discovered Susan is having an affair with a former mutual friend. The affair began after Michael's harsh and repeated criticism of Susan for excessive drinking and abuse of prescription drugs. The two have had a few violent incidents that arose out of shouting matches between them. Michael sometimes hits Susan after Susan criticizes him. Susan sometimes hits Michael first after he makes a negative comment about her, then Michael hits her back even harder. Neither has ever sought medical attention for injuries caused by the other. Michael's violent behavior is not accompanied by any other manifestations of an attempt to control Susan's life. He never threatens Susan with violence and never tries to control her finances, her relationships with friends, and so on. The last violent episode was a year prior to the date Susan filed her complaint for divorce.

Justin and Christina were inadvertently exposed to two incidents of parental violence. Both incidents occurred when they returned home from school activities while a fight was going on. Both children were terrified.

Parents and children continue to live in the same house. Susan and Michael each blame the other for their marital difficulties. Michael is deeply remorseful about his role in the violence and the fact that the children have been exposed to it. Susan blames Michael for the violence and has little insight into her role in it. Both children express great love for their parents. Christina is withdrawn, depressed, and has spoken of suicide. These problems are piled on top of a learning disability. Justin does not demonstrate any emotional problems at the moment, but his schoolwork has recently taken a precipitous decline. Justin is very protective of his mother, whereas Christina is not obviously aligned with either parent.

Principles of DCM

Susan files for divorce from Michael and seeks sole custody of the children. Michael wants joint custody. The family now comes to the attention of the local child custody court. How should a DCM-oriented court handle it?

- *Unified treatment* – a single judge and support team is assigned to the family, develops the family's service plan, and ensures their compliance with it.
- *Screening* – court personnel take a family history, match family members' needs with appropriate services, and present a service plan to the court for its approval.
- *Service plan* – service plans are tailored to the individual needs of parents and children. Low-conflict, less dysfunctional families are referred to less intensive, time-limited services such as traditional education and traditional mediation. High-conflict families are referred to education, mediation, and therapeutic services that integrate screening, violence prevention, and safety precautions. Services are mandated if parents do not agree to attend them.
- *Case management and review* – a case manager is assigned to communicate with the family and service providers to ensure that the family meets court deadlines and attends mandated services. The case manager also informs the court if a change in the service plan is

Figure 9.1 DCM case flow

necessary because of a change in the family's level of dysfunction or conflict (e.g., an incidence of violence, a suicide attempt by a child). The court regularly reviews implementation of the service plan at status conferences. Firm deadlines are set and adhered to.

- *Development of a parenting plan* – the parents are given structured opportunities and forums to negotiate their own parenting plan. If that fails, a hearing is scheduled.

The management of the Wilson's dispute under a DCM system is shown in Figure 9.1.

Unified Treatment

The Wilson family should be assigned to a single judge, aided by a single services team, which supervises the family the entire time it is engaged with the child custody court. "One judge, one support team, one family" is the central tenet of the unified family court.[387] A DCM plan for child custody cases is, in effect, a subset of the unified family court concept.

Most child custody courts do not at present follow the one-judge, one-family model. The courts instead fragment the case of a divorcing family between different courts depending on the legal issue that the case raises. A recent survey found that unified family courts have been enacted on a permanent basis in 13 states.[388] Reform activity to develop unified family courts has been reported in many other states.[389] Florida, for example, has recently undertaken the task of establishing a model unified family court on the recommendation of a statewide interdisciplinary advisory committee.[390]

In non-unified family courts, the same family problems can easily be raised in different cases in different courts, with conflicting results. It is entirely conceivable that Michael will seek an order of protection against Susan for domestic violence in one court that is authorized to grant such relief, while Susan will seek a similar order from a different judge in a different court in which she files her divorce action. It is also possible that a criminal domestic violence or child protection charge can be brought in one court while the divorce and custody action proceeds in another court. The judges may disagree, with the result that an appellate court will have to sort out the conflict. The children may be assigned lawyers in one court, but not in another. One court may order a forensic evaluation; another court may not, or might order a duplicate evaluation. Child protective services may be involved in one court proceeding but not in another.

The Colorado court system recently reported that as a result of a court structure that fragments family disputes between different courts:

[F]amilies who face multiple court filings frequently find themselves appearing before several judges on several different dates. Consequently, judges who preside over each case are unaware that there are other matters pending before other judges . . . The absence of critical information too often results in judges entering orders that conflict with those of one or more judges in other cases involving the family . . . When family cases are resolved in court, families are generally required to undergo multiple assessment and complete treatment plans . . . These requirements frequently overlap, are duplicative of requirements in other cases, or conflict with the requirements in other cases.[391]

Fragmentation between courts is an irrational and inhumane way to treat families in crisis.[392] Judge-shopping within the same state in family cases serves no discernable social purpose. It reflects a court structure organized around the legal issues presented rather than around the problems of the parents and the children. Families have complex needs and interdependencies – judges who oversee their reorganization need to know their histories, including what has transpired in court in the past, as well as be able to address all of their problems. The need for continuity and efficiency makes the single-court, single-judge system standard operating procedure for complex business cases in most court systems. The same need is even more important in the child custody court, where human relationships are at stake.

Lawyers and parents nonetheless worry that a single judge permanently assigned to the same family will wield enormous discretionary power arbitrarily, will have access to information that would not be admissible in court, and will fail to make distinctions between civil and criminal family matters for burdens of proof and other procedural matters.[393] These are important concerns, but they should not delay the creation of unified family courts. The risks that an overreaching and incompetent judge in a unified family court creates for a given family pales by comparison with the chaos created for families already in crisis by a court system that organizes judicial services by legal issue rather than by addressing the needs of families as a whole.[394] No state that has created a unified family court has ever found the risks created by the one-judge, one-family system so pervasive that it had to reinstate a more fragmented system of judicial assignments. Appeals are available to remedy injustice in individual cases. Judicial selection and retention procedures can improve the quality of judges in a unified family court, and judicial education can help those judges make distinctions between the procedures in different types of cases.

There is no doubt that DCM plans and unified family courts call for sophisticated, committed judges who are experts not only in family law but in mental health, dispute resolution, social services, and case management. Unfortunately, judicial assignment to the child custody court tends to be at the bottom of the judicial prestige hierarchy. Many judges do not want to be assigned to the child custody court. Caseloads are overwhelming and judges have to deal with emotionally distraught parents all day. Many judges have no background or experience in family law, let alone psychology or social services. Many view the child custody court as dealing with "non-legal" emotional matters. Newly appointed judges are often sent to the child custody court, and cannot wait to be replaced so that they can move up to auto accident and contract cases. They do not invest the time and effort necessary to become the experienced child custody court judges that DCM requires. The difficulty of attracting and retaining excellent judges for the child custody court is just another manifestation of the problem that our society has in attracting and retaining other professionals who work with children – teachers, pediatricians, nurses, day-care providers.

There is no greater challenge for judicial administrators than attracting and retaining well-qualified judges of appropriate background and temperament for the child custody court. Judges assigned there should want to make a career working with families and children, and have the disposition to do so. Administrators need to create incentives for new judges to join the child custody court and afford them the professional respect and recognition they deserve. Perhaps judges in the child custody court should be paid more than those who deal with less emotionally and legally challenging matters such as automobile accidents and contracts. In many states today, they are in fact paid less than other judges. Every experienced judge who leaves the child custody court should be viewed as a serious loss to the community, and administrators should explore what could have been done to keep him or her on the bench.

Developing a Service Plan

Screening the Wilson family and creating a service plan for it is a significant challenge. There is a great deal we do not know about high-conflict divorce involving children. Indeed, there is as yet little consensus about what constitutes a high-conflict divorce, with some believing it should include families that experience family violence, while others believe it should be limited to those involved in repetitive litigation.[395] We do not know a great deal about how much overlap there is between the types of dysfunction and conflict that divorcing parents and children can exhibit. The art and science of evaluating parental conflict levels, mental health, and risks to safety is in its comparative infancy. The available information is imperfect, and experts differ about how to interpret and apply it to particular families – any prediction about the future for human behavior is hazardous.

Recognizing the limitations of what we know and can know does not mean that DCM screening is impossible, just tentative. Essentially, families with higher service needs must be identified as early as possible after their custody dispute comes to the attention of the child custody court. As a starting point, those families can be defined to include those in which there are allegations or a history of:

- domestic violence
- child abuse or neglect
- repetitive litigation
- substance abuse
- mental illness
- suicide threats
- abduction threats
- children who refuse to visit a parent

The Wilsons qualify under several of these categories – domestic violence and substance abuse allegations being the most prominent. Their children, furthermore, are troubled, as the girl has contemplated suicide.

The child custody court has a structural problem in screening the Wilson family and devising a service plan – the information necessary to classify the Wilson's level of conflict and dysfunction is not necessarily available or reliable at the time Susan files her divorce complaint. How is the court to learn about the violent incidents, Susan's alleged substance abuse, and Michael's gambling in order to create a viable service plan at the earliest possible moment? How can the screening process assess how Justin and Christina are coping with their parents' conflict? Suppose the facts that result in the conclusion that the Wilsons need intensive intervention are contested (e.g., Susan denies Michael's accusations about her substance abuse problems and Michael denies gambling and drinking)? Susan may be reluctant to disclose Michael's violence or her violent behavior for fear of embarrassment or retaliation.

Child custody courts have historically relied on contested pleadings (sworn, written allegations by parents) to identify the nature of the dispute between parents and on trials to sort out their validity. Reliance on what the parents present to the court without independent investigation and verification is not an adequate basis on which to screen and create a service plan. Parents (or their lawyers) determine what to include in the pleadings. Pleadings and parents' allegations generally run a risk of both over- and under-disclosure. Some pleadings may contain truthful allegations of violence and dysfunction, but those allegations may also be false, overblown, or designed for tactical advantage, and will simply further inflame parental conflict. On the other hand, some victims of violence are reluctant to disclose what happened to them in court pleadings because they fear for their own or their children's safety or because of their economic dependence on a batterer. Many parents do not have legal representation to help them draft an appropriate pleading. Previous or related court proceedings involving the family are not disclosed in most pleadings, nor are mental health or substance abuse problems always disclosed. The children are not always consulted in pleadings drafted by parents and their condition is rarely fully described in pleadings. Parents may have dramatically different perceptions of how well their children are coping that pleadings do not reveal.

Pleadings and the voluntary parental disclosures they contain are simply not designed to create a family history for diagnostic purposes. DCM screening and development of a service plan requires more-detailed information than is typically contained in the information parents voluntarily present to the court. The court, however, generally does not conduct its own investigation of the family's situation until it appoints a custody evaluator, a relatively late stage of the dispute resolution process discussed in Chapter XII.

DCM may thus require the child custody court to move to an inquisitorial model of fact gathering in which its staff proactively gathers the necessary information much earlier in the process of dispute resolution rather than simply relying on what the parents tell them.[396] Fully functional DCM screening protocols must include dispute resolution criteria (such as repetitive litigation), mental health criteria (such as mental illness and drug and alcohol abuse), and safety criteria (is either parent a danger to the other parent or to the children or to himself or herself?).

At the very least, both parents should be required to fill out a detailed family joint history in writing, or separately if they disagree. The written form would be much like those used in a doctor's office for a new patient, and request information about previous court proceedings, violent incidents, how the children are doing, and so on. Additional screening should be required in some cases. Court staff may, for example, have to conduct confidential interviews with a parent to determine if family violence exists if the facts are in dispute. Screening may require that the children be interviewed in selected cases to assess their mental health. It may also require examinations of school records and consultations with key figures in the children's lives, such as teachers.

Developing reliable and efficient methods to gather the information necessary to screen families for the purpose of developing a service plan in a DCM system is a major challenge for the child custody court. A fundamental problem with an extensive inquisitorial type of screening is that it may have to proactively gather information for hundreds of families. The expense of the screening process can be substantial. A screening protocol that can be administered in a reasonable amount of time with reasonable accuracy needs to be developed to identify which families need intensive intervention and which do not.

The task of creating a reliable, efficient screening protocol to help a child custody court develop appropriate service plans is not impossible. There are some screening tools now available to determine the existence of domestic violence between intimate partners that can be adapted and expanded.[397] Repetitive-litigant families should be relatively easy to identify if courts have coordinated information systems that can identify a litigant's history in the court system.

The information-gathering that is necessary for effective screening also creates legal concerns about when, how, and to whom information will be revealed. Lawyers for parents will no doubt be concerned about protecting their clients' rights during the screening process. The clients will have to disclose information to the screeners, and will be penalized for providing false or incomplete information. The screeners will also need access to records – other court cases involving the family, hospital records, school records, and so on – that many lawyers may want to keep confidential. Lawyers will also be worried about the screeners' making recommendations to the court based on information whose reliability has not been vetted through the adversarial procedures of a contested hearing.

These are legitimate fears that need to be acknowledged and addressed. Judicial oversight of the screeners, and extensive training for them, will alleviate many of these fears. Conceptually, screeners would be asked to conduct shorter, more efficient neutral evaluation of the family, similar to that typically undertaken at later stages of child custody litigation by a court-appointed custody evaluator as described in Chapter XII. Custody evaluators interview parents and children and routinely access collateral sources of information such as hospital and school records for their reports.[398] No adversary hearing is required before the evaluator makes a recommendation to the court, though the evaluator is available as a witness if either parent contests the recommendations. A similar procedure could be created for parents contesting the recommendations of the screeners.

Procedures for DCM screening must satisfy due process of law. As a matter of fundamental fairness, and to ensure the accountability of the screeners, Michael and Susan must have the right to contest any of the recommendations for mandatory services made as a result of the screening process at a hearing before the court. The screening process can only result in recommendations to the court for a service plan. Those recommendations must be reviewed and approved by the court, which maintains authority and supervision over the screening process and the service plan.

Mandated Services and Judicial Supervision

The Wilsons will benefit if the court and the screening team have a rich variety of options to call on in developing a service plan. The options are extensive and might include:

- Supervised visitation for Michael (discussed in Chapter VIII).
- Appointment of a lawyer or guardian for Justin and Christina (discussed in Chapter XI).
- An expedited neutral forensic evaluation (discussed in Chapter XII).
- Individual therapy for either or both children.
- Family therapy.
- An educational program for the children in which Justin and Christina can learn about the legal process, and what they and their parents are experiencing (discussed in Chapter VI).
- Substance abuse treatment for both Michael and Susan.
- Counseling for domestic violence victims for Susan, and perhaps for Michael.
- An anger-management program for Michael.
- A compulsive gambling program for Michael.
- An educational program specially designed for high-conflict families promoting parallel, as opposed to cooperative, parenting (discussed in Chapter VI).
- Mediation with specially trained mediators who take safety precautions and are especially aware of the problems of family violence

to help Susan and Michael develop a parenting plan for Justin and Christina (discussed in Chapter VIII).
- A special master, if parental conflict continues (discussed in Chapter VIII).

Not all of these services will be affordable or necessary. What is more important than the specific elements included in the service plan is that the court develop one that addresses the Wilsons' dispute resolution and therapeutic needs comprehensively. The court will have to make judgments about which of the available services best fits the family's needs, and, if resources are limited, that are the most important. The parents must be able to pay for any of the services that are not provided free of charge. If mandated services are absolutely essential to the best interests of the Wilson children, or any other child, the court must make them available (without regard to a parent's ability to pay) from taxpayer funds. Some of the elements of the service plan, such as supervised visitation, touch upon a parent's legally protected interests, and require due process and a judicial hearing before being ordered, even temporarily, over a parent's objection.

Case Management and Review

The service plan approved by the court must be implemented by careful monitoring and evaluation. Children must feel that the state, through its court system, is looking out for their interests; parents must feel that the plan is a rational progression toward resolution of their dispute. Children have a unique sense of time – a day can seem like a month and a month a year, depending on their developmental stage. The court process should take place in accordance with the child's sense of time, not the adults'. In addition, the imposition and enforcement of time deadlines will help convince the Wilsons that the court system is serious about protecting their children and will hold them accountable for their welfare.

One way the court can achieve these goals is to appoint a case manager to supervise the service plan's implementation. The case manager will be responsible for regular conferences with the Wilsons and their lawyers to ensure that deadlines are met and to inform the court if they are not. The case manager can also recommend modifications of the service plan to the court as they become necessary. Implementation of the service plan can also be improved if the court keeps the case on its docket for regular status conferences.

Does DCM Work? A Report from Australia

Research findings show that DCM can make a significant difference in the lives of highly conflicted parents and children, including those who have been victimized by violence. For example, the Family Court of Australia initiated a multi-disciplinary DCM program in 1998 called Project Magellan for managing custody disputes involving allegations of child abuse.[399] The Project involved 100 families and a coordinated effort between Australian state and federal agencies and human services organizations. The Project's findings on the incidence of child abuse allegations in child custody disputes are discussed in Chapter VIII. What is significant here is the DCM plan the family court developed to manage these cases that cross the borderline between child custody and child protection, and how well it worked.

An earlier study of child custody disputes that included child abuse allegations established the baselines to which the cases in Project Magellan were compared. The earlier study found that these disputes took an average of five judicial hearings over a period of 18 months.[400] The average age of the children involved was 4 years. Mental health staff considered more than one-quarter of the children to be suffering from serious distress, which increased as the court process went on. Domestic violence allegations were made in addition to child abuse allegations in 40% of the families. Child protection services and the family court had significant difficulties coordinating their efforts on the children's behalf.

In response to the results of the study, the family court created a steering committee to develop a new protocol to address the problems the study revealed. The result was a DCM system, including family group conferencing – a carefully structured form of mediation for families with violence in their histories.[401] What happened?

- Child protection authorities created reports more quickly and provided much more relevant detail.
- Disputes were resolved more quickly (whether by private agreement, mediated agreement, or court order), with the average time to resolution falling from 17.5 months to 8.7 months.
- The number of court hearings dropped from an average of five to an average of three.
- A smaller number of cases went to trial (13% as opposed to 30%).
- Only 5% of the court's orders, down from 37%, were the subject of further litigation in a 1-year period.
- The percentage of highly distressed children in the sample dropped from 28% to 4%.

A similar DCM project – the Wisconsin Unified Family Court Project – reports comparable results to Magellan.[402] So does a pilot program for child protection and welfare matters in a Canadian court.[403] Specialized domestic violence courts that integrate the handling of the civil protection orders and criminal domestic violence cases with DCM and therapeutic justice values show similar positive results.[404]

In short, DCM works if implemented with commitment and energy. The child custody court can serve as a spoke in a wheel of services for the family and ensure that rights are protected and mandatory service plans adhered to. It can identify families in need of greater intervention and develop individualized family service plans that expedite and rationalize the child custody dispute resolution process. These troubled and violent families can participate safely in mediation programs that allow them a greater measure of self-determination than the court process typically provides.[405] The child custody court can coordinate community resources to provide help to parents and children. What is needed is the will and the way.

X Lawyers for Parents

Discourage litigation. Persuade your neighbors to compromise
whenever you can. Point out to them how the nominal winner is
often a real loser – in fees, expenses and waste of time. As a
peacemaker, the lawyer has a superior opportunity of being a good
man. There will still be business enough.

Abraham Lincoln (1846)[406]

My joy was boundless. I had learnt the true practice of law. I had
learnt to find out the better side of human nature and to enter men's
hearts. I realized the true function of a lawyer was to unite parties
riven asunder. The lesson was so indelibly burnt into me that a large
part of my time during the twenty years of my practice as a lawyer
was occupied in bringing about private compromises of hundreds of
cases. I lost nothing thereby – not even money, certainly not my soul.

Mohandas Gandhi (1954)[407]

When parents get married or give birth or a spouse dies, socially recognized
guides such as a rabbi, a priest, a doctor, a midwife, or a nurse remind them of
the kind of behavior that is expected of them. When parents divorce, lawyers
greatly influence how the parents think about the divorce process and how
they relate to each other and to their children. Parents turn to lawyers because
they need to get through the legal aspects of divorce. But they seem to expect
something more from their lawyers – advice and counsel equivalent to that
provided by the rabbi, doctor, or midwife at other critical times in their lives.

What lawyers actually tell parents varies greatly depending on how the
lawyers see themselves as professionals.[408] Some lawyers view themselves
as technical experts on the process of divorce, not on the parent's overall
life situation or the child's best interests. Some lawyers define their job as
helping their clients reach a reasonable settlement and trying to reduce the
conflict surrounding the children.

Other lawyers define their job as representing their client's interests, as the
client defines them; these lawyers believe that the judge protects the child's

125

best interests. The lawyer who takes this view believes the client is the *parent*, not the *child*. This view has support in existing law. "In a malpractice context, some courts have held that a lawyer in a divorce action owes no duty to the child(ren) of the client, on the rationale that the lawyer does not represent the child and that any duty to the child is inconsistent with the duty of zealous representation that the lawyer owes to the client."[409]

The client's goal may be to limit or to sever the relationship between the other parent and the child, regardless of whether that goal is in the child's best interests. A lawyer who takes the "zealous advocacy" view of representation may believe he or she is obligated to present what the parent desires, even if those desires inflame the conflict further. This is a troublesome problem for a legal system that is supposed to protect the child's best interests. Indeed, some have argued that the adversary system is simply incompatible with children's best interests because it is based on the assumption that one parent will win and the other will lose.[410]

As discussed in Chapter III, there are indications that the public is increasingly skeptical of the role that lawyers play in the divorce process. Many parents complain that lawyers advise them to litigate rather than to compromise on parenting issues, and emphasize short-term aggression over long-term relationships. Such advice, they feel, prolongs the conflict and thus increases the lawyer's fees.

These problems suggest two basic strategies to improve the legal representation of parents in the child custody court. In essence, courts should encourage lawyers to create models of practice that promote

- a collaborative approach to the representation of parents in child custody disputes that (1) emphasizes the parents' long-term interests in having a parenting relationship with each other, and (2) seeks to minimize harm to the children;
- widespread access to legal information and diversified forms of representation that reduces the cost of the traditional full-service model.

This chapter will propose changes in the ethical rules that regulate lawyers in order to make divorce practice more child-oriented. It will also define and discuss "collaborative law" and "unbundled" legal services – two models of legal practice that promote reform goals. Finally, the chapter will propose certain changes in the way family lawyers are educated that aim to improve the quality of representation for parents in the child custody court by promoting interdisciplinary collaboration and understanding.

Adversarial Attitudes and Advice

Raoul Felder, the divorce lawyer for former New York Mayor Rudolph Giuliani, told reporters for the national media that they would have to "pry [Donna] Hanover's [Giuliani's estranged wife] fingers off the chandeliers as she is dragged out of Gracie Mansion [the Mayor's official residence]."[411] On May 11, 2001, two days before Mother's Day, after the judge in the case had made an adverse ruling for Giuliani, Felder told the press that Hanover "doesn't care what happens to the children. She cares about getting her name in the paper and embarrassing the mayor and getting movie roles and getting a better job. And if it hurts the kids, so what?" For emphasis, he said on Mother's Day that Hanover was like "a howling stuck pig. She reminds me of the little kid who murders his parents and complains he's an orphan." Felder also let the media know that Guiliani's hormone treatments and radiation for his prostate cancer left him impotent. Felder complained that Hanover never helped the Mayor when he vomited after chemotherapy. Instead, she disrupted his sleep with early-morning workouts. At 5 AM, "she started with the machines, with the exercising," he said.[412]

Felder apparently made these remarks as part of a conscious strategy to aggressively influence public opinion to take a favorable view of his client. Hanover's lawyers too were "spinning" the media. Consultants have been known to advise divorce lawyers that "[t]he media can be a strong ally in a high profile case, and proper use of the media can strengthen one's case tremendously."[413]

Felder's media strategy took emotional risks with the Giuliani-Hanover children. These children, their friends, and those around them will read Felder's remarks and may believe that they represent what their father thinks of their mother. Even if they are not to blame, children often take responsibility for parental conflict. A child who hears one parent (or that parent's lawyer) insult another during an adversarial battle may think that he or she is responsible for the shame and humiliation the parent must bear. A child also sees such statements by a parent's lawyer as a very unattractive method of conflict resolution for his or her parents to use as a model for the future.

Felder's advocacy, while counterproductive and distasteful, does not violate the ethics of the profession. Indeed, some will justify his behavior as zealous advocacy on behalf of a client. The difference between the Giuliani-Hanover custody dispute and others is that the battle was fought in the media and the courtroom, whereas in most cases it remains in the courtroom and the law office. Rather than negotiating or mediating a solution, some lawyers respond to a weekend visitation dispute by filing a motion that includes derogatory comments about the other parent. This combat mentality makes it difficult for lawyers and their clients to resist the temptation to attack aggressively.

The Lawyer as Counselor

There is a tradition of civility and rational discourse in the legal profession that the contentiousness of modern American society and the passion and anger of custody disputes sometimes conceals. That tradition is reflected in Lincoln's and Gandhi's comments on the meaning of law practice given at the beginning of this chapter. As two of the greatest lawyers who ever lived, despite differences in culture and background, they recognized that lawyers have a primary obligation to encourage clients to compromise.

A great myth exists in both popular culture and in the legal community that the "better" lawyer is the one who is more adversarial and combative. Every study of legal negotiation approaches leads to the opposite conclusion – the problem-solving mentality expressed by Lincoln and Gandhi is better respected and more effective than the adversarial and combative mindset expressed by Felder. Preparation, the ability to create options for solving issues, forthrightness, and ethical behavior are the keys to effective lawyer behavior.[414]

The spirit of Lincoln and Gandhi is particularly important for disputes involving children. It also has support in the formal codes that describe a lawyer's ethical responsibilities to his or her client. Under the ABA's *Code of Professional Responsibility* (CPR), as enacted in 1969, an attorney was instructed to represent a client "zealously within the bounds of the law."[415] Many lawyers apparently confused "zealousness" with "over-zealousness." When the profession changed the format of its regulatory code to the *Model Rules of Professional Conduct for Lawyers* (RPC) in 1983, the word "zealously" was omitted from the governing rules and the lawyer was instructed to be "competen[t]" and "reasonabl[y] diligen[t]."[416] The concept of "zealousness" in representation was relegated to the preamble to the *RPC* and commentary.[417]

The distinction between representing a client "zealously" and representing a client "competently" and "diligently" is an important one – defining a lawyer's duty as competent and diligent representation certainly suggests more strongly that the lawyer should advise a parent to distinguish between times when aggressive litigation tactics offer short-term advantage but defeat a child's and parents' best interests in the long run. It also strongly suggests that the lawyer for a parent should try to convince the client to forgo a custody dispute because it is in the best interest of the child.

A Divorce Lawyer's Pledge for Children

Conversations with many divorce lawyers reveal that they are concerned that their own client or opposing counsel will perceive them as "weak" or "unduly conciliatory" if they recommend mediation or parent education rather than litigation to their clients. A taboo about appearing too eager for a settlement is deeply ingrained in our adversarial legal culture.

The best way to change the state of mind that creates that taboo is to create a professional norm that makes discussion of conflict reduction with parent/clients a routine part of the divorce lawyer's function – conduct that clients can expect. If parents expect every lawyer to be able to discuss conflict management mechanisms with them, no lawyer will be reluctant to do so.

Divorce lawyers can voluntarily borrow a creative idea from the corporate bar to facilitate discussion with parents and each other about how to reduce and contain conflict. About 850 of the nation's largest companies, and 2,000 of their subsidiaries, have voluntarily subscribed to a policy statement promulgated by the Center for Public Resources committing them to explore alternative dispute resolution (ADR) procedures with each other before filing suit. Nearly 1,150 U.S. law firms have committed themselves to becoming knowledgeable about ADR and to counseling clients about its availability.[418]

Divorce lawyers' groups could develop a similar pledge committing divorce lawyers to discussing conflict reduction programs with their clients before filing suit. A neutral organization could keep a list of all lawyers who sign the pledge, and inform anyone who inquires as to whether a particular lawyer has signed it. In addition, lawyers who sign the pledge could attach a statement prominently to their client retainer agreements and display a plaque in their offices stating something along these lines:

There are programs in our community that can help parents help children through the difficult transitions of divorce. Please discuss with me whether they are appropriate for your family's situation.

The list of signers and the pledge will provide significant benefits to lawyers and clients. By displaying the statement where a parent/client can see it, the lawyer invites the parent to discuss conflict-management programs with that lawyer. The display indicates that both the lawyer and the parent are concerned about the welfare of the children and will work together to build a responsible post-divorce parenting plan.

The statement makes conflict management about the children a legitimate subject of lawyer-client dialogue. The lawyer becomes the client's guide to the dispute resolution process and encourages the client to consider the interests of children carefully before litigating aggressively. If a parent hires a lawyer who does not display the statement, he or she will be aware that this lawyer is likely to try to resolve problems through litigation rather than through ADR.

Prospective clients can also consult the list to determine something about a prospective lawyer's orientation. A lawyer can consult the list to determine if the lawyer for the other spouse is also on it. If so, both counsel can be confident that each will discuss conflict reduction methods with their clients.

Child-Friendly Ethical Rules

The profession should ultimately resolve its ambivalence about the kind of representation that should be encouraged in child custody cases, and amend its rules of professional responsibility to formally recognize an ethical duty to prevent harm to children while representing parents.[419] The ethical rules of lawyers symbolize the profession's commitment to shared values, and their enforcement indicates the boundaries of acceptable conduct by counsel.

Some states have recognized an ethical duty for lawyers to advise clients about alternatives to litigation, a duty that applies especially to custody litigation.[420] Courts can also create procedural rules that require lawyers to certify that they have discussed alternatives to litigation with their clients before they file a complaint for custody with the court. These formal rules will enhance the standing of lawyers who give child-sensitive advice to parents even if the parents do not wish to hear it; lawyers who do not give such advice will face court sanctions and appropriate professional censure.

The American Academy of Matrimonial Lawyers (AAML – a voluntary and selective national organization of divorce specialists) has already adopted such child-oriented provisions in its *Bounds of Advocacy*, a supplementary code of aspirational standards for divorce law specialists who are members of the AAML.[421] The AAML should be commended for its recognition of the harm that aggressive custody litigation can do to children. However, the general rules regulating professional responsibility of all lawyers should be expanded to include the concepts in the *AAML Bounds* because many lawyers who provide representation to parents in custody disputes do not belong to the AAML and are not bound by its aspirational guidelines. In most jurisdictions, any lawyer, even one with no special training or experience, can represent a parent in a divorce. More importantly, the state processes that regulate lawyers – such as continuing education requirements, disciplinary sanctions, and potential malpractice liability – do not include the AAML's ethical standards. If lawyers are to profit from representing parents, the lawyer's ethical code and its enforcement mechanisms should recognize the unique interests of children.

Lawyers should thus amend their governing code of professional responsibility to include a rule along the following lines:

Duties to Children

An attorney representing a client in an action against the other parent concerning their child shall advise the client of the potential harm protracted conflict is likely to have on the child and discuss how to contain and manage the dispute to reduce the effect on the child. An attorney shall not allow a parent to contest child custody for purposes of financial leverage or vindictiveness. An attorney shall encourage settlement of custody disputes through referrals for education, mental health therapy, negotiation, mediation, or arbitration, except where domestic violence or child abuse or other serious contrary indication is present. In such an instance, an attorney should consult with appropriate experts in the area about how to proceed.

If such a rule were adopted, a lawyer who advises litigation over custody without seriously discussing ADR and probing a client's motivation for litigation would be subject to sanction by the regulatory machinery of the profession. Sanctions already exist for lawyers who encourage frivolous litigation by clients.[422] An ethical rule of the type described here would simply be a more concrete and specific articulation of the proposed ethical code for child custody litigation and a symbol of the profession's commitment to the welfare of children.

Changes in the ethical rules of the profession to promote greater sensitivity to the risks that prolonged parental conflict creates for children might have unintended consequences that policymakers should try to anticipate and guard against. For example, an unintended effect of the kind of ethical rule advocated would be to empower a child to sue a parent's lawyer if the lawyer advises litigation when mediation might have resolved the conflict. No one wants to create more opportunities for satellite civil litigation in an already heated child custody dispute. Rule drafters should be able to figure out ways to foreclose this possibility. Such potential collateral consequences should not deter discussion and implementation of a change in the ethical rules of the profession to reflect its commitment to children's needs.

Collaborative Law

"Collaborative law" is a movement among attorneys to formally implement the spirit of Lincoln and Gandhi in divorce practice. There are groups of divorce attorneys in many states who adhere to collaborative law principles. Many highly experienced matrimonial lawyers are adopting collaborative law principles, and report great benefits to their clients and improvements in their own professional satisfaction.[423]

In 2001, Texas enacted a collaborative law statute that authorizes "a suit affecting the parent-child relationship" to be "conducted under collaborative law procedures ... on a written agreement of the parties and their attorneys."[424] The Texas statute defines collaborative law as

a procedure in which the parties and their counsel agree in writing to use their best efforts and make a good faith attempt to resolve the suit affecting the parent-child relationship on an agreed basis without resorting to judicial intervention except to have the court approve the settlement agreement, make the legal pronouncements, and sign the orders required by law to effectuate the settlement of the parties as the court determines appropriate. *The parties' counsel may not serve as litigation counsel except to ask the court to approve the settlement agreement.*[425]

The Texas statute authorizes and captures the critical features of collaborative law. Parents retain lawyers for a limited purpose – settlement negotiations. Lawyers and clients agree in writing that the lawyers who try to negotiate the settlement will not represent them in litigation if negotiations fail. By mutual agreement, both lawyers are thus disqualified from representing their clients if either parent chooses to end the collaborative law negotiations. In essence, if the lawyers and clients cannot settle the case, the lawyers withdraw, and the clients must hire new counsel for the litigation.

Collaborative law thus realigns the incentives in the lawyer-client relationship to give both the lawyer and the client a stake in settlement rather than litigation. If a case is not settled under traditional representation, the lawyer still gets paid additional fees for litigation. In a collaborative law model, the lawyer loses the projected additional fees if the case is not settled, and the client has to pay the additional costs both of new counsel and further litigation.

Collaborative also law removes settlement negotiations from the traditional adversarial shadow of litigation. Collaborative law ground rules aim to contain and manage conflict responsibly. The traditional accusations and counter-accusations of pleadings, motions, and court hearings are banned. Collaborative law practitioners promote an atmosphere in which counsel and parents actively engage in problem-solving negotiations on post-divorce parenting issues. "By establishing norms and practices promoting cooperation, [collaborative law] provides an opportunity to avoid launching adversarial reaction cycles and suppressing them soon after they begin."[426]

In contrast to typical settlement meetings in the adversarial process in which the lawyers talk to each other and then each talks to his or her own client, collaborative divorce settlements emerge from "four way" meetings between spouses and their lawyers, who agree in advance to the ground rules, including civility and voluntary disclosure. Lawyers prepare the agenda and their clients for the four-way meetings. The meetings are designed to make parents become active participants in shaping their own futures. Four heads, particularly when two of them are very experienced in the problems facing divorcing parents, are better at problem-solving than two. Lawyers add value to the negotiation by bringing their knowledge, resources, skills, and strategic considerations to bear on solving the problems of the divorce and the reorganized parenting.[427] If both parents agree, they can retain an expert as a consultant, but the expert does not testify if settlement fails.

The goals of collaborative law and mediation are thus the same – to promote voluntary, informed agreements by problem-solving negotiations and parent self-determination. Lawyer participation in the processes is different. During mediation, lawyers generally play a consulting role for clients. They are often not present at mediation sessions, and simply review the agreements generated by parents and the mediator. Since they do not participate in the mediation, the reviewing lawyers may not be committed to the trade-offs and compromises embodied in every agreement. Some reviewing lawyers believe that they should promote informed consent and careful deliberation before agreements resulting from mediation are signed, a role that some have described as a "more or less reluctant hired sniper."[428]

Unlike lawyers in mediation, collaborative lawyers actively advise and negotiate alongside their clients "at the center of the dispute resolution process, rather than on the sidelines..."[429] Lawyers, not parents or non-lawyer mediators, take the lead in structuring the four-way meetings. Collaborative law is thus a particularly useful option for a parent who is reluctant to mediate because he or she fears the other spouse, feels disempowered, and needs the benefit of an advocate and adviser in the room as settlement negotiations proceed.

Limitations and Uncertainties of Collaborative Law

Collaborative law has not been empirically studied. We simply do not know much about the effect it has on parents and children. Collaborative law should not be an option for all parents. Its limitations are similar to those for mediation. A parent divorcing a violent parent, a mentally ill parent, or one who is fundamentally dishonest and cannot be trusted may not be a good candidate for collaborative law.

Collaborative law requires both parents to retain lawyers, an expense that is beyond the reach of many parents. In addition, it requires them to take the risk that if the collaboration breaks down, new lawyers will have to be hired at significant additional expense. Collaborative law will thus likely be an option for only a small segment of the divorcing population, mostly the upper-middle class and the wealthy. Collaborative law does not, for example, address the needs of *pro se* parents and their children in the child custody court. It should not be viewed as a competitor or alternative to the education and mediation programs of the child custody court. These programs should be open to all divorcing parents, regardless of income or willingness or ability to pay or to retain a lawyer.

Furthermore, collaborative lawyers face difficult practical and ethical issues, which its theory and the ethics structure of the organized bar have yet to fully clarify.[430] Collaborative lawyers are, in a phrase used by one of its main proponents, "engaged moral agents" who should insist on clients' "taking the long view and the high road."[431] They will inevitably face difficult moral and ethical dilemmas, particularly in deciding when to withdraw and when to recommend that a client pursue litigation, particularly because the client will have the additional burden of finding and paying for new counsel. "By withdrawing, lawyers can harm clients when they trust their lawyers and/or do not want to invest the time and money required to find, hire and educate new lawyers about their case."[432]

For example, does the requirement that a collaborative lawyer withdraw rather than litigate if negotiations break down give the lawyer too much power over the client? In general, lawyers are generally prohibited from requiring clients to agree in advance that the lawyer can withdraw from representing them.[433] This prohibition is designed to prevent lawyers from using the threat of withdrawal to pressure a client to accept a settlement that the client does not want. Furthermore, what happens when a client begins by seeking collaborative representation, but then needs representation in court because of unexpected developments (e.g., an incident of violence)? Will the collaborative lawyer abandon him or her? Collaborative law works effectively only if the lawyers and parents involved all share its values. What happens if the client acts duplicitously (e.g., by withholding or distorting critical financial information)? Will the collaborative lawyer threaten to withdraw and thus exert pressure on a client to take the high road? How will collaborative lawyers work with lawyers who say they want to collaborate but actually operate in a more traditional adversarial framework?

Suppose, for example, in the middle of what are purportedly collaborative settlement negotiations, one lawyer makes a motion to restrict the other parent's visitation rights in order to secure a strategic advantage in the bargaining. The lawyer thinks that that parent will be intimidated into making greater financial concessions out of fear of losing contact with his or her children. How should the lawyer representing the parent who is dedicated to collaborative principles respond? Is it fair to the truly collaborative lawyer's client to withdraw now, causing anxiety, delay, and expense in responding to the motion simply because the other lawyer refuses to abide by the collaborative law agreement?

Despite these problems and uncertainties, collaborative divorce lawyers are asking the right questions. They offer a valuable conceptual alternative to the adversarial process for parents who want their divorce without the warfare but still want the expertise and support of counsel. In 21st century America, a significant number of upper-income parents can afford counsel for divorce, but have less and less confidence in the ability of the divorce bar to protect their interests. Collaborative law promises to provide them with the expertise of lawyers to navigate a complex legal system and to make long-term economic and parenting decisions without the baggage of combat.

Collaborative law should gradually influence mainstream divorce practice, particularly if it is incorporated into legal education. Full disclosure, client consent, and the legal profession's tradition of civility and compromise hopefully will help resolve the professional responsibility issues this new form of practice presents, and allow collaborative law to grow and to prosper.

Unbundled Legal Services

Forms of legal representation that provide *pro se* parents with greater access to legal information and advice are also long overdue. *Pro se* parents need educational programs if they are to represent themselves, and, as discussed in Chapter VI, courts are beginning to provide them. Policymakers also need to address the question as to whether a *pro se* litigant in the child custody court is better off obtaining as much legal advice and representation as he or she can afford, or is willing to accept, or whether the legal system should insist on traditional full-service (bundled) representation.

In traditional representation, the lawyer enters an appearance in court for a client and represents that client in all aspects and phases of the dispute – office counseling, drafting court pleadings, representation in settlement negotiations, and drafting agreements. In contrast, lawyers engaged in providing unbundled legal services provide legal representation on a task-by-task basis.[434] In an unbundled representation, the lawyer and client collaborate in defining the scope of the lawyer's tasks. The lawyer guides and informs the client, but does not direct the client's actions or substitute for the client in negotiations or the courtroom. Examples of unbundled services are coaching a client in mediation but not attending the mediation sessions or advising a client on what should go into a pleading rather than drafting it for him or her.

Rather than structuring family courts and family law on the assumption that litigants will have lawyers, unbundling organizes the dispute resolution process around the assumption they will not. Instead, lawyers educate their clients as much as possible on how to handle their dispute themselves.

Unbundling has a long tradition in legal circles. Corporate lawyers have responded to client phone calls for years, provided second opinions, or given clients advice on how to accomplish a particular task. "What is really new about unbundling is the mind-set of lawyers to proactively make such limited services available and to tell Jane Q. Public how to get them."[435] Unbundling is especially necessary for family law disputes, as many parents simply cannot afford and do not want the full-service model.

The unbundled model of services raises many important ethical issues.[436] For example, informed client consent needs to be secured for limited representation. Clients need to fully understand what their lawyers will and will not do for them. Limited legal advice where the lawyer is not fully aware of all relevant facts and does not take time to research applicable law may be misleading or incomplete, leading to malpractice claims. Some states require clients to disclose whether a lawyer helped them prepare a document they filed with a court. The bar needs to address these problems, and design, promote, and carefully evaluate unbundling initiatives to make sure they provide help when most needed, remain true to the core values of the profession (client loyalty and confidentiality), improve access to justice, and do not lead to more litigation.

The critical policy question is whether some legal advice is better than none at all. The traditional full-service model of representation is the exception rather than the rule for litigants in the child custody court. The number of lawyers has increased in recent years. Yet, because of both poverty and consumer choice, the number of *pro se* child custody litigant parents has grown, with no end in sight. There is thus a fundamental disconnect between what lawyers currently deliver to parents and what those parents can afford and are willing to pay for. Something is wrong in this marketplace. Just asking whether unbundling is a good idea is a step forward in providing access to justice in the modern child custody court.

Changes in Legal Education

Changes in the way parents are represented will also require changes in the way future divorce lawyers are educated. The typical law school curriculum emphasizes adversarial models of dispute resolution. The basic educational material for most law school courses is judicial decisions in intensely litigated cases. In most law schools, family law is not a required course. Most law professors believe that most of their students take the course because it is on the bar examination. Where it is required on the bar, enrollments in family law seem to be substantial; where it is not, enrollments are lower. The basic family law course focuses on statutes and cases in a large group setting. It teaches almost nothing about when it is appropriate for lawyers to collaborate to serve children's best interests, how to work with angry and conflicted parents, and whether and how to encourage clients to participate in mediation. It does little to introduce future lawyers to interviewing and counseling skills.

The same criticisms can be made with great force of legal education in all fields – from corporate to criminal law. These criticisms are particularly powerful when applied to the training of future family and divorce lawyers, who, by definition, have to be comfortable working with clients under great emotional distress and in an interdisciplinary environment.

Law schools are beginning to address the need to train future divorce lawyers in collaboration and problem-solving, and to give them the interdisciplinary tools they need in order to work with clients under emotional distress. Law students around the world, for example, now participate in client counseling competitions in addition to competitions for best courtroom performances.[437] Hofstra Law School on Long Island, New York, offers two courses in which law students receive joint education with child psychiatry fellows and child psychology trainees from North Shore-Long Island Jewish (LIJ) Health Systems. The faculty consists of lawyers and mental health professionals. The first course focuses on negotiation and mediation, while the other focuses on the role of lawyers and mental health experts in child custody disputes. The focus is on how lawyers and mental health professionals can work together and solve problems for families and children. The law and mental health students, for example, read the same books on problem-solving behavior and discuss how they can implement the concepts in particular cases.[438] The courses conclude with simulated mediation sessions conducted by actual mediators, or simulated child custody trials based on real trials presided over by an actual judge.

Hofstra Law School and North Shore-Long Island Jewish Health System also jointly staff a Child Advocacy Clinic where law faculty and students work with North Shore-LIJ faculty and mental health trainees to represent some of the most troubled children in American society as law guardians in child protection cases. Faculty and students participate in a joint weekly seminar and in weekly case-review conferences. Under senior staff supervision, mental health trainees help the law students develop techniques for client interviews, read case files and child and family case histories, prepare children to testify, develop service plans, and so on.

Other law schools have similar joint programs with mental health teaching institutions.[439] Joint degree programs in law and mental health disciplines (law, psychology, psychiatry, and social work) are also offered, and their faculty and graduates can help provide leadership in integrating legal and mental health systems for the benefit of children.

Governmental bodies that establish criteria for admission to the bar and legal educators have to progress beyond the idea that any lawyer who graduates from law school is capable of representing a parent in a child custody dispute. It is a complex, demanding task that requires difficult ethical judgments, people skills, and legal and mental health knowledge. This kind of education cannot be provided in a large classroom or from a traditional casebook. If society wants higher quality representation of parents and more lawyers concerned about the best interests of children, it will have to invest resources and imagination in training lawyers appropriately.

XI The Voice of the Child, the Lawyer for the Child, and Child Alienation

It is an appealing and humane idea to insist that a child's voice be heard as part of the process of deciding a custody dispute. A child is, after all, the person most affected by the court's decision. The court's order will determine where the child lives and who will be responsible for making decisions for him or her. The order may determine everything from after-school activities to relationships with friends. A child may also have strong preferences as to which parent he or she wants to live with and how he or she wants his or her post-divorce life to develop.

In an editorial in a California legal newspaper, Alanna Krause, an honor student, the daughter of a prominent and wealthy California attorney, and the subject of a bitter custody dispute, articulates the rationale for hearing children's voices in custody cases:

Hundreds of years of legal history have led the United States to implement a system that ensures that every party in a legal proceeding gets a voice. We rest assured that, unlike in other nations, we cannot be incarcerated, so well thought out: God Bless America.

But there is a forgotten minority that is not afforded those basic rights. They are not criminals or foreign aliens. In contrast, they are a group we hold dear – one innocent and well meaning, with no hidden agendas or twisted motives – children.

Instead of being actually represented, children get their "best interests" represented by adults. We children have no choice and no recourse when those adults have their own agendas. A case in point? Mine.

Alanna goes on to state that her court-appointed Guardian Ad Litem (Guardian) ignored her complaints that the father with whom she was forced to live was abusing her. She wanted to replace her Guardian with someone who saw the custody dispute the same way she did, but could not do so. Alanna also complained she could not personally cross-examine the court-appointed mental health professionals who also disagreed with her. Alanna concludes:

Yet, at 11, I could speak for myself. I had a mind and set of opinions, but no one seemed to care. The judge denied my right to legal representation, especially when the court-appointed lawyer wouldn't speak the truth. Granted there is no guarantee that hearing me would have inspired the judge to untwist her motives and unclench her hold on personal allegiances and biases, but who knows? At least it would have been in the court record.[440]

Children like Alanna occupy an ambiguous status in American law and culture, and the debate over the extent of their participation in child custody disputes reflects that ambiguity. Many adults are concerned that a child needs to be protected from parental conflict rather than enmeshed in it, and one parent will try to bribe or persuade the child to have a preference in that parent's favor. Children can feel inappropriately responsible or omnipotent if asked to choose between their parents. On the other hand, some argue that "the tradition of not listening to children's voices during the divorce process has unintended negative effects. Extensive research literature indicates that the perception of control over decisions is related to positive mental health. This seems to be true in the case of children who have no control over the outcome of divorce proceedings. As a result of their exclusion, children complain about feeling isolated and lonely during the divorce process, and many older children express anger and frustration about being left out."[441]

As a legal matter, however, although parents' constitutional rights may be at stake in a child custody dispute, the constitutional rights of minors are not. Children are not full formal parties to custody litigation between their parents. They have, for example, no legal right to review court papers and make appearances in court proceedings. This is a reflection of the larger proposition that the legal system does not treat children as fully competent to make critical decisions such as whether or not to sign a contract or whether or not to have surgery." [E]veryone acknowledges that children are different and that age is not an entirely spurious measure of children's capacity for equality or right to equal treatment."[442]

Furthermore, the legal system is concerned about undermining parental authority by empowering children. The legal system generally allows parents a great deal of autonomy to make decisions for their children based on the premise that the decisions parents make are likely to be better than those made by the state. In holding that a minor does not have a constitutional right to a hearing when his or her parents want to commit that minor to a mental institution, the U.S. Supreme Court stated:

The law's concept of a family rests on a presumption that parents possess what a child lacks in maturity, experience, and capacity for judgment required for making life's difficult decisions. More important, historically it has recognized that natural bonds of affection lead parents to act in the best interests of their children . . . That some parents 'may at times be acting against the interests of their children' creates a basis for caution, but is hardly a reason to discard those pages of human experience that teach that parents generally do act in children's best interests . . . [443]

Some advocates for children give more weight to some of these competing considerations than others. There is thus a full panoply of positions on the role of children in a custody dispute "from the notion that children have a right to be protected from the trauma of the court process to the position that children have a right to be heard even if they lack the full capacity to make the ultimate choices to the position that children have an autonomy right to make the ultimate decision on custody and visitation."[444]

This chapter will not attempt to resolve the question of what weight a child's preference should have in a custody dispute; a full discussion of that topic would take another book. Rather, it simply provides an overview of some aspects of a child's preference to demonstrate its complexity in the modern child custody court. The chapter first addresses the extent to which the child custody court at present considers a child's preference as to which parent to live with and the role mediation can play in resolving the dilemmas that the child's preference presents. It then discusses the role of the child's lawyer in a custody dispute, a topic that demonstrates the ambiguities of the role a child's preference plays in the custody court from a different perspective. Finally, the chapter discusses the problem of the alienated child – what can a court do when a child wants nothing to do with a divorcing parent?

The Role of a Child's Preferences in Custody Disputes

Child custody courts consult children not because they believe children should decide custody issues, but because the consultation informs the wise exercise of the court's discretion in fashioning a custody order. Most state statutes provide that the court should consider a child's preference only if it reflects a "mature" judgment. Florida's statute is typical, requiring the court to consider the "reasonable preference of the child, *if* the court deems the child to be of sufficient intelligence, understanding and experience to express a preference."[445] Judges thus have great discretion to count or discount a child's preferences.

We do not know how many judges actually consult children. There is conflicting evidence about how much weight judges actually give to children's preferences, though the critical variable seems to be the child's age; the older the child, the more weight the court gives his or her preference in determining the ultimate parenting plan.[446] Judges (and parents) tend to defer to the custody choices of adolescents.[447]

Judges who do consult children usually do so in a closed-door (*in camera*) interview.[448] Even the most vigorous advocates of considering a child's preference in a custody dispute do not suggest that the child should be sworn as a witness and cross-examined by his or her parents' lawyers in front of his or her parents. They recognize that a courtroom confrontation of this sort could irreparably poison the parent-child relationship.

For some children, judicial interviews are an important opportunity to have direct access to a decision-maker who has extensive power over their future; judges can, presumably, also learn something valuable about the child from these encounters. Many experts believe, however, that judges acquire very little information of value to a custody decision in a brief interview with a child, and recommend that the interview be conducted only if required by statute.[449] Clinicians also report that for many children, an interview with a judge is a very stressful experience in which a child experiences loyalty conflicts, guilt, and fear of retribution. Judges are not generally trained in the child-interviewing skills that might reduce the problems children experience in these interviews.[450]

Moreover, such an interview may expose the judge to unreliable evidence that may influence the decision in the case, evidence that the parents will not have the opportunity to confront. For example, one parent can convince a child to exaggerate to the judge a story about mistreatment, and the other parent will not have any way of challenging the accuracy of the child's story. This danger is particularly acute in a small number of cases when a child is alienated from one parent because of the other parent's deliberate plan to remove the target parent from the child's life, a subject discussed later in this chapter.

Children in Mediation

The best solution to the dilemma of including the child's voice in the custody decision-making process is to take the process out of an adversarial framework and place the child's voice into the safer setting of mediation. Many children want only the right to express their thoughts and feelings, and do not want to be in the position of choosing between their parents. When offered the opportunity, most children willingly participate in mediation.[451]

Most parents seem receptive to the idea of a child's participation in mediation. In a pilot study in Australia in 2000, 80% of parents agreed to have their children interviewed by the parents' mediator, who conveyed the results to the parents. Other pilot studies also suggest that most children are grateful for the opportunity for a voice in the process, and that a child's participation in mediation generally has a positive effect on the parent-child relationship.[452] It is questionable whether the same can be said of the child's participation in child custody decision-making in the courtroom.

There are several models of mediation practice for a child's involvement in the process. In one model, for example, a child participates in the final mediation session, at which time the child learns firsthand what agreements were reached and why. In another model of mediation, the mediator or a mental health professional interviews the child and reports the results to the parents.

The emotional strengths and vulnerabilities of children are highly individual, and respect for differences should prevent creation of a rigid rule that children should or should not participate in mediation. Some children may benefit, whereas others may feel the same kinds of anxiety and conflict that occurs when a judge interviews them. The *Model Standards of Practice for Family and Divorce Mediation* make the child's involvement in the mediation process an issue that the parents and the mediator should discuss together. The *Model Standards* do not require the child to participate in the mediation process. Rather, they allow the parents, in consultation with the mediator and the child, to decide that question themselves. The *Model Standards* require the mediator to inform the parents about the ways in which a child may participate (e.g., in person, in an interview with a mental health professional or the mediator, or in a videotape statement), and the costs and benefits of each.[453] The *Model Standards* specify that, except in extraordinary circumstances, children should not participate in the mediation unless both parents consent.[454]

The Ambiguous Status of a Child's Lawyer: Guardians and Attorneys

Though framed differently, the underlying questions concerning the role of a child's lawyer in a custody dispute are the same as the question of how much weight a judge should give a child's preference in fashioning a custody order.[455] The key issue in both settings is the weight the adult – this time a lawyer instead of a judge – gives the child's views.

Some background is necessary in order to understand the problem. There are two types of children's representatives in a custody dispute, though the nomenclature for these types of representatives varies in different states – Guardian (sometimes called Guardian Ad Litem, or GAL) and Attorney. In theory, an Attorney for the Child acts as an advocate for a client (a minor child) and essentially treats the child as if the child is a party to the custody dispute of the child's parents. An Attorney advocates for the custody arrangement that the child wants as forcefully as if the child were an adult client. An Attorney has a confidential relationship with the child, and participates fully as an advocate in all phases of the legal process.

A Guardian, unlike an Attorney, protects rather than empowers the child. A Guardian's principal allegiance is to the court and not to a child client. A Guardian is an investigator and a reporter, bound to determine and advance the child's "best interests" even if those interests conflict with the child's preferences. Although a Guardian may – and generally should – consider the child's preferences in making his or her recommendations to the court, those preferences are but one fact to be investigated and reported. A Guardian will thus report to the court that a child wants to live with his or her father, but has the right and the obligation to present reasons as to why that parenting plan may not be in the child's best interests – if that is the Guardian's opinion. A Guardian can be called as a witness, and cross-examined at trial, and has a non-confidential relationship with the child.

A Guardian need not be a lawyer. In many states, mental health professionals can be (and are) appointed as Guardians. The fundamental difference between a lawyer and a non-lawyer Guardian is that a lawyer Guardian can call and examine witnesses and make legal arguments to the court, while a non-lawyer Guardian cannot.

The conflict in roles between a lawyer Guardian and an Attorney is most acute when the child expresses a preference for a parenting plan with which the representative disagrees. In settlement negotiations and in the courtroom, an Attorney pursues the lawful objectives of the client whatever they may be. An Attorney appointed to represent Alanna (the honor student quoted at the beginning of the chapter) will argue that she should not be in the custody of her father, as that is what Alanna wants, and her objective is not unlawful. The Attorney can, of course, counsel the child against taking a position that the Attorney believes is not in the child's best interests. The Attorney can try, for example, to persuade Alanna that she should have a relationship with her father for her emotional and economic well-being. In the end, the Attorney must accept the child's definition of the objectives of the representation as long as the child has the mental capacity to understand his or her options, and to articulate an opinion.

A Guardian, unlike the Attorney appointed to represent Alanna, can override the child's preferences and take a different position from the child's. The Guardian treats Alanna as potentially incapacitated, and can make decisions for her.[456] The Guardian could thus argue to the court that Alanna should be in the custody of her father even if she does not want to be.

In many states, governing law sends an ambiguous message to judges, lawyers, parents, children, and to the child's representatives themselves about their role in child custody disputes. Indeed, the New York term for the child's representative – "Law Guardian" – fuses these ambiguous roles. The word "law" in the title conveys the idea of an Attorney, while the word "guardian" conveys the idea that the law guardian has the right to substitute his or her judgment of "best interests" for the child's preferences. The governing statute increases the ambiguity by defining Law Guardian as a lawyer whose position is created for minors "to help protect their interests *and* to help them express their wishes to the court."[457]

In the absence of clear guidelines from a statute or the court, individual attorneys appointed to "represent" a child in a particular case, like judges in the child custody court, have great discretion to decide whether to view their role as that of a Guardian or an Attorney. One lawyer may exercise discretion to advocate for the child's preferences, whereas another may override those preferences. Different lawyers may treat similarly situated children differently, often perplexing parents and children as to what role the lawyer is playing.

Carballeira v. Shumway,[458] a 2000 New York case, illustrates the ambiguous role of the child's representative. The parents' 1995 judgment of divorce, entered after a lengthy trial, granted them joint custody of their only son. In March 1997, when the child was approximately 10 years old, the mother filed a modification petition seeking sole custody. The child custody court appointed a Law Guardian for the child and conducted a 10-day trial, during which the father also requested sole custody.

The trial court eventually dissolved the joint custody arrangement because of the continuing acrimony between the parents. It modified the divorce judgment to grant sole custody to the father, with the mother maintaining both visitation rights and a consulting role in major educational and medical decisions.

On appeal, the mother did not challenge the modification of the divorce judgment nor directly contest the merits of the court's decision. Rather, she argued that a new hearing was required because the Law Guardian did not provide adequate representation to the child. The mother argued that the Law Guardian advocated a position contrary to the expressed wishes of the child, was biased against the mother, and revealed the child's confidences to third parties.

The New York appellate court rejected all of these arguments. The court reasoned that even though the Law Guardian disagreed with the child, he acknowledged and repeatedly communicated to the trial court the child's preference to live with the mother. The court noted that in a custody determination, a child's preference is just one factor that a trial court considers, and not necessarily a dispositive one. The Law Guardian was thus free to advocate his own vision of the child's best interests rather than simply advocating for the child's preferences.

On the bias claim, the court held that "[a] Law Guardian should not have a particular position or decision in mind at the outset of the case before the gathering of evidence . . . On the other hand, Law Guardians are not neutral automatons. After an appropriate inquiry, it is entirely appropriate, indeed expected, that a Law Guardian form an opinion about what action, if any, would be in the child's best interests."[459]

The court next held that the Law Guardian properly disclosed the child's confidential communication by telling the father the child made a suicide threat. For unexplained reasons, the court stated that the Law Guardian did in fact have a duty of confidentiality to the child, but that the child had voluntarily waived that duty. The opinion does not reveal any facts about how the Law Guardian obtained the child's consent to the disclosure.

Carballeira thus holds that a child's representative has the power to decide to act as a "Guardian" rather than an "Attorney." Concerns about the child's capacity to make wise decisions defining the objectives of the representation may have influenced the *Carballeira* court. The child was 11 years old at the time of the hearing. He suffered from several neurological disorders, including Tourette's Syndrome, Obsessive Compulsive Disorder, and Attention Deficit Hyperactivity Disorder. The child wanted to live with his mother. The psychologist who conducted an evaluation of the child opined "that the child was certainly intelligent, but somewhat less mature than average and could be easily manipulated by adults. The record further indicates that the child may have been blinded by his love for [his mother], that she exerted influence on his thoughts concerning custody, and that he did not articulate objective reasons for his preference other than his dislike of discipline at [his father's] home and the lack of rules and discipline at [his mother's] home."[460]

These concerns about the quality of the child's judgment explain why the concept of the child's representative is so ambiguous and problematic. Though the concerns are serious, nobody would look favorably on a lawyer for an adult in similar conditions taking a position in court contrary to his or her client's wishes.

The decision in *Carballeira* is a Catch-22. The *Carballeira* court treated the child as an adult when it held that the child had the capacity to make the serious, informed decision necessary to waive the attorney-client privilege that allowed the Law Guardian to disclose the child's suicide attempt to his father. The court did not deem the same child to be old enough and capable enough to establish the objectives of the Law Guardian's advocacy. Children, apparently, cannot win in a courtroom world dominated by adults.

Redefining the Role of a Child's Representative

This chapter cannot resolve the long-standing debate about whether a child's lawyer should be an Attorney, a Guardian, or something in between. As this is being written, a Task Force of the Family Law Section of the ABA is engaged in a comprehensive and thoughtful attempt to set standards of appointment and practice for lawyers representing children in custody and visitation disputes that hopefully will provide models that child custody courts can draw on.[461] For now, this chapter takes the position that the judge in a child custody dispute has the responsibility for making the Attorney or Guardian determination. The court should appoint a lawyer for a child in a custody dispute only after clearly defining what role the court wants the child's representative to play. All actors in the child custody dispute resolution system, including the appointee and the parents, should be clear about what this critical participant's job description is.

Through legal arguments, calling of witnesses, and conducting out-of-court interviews and discovery, a Guardian may bring perspective to the child custody court's decision-making process that parents do not. Many lawyers who represent children in custody disputes as Guardians appropriately recognize that an adversarial orientation to their task is inappropriate for these intra-family conflicts. Instead, they attempt to reduce the antagonism between the parents, help resolve the dispute in accordance with the child's sense of time, investigate and advocate for a particular result, collect data and recommendations about the fitness of the parents, and propose custody plans to the court. A Guardian can also help the child outside the courtroom by explaining the legal process and providing emotional comfort, counseling, and referrals to services.[462] Many poor children have no ally other than a Guardian who performs these valuable functions, often for little or no compensation.[463]

A Guardian is, nonetheless, an unpredictable factor in the child custody decision-making process, unaccountable to anyone but the court, and thus needs careful judicial control to be sure he or she acts in the best interests of children. A Guardian is a stranger to the family, and has no clear guidelines about how to perform his or her task. Appointing a Guardian creates a presumption for the court and the parents that the lawyer appointed has some kind of special insight or wisdom to perform the complex task of ascertaining the child's best interests. The court gives great weight to what a Guardian has to say, and the Guardian thus assumes great power to resolve the parents' dispute. As some critics have argued, "[M]ost courts...ascribe to the [G]uardian and his or her opinion a level of competence, validity, wisdom, credibility and objectivity richly undeserved."[464] A Guardian is immune from suit by either the parents or the child.[465]

It has been estimated that 1,100 Guardians are appointed each week to represent children in child custody disputes in the United States.[466] The routine appointment of Guardians poses significant practical problems that suggest that the practice be limited to very few cases.

First, the Guardian's role can overlap with the functions performed by other professionals in the child custody dispute resolution process, sometimes forcing financially strapped parents to pay twice for about the same service. The well-financed child custody court has professionals (many of whom are not lawyers) trained to perform many of the same functions as a lawyer Guardian. Trained mediators mediate, mental health experts appointed by the court investigate and report, and educators and therapists provide counseling and referrals. There is little reason to routinely appoint a lawyer as a Guardian to duplicate what other trained professionals do, especially since it adds to the expense and delay in already expensive and lengthy custody cases. Guardians should be reserved for those children for whom courtroom advocacy is required.

Another problem is financial compensation for Guardians. It must be large enough to recruit hundreds of competent lawyers each year since it is unlikely that enough will volunteer to do the job on a *pro bono* basis. Fees for

Guardians in hotly contested cases can be $35,000 or higher. Guardian's fees are generally based on the parents' income. In the small number of cases in which the divorcing parents are well-off financially, this arrangement adequately compensates Guardians. For most families, paying three lawyers instead of two puts a strain on their financial resources. On the other side of the financial ledger, many poor children who could benefit from Guardians do not have one appointed for them as there is no public money to pay the not insignificant costs of providing Guardians to them.[467]

Numerous complaints and studies also indicate that Guardians are poorly trained.[468] Most lawyers appointed as Guardians have no particular ability to assess family dynamics or family violence, nor do they have special training to do their jobs competently. A multi-disciplinary commission established by the Florida bar recently examined the quality of representation provided to children in that state – and found it wanting.[469] The court system that appoints Guardians must create procedures to ensure their competence and accountability for poor performance. Perhaps the only way to address this problem is to limit the appointment of Guardians to those lawyers in a public service office who have received special training and devote their professional lives to working with children.

There are circumstances in which a child should have a specially trained Attorney to represent his or her views to the court in the same manner as an adult. Attorneys for children should be appointed in custody cases involving family violence or child protection concerns, parents with diminished capacity, or older children with very strong views about what their parenting arrangements should be. However, routinely appointing an Attorney for a child runs the risk of making the child the courtroom adversary of one parent or the other. The need to avoid encouraging a child to choose between parents and assuming an adversarial posture toward them suggests that a child custody court should appoint Attorneys to represent a child's preferences in a custody dispute only with caution and only after defining the specific reasons that appointment of an Attorney is necessary to protect the child's best interests.

Alienated Children

The problem of a child custody court's taking account of a child's preferences is most acute when an older child refuses to visit a parent, a so-called "alienated child." Do we view the feelings of an alienated child as determinative, or as a voice to be heard in the courtroom with his or her own Attorney? Or do we view an alienated child as one who is in need of sympathy and therapy? Do we accept an alienated child's allegations of abuse by the rejected parent, which, though often true, can also be false or manipulated by the other parent (as discussed in Chapter VIII)? What limits are there on the legal system's ability to compel a child to have a relationship with a parent when that child adamantly refuses to do so?

At least one court has resolved these questions by treating a child who refuses to visit its parent as a criminal. No parent has ever been put in jail for refusing to visit with his or her child during a court-ordered visitation. Yet at least one court placed children in jail when they refused to visit with their non-custodial parent.[470]

In re Marshall is a highly publicized Illinois case in which the trial judge sent a 12-year-old girl (Heidi) to a juvenile detention center shackled in leg irons and "grounded" her 8-year-old sister (Rachel) for refusing to visit with their father.[471] The girls visited their father during the summer of 1993 and for about a week at Christmas. They did not want to visit during their spring break in April of 1994. Their mother contacted a psychologist. After several visits with the girls, the psychologist recommended that neither child go to visit with their father for their next scheduled visit.

Both girls said they were afraid of their father. Both said their father had hit them and both said they worried that if they went to visit their father, he would not allow them to see their mother again, as he had threatened in the past. When the girls did not show up on schedule, the father brought a contempt action for violation of the visitation agreement; the mother filed a petition to modify and restrict the father's visitation rights.

The trial court denied the mother's petition to modify visitation, finding that there was no evidence that visitation with the father would seriously endanger the children's physical or moral health. The court appointed a counselor to help facilitate visitation and repair the parent-child relationship. But after several extended sessions with the counselor, the children still refused to visit with their father.

The trial court then found both Heidi and Rachel in civil contempt. The court grounded Rachel and ordered her not to leave her mother's home. She could not watch television or have friends over to the house, but she could read and do crafts. The court reprimanded the mother for not being able to induce the girls to attend scheduled visits, and ordered her to enforce these measures strenuously. The court then placed Heidi, the older of the two children, in a juvenile detention facility until she agreed to visit with her father. Heidi was not handcuffed, but she was shackled with leg irons as she was transferred from the courthouse to the juvenile jail to serve her sentence.

The appellate court held that although Heidi and Rachel were in civil contempt, the trial judge should have considered alternatives before restricting their liberty for violation of a visitation order. The appellate court suggested that, as an alternative, contempt proceedings be brought against the mother who was influencing the children not to visit.

When the trial court told Heidi and Rachel that they had to visit with their father under threat of punishment, Rachel responded, "You [the trial judge] ... just made the biggest mistake probably ever you could have made." Heidi, the older child, cautioned, "It's not that simple."[472] They were right. By holding the children in contempt, the trial court aligned itself with the non-custodial parent and pushed the children further away from reconciliation or, at the very least, from meaningful negotiation with their father.

As a child psychologist said at the time, "The children may well be inclined to blame the [non-custodial parent] for their punishment, since in their minds [he or she] is the reason it's all happening."[473] In the eyes of the children, the judge essentially became an agent of the non-custodial parent, aggravating the anger and distance they felt toward their father. The judgment of the court reinforced the children's hatred for the father because the judge reinforced the family polarization. There is no way out of this dilemma if the child custody court punishes a child for refusing to visit a parent.

What should the legal system do with children like Heidi and Rachel who are so alienated from their father that they are willing to risk serious punishment in order to avoid him? The first thing is to diagnose their position carefully and to listen carefully to their concerns. An alienated child has been defined recently as "one who expresses, freely and persistently, *unreasonable* negative feelings and beliefs (such as anger, hatred, rejection and/or fear) toward a parent that are significantly disproportionate to the child's actual experience with that parent . . . [T]he problem of the alienated child begins with a primary focus on the child, his or her observable behaviors, and parent-child relationships."[474]

Defining what are "unreasonable negative feelings and beliefs toward a parent" is difficult in particular cases, as theories and clinical judgments vary. Observation suggests that a significant number of divorcing children are alienated from a parent, but there is no empirical data that establishes the number of children who have those feelings, or whether the reasons for them are reasonable or unreasonable by any definition. Different emotional patterns may be the basis of a child's alienation. A child may, for example, choose sides simply to reduce stress – it is easier to ally with one parent than defend each parent against the other. Even if one parent is an enemy, by making a choice at least a child has an ally. Child alienation may also be the result of a deliberate scheme of brainwashing by one parent.

Some mental health professionals and courts look at the problem of child alienation as a diagnosable mental health disorder, Parental Alienation Syndrome (PAS). PAS symptoms appear when one parent deliberately alienates the child from the other parent. The alienating parent's purpose is to use the child's feelings and behavior to eliminate the other parent from the child's life. The alienating parent often accuses the target parent of sexual abuse, an accusation that, as discussed in Chapter VIII, transforms the child custody dispute into a criminal or child protection proceeding, with great risks to parents and children.[475]

A PAS "diagnosis" justifies a court's decision to discount the child's reasons for not wanting to visit the target parent, and can give the target parent a significant victory. Some believe that if PAS is found, the best remedy is to shift custody of the child to the target parent, regardless of the child's feelings or relationship with that parent. The custody shift is a kind of "shock therapy" for the child affected by the alienating parent's PAS.

On a political level, PAS further fuels a gender war in custody cases. Fathers' groups view it as an antidote to an alleged epidemic of false accusations of domestic violence and child abuse. Women's groups view it as "junk science," a plot by fathers' groups to counter the protections and transformation in social attitudes that have emerged in recent years to improve the legal system's treatment of domestic violence and child abuse.

There is no systematic empirical data that establishes conclusively that parents who make allegations of child abuse, even false ones, and children who believe them have a recognized mental health disorder justifying a particular custody arrangement or course of treatment. PAS does not appear in the DSM-IV, the diagnostic manual for mental health professionals. Recent commentary has argued that courts should not consider expert findings of PAS.[476]

The battle over PAS focuses on the behavior of the parents, not the reactions of the child. Above all, courts need to know why the child rejects a parent. In some cases, a child has a rational reason for not wanting to visit, such as abuse or neglect. Regardless of accusations of PAS, these claims must be investigated carefully, not dismissed out of hand. The child's safety must be protected.

There is no magic bullet to cure alienated children. Child alienation is a symptom of a high-conflict family, and calls for differentiated case management and mandated services, including therapy for the child. Alienation of a child may have a serious factual basis, or it may be the result of a plot by one parent to poison the relationship between the other parent and the child. It should not be thought of as a unitary phenomenon – the child is either alienated or not – but rather as a matter of degree. It fluctuates in intensity from child to child and changes over time with positive and negative interventions.

Therapy may help children like Heidi and Rachel to develop a relationship with their father, as might a period of supervised visitation. In addition, the entire family's participation in an educational program for high-conflict parents and children might also help. Custody arrangements for alienated children should be changed only with the greatest care and with therapy to aid the children in any forced transition, not because of a diagnostic label without empirical support.

Ultimately, if the court's efforts to nurture a relationship between the alienated child and the rejected parent fail, the court should not punish the child, no matter how irrational the child's feelings. Punishment, if any, should be focused on the parent who deliberately causes the alienation and makes deliberately false accusations. Courts can only encourage children, but not force them, to have relationships with their parents. It is hard to conceive of a situation when it is in a child's best interests to be treated like a criminal because of his or her negative feelings toward a parent. We simply have to accept the reality that there are some things that are beyond the power of child custody courts to correct, even if they are contrary to a child's best interests in having a relationship with both parents.

XII Neutral Mental Health Evaluators

Mental health professionals play a variety of roles in child custody disputes. Many provide confidential therapy for parents and children. Sometimes they mediate, although, as discussed in Chapter V, not all mediators are mental health professionals. Mental health professionals sometimes serve as expert witnesses, and are paid by one parent. This chapter focuses on the mental health expert as a neutral evaluator (sometimes called a "forensic evaluator" or a "neutral expert") appointed by the court.

The Role of the Neutral Mental Health Evaluator

Child custody is one of the few areas in which our otherwise adversarial, party-driven courts routinely appoint a neutral expert to conduct an investigation on its behalf. In the typical auto accident or medical malpractice case, for example, courts rely on parties to a dispute to present and pay for partisan expert testimony. In contrast, courts in child custody disputes regularly appoint a neutral mental evaluator to report on the functioning of parents and children and family dynamics and to make recommendations for custody arrangements that the court should order in the child's best interests.[477] The evaluator's report focuses the court and the parents on the children's best interests, not on the perspective of either parent. The evaluator also brings information and perspective to the court's attention that neither parent might produce on his or her own initiative.

The neutral evaluator proactively interviews parents and children, reviews relevant records, and seeks information from "collateral sources" (e.g., a child's teacher or therapist). The neutral evaluator can be a psychologist, psychiatrist, social worker, or a staff member of the local family court services bureau. He or she has no financial allegiance to either parent, as the court usually orders the parents to pay for the expert's report in proportion to their ability to pay. The neutral evaluator can insist on an interview with both parents and children to review relevant records, and can use the compulsory process of the court to enforce these ground rules. Nothing that anyone says to the evaluator is confidential. The evaluator submits a written report to the court before trial. The evaluator is available as a witness at trial and can be cross-examined by either parent.

The fundamental dilemma the child custody court faces in appointing a neutral mental health evaluator is that he or she can be too influential in shaping the court's decision. Neutral forensic evaluators are aides to judges, but they are not the judges themselves. The judge – the accountable public official – must make an independent determination of the child's best interests. The judge can, but is not required to, rely on the evaluator's report and recommendations in making a custody determination.

The Benefits of the Neutral Mental Health Evaluator

Neutral mental health evaluators generally perform a valuable service for the court, parents, and children by providing a holistic assessment of how well family members cope with the stress of divorce. Their report and recommendations focus the court, the parents, and their lawyers on the emotional functioning and well-being of the child and other family members at a very stressful and difficult time in their lives.

The neutral mental health evaluator also serves as a check on the biases and motivations of the judge in a child custody case. Every professional involved in a child custody dispute has potential biases and different theories on how children best develop and thrive, based on his or her experiences and values. A judge can, for example, be subconsciously biased against working mothers or against fathers having the ability to care for infants. The report of a mental health evaluator that a judge disregards in making a custody determination can provide a useful signal to an appellate court that it should pay careful attention to that particular case.

A court-appointed mental health evaluator may also favorably affect the behavior of the parents before the trial. "In some cases, evaluations can provide families with assistance in their decision making."[478] The evaluator's report encourages settlement by stimulating the negotiation process with a vision from a credible source of what custody arrangements are in the child's best interests. The expert's report informs parents distracted by the divorce about their child's emotional health and encourages the parents to look at their continuing conflict from the child's perspective. The evaluator's explanation of recommendations enhances their understanding of the child's needs and their strengths and weaknesses as parents. The evaluator's scrutiny motivates parents to control their most aggressive actions and impulses toward each other for fear that the expert will draw unfavorable inferences.

The parents also know that the evaluator's report is, in effect, a preview of the court's ruling. The parent who receives a less than favorable report will think seriously about settling rather than pushing the dispute to trial, where the outcome could be even worse. "Litigants are cognizant that a judge has chosen or endorsed a court-appointed expert. Therefore, an expert's report serves as a predictor of a judge's decision and a blueprint for settlement negotiations."[479]

A mental health expert paid by one parent and selected by that parent's lawyer will always be suspected of being a "hired gun." Often, he or she will not have the opportunity to interview the other parent before reaching conclusions, because one parent has no incentive to cooperate with an expert chosen by the other side. In all likelihood, the reports and testimony of party-paid mental health experts will be incomplete and subject to attack for partisan bias.

Courts thus appropriately tend to consider reports of neutral experts more seriously than those of a party-paid expert. After a neutral expert has reported, courts usually do not require parents and children to be examined by an additional party-paid expert.[480]

Party-paid mental health experts do still participate in child custody disputes. Their remaining major role is to provide a critique and evaluation of the report of the neutral mental health evaluator. Thus they serve as a valuable check on the quality and influence of the neutral evaluator and help ensure that the court does not rely on the neutral evaluator's report and recommendations without critical evaluation. Many parents, however, cannot afford to pay for both a neutral evaluator and for another expert to critique the neutral evaluator, so the number of disputes in which both neutral and party-paid experts are involved is probably quite small.

Accountability and Quality Assurance

The advent of neutral mental health evaluators is a desirable movement away from exclusive reliance on the adversary process in the child custody court. It is a young and evolving profession, having entered the child custody dispute resolution process in great numbers and influence only since the 1980s, when emotional rather than moral concerns increasingly came to be viewed as the core of what was before the court for decision.[481]

Like lawyers for children, neutral evaluators are an unpredictable factor in the child custody system. As professionals, they can help tip the balance in favor of the child by illuminating his or her best interests for parents, counsel, and the court from a dispassionate, neutral perspective. An evaluator's acting unprofessionally, or providing opinions and recommendations to the court from an ideological bias or without adequate supporting data, can further inflame an already difficult situation. To reduce that risk, child custody courts need to be critical consumers of the reports of neutral evaluators, and devote attention to ensuring their quality and accountability.

The critical attitude that courts should take in considering an expert's report is exemplified by the actions of the trial court in a 1999 California case, which modified the recommendations of a neutral evaluator on physical custody, and was attacked by a disappointed parent on appeal for doing so. The appellate court nonetheless affirmed the trial court's critical review and modification of the expert's report by stating:

Although the court's order does not comply with the court expert's recommendations, it does address itself to the problems found by the expert and should be of benefit to the minor. This appears to be the essence of intelligent judging. Not willing to be a mere rubberstamp for what the sole expert thought was best, the court came up with its own modification, one that would answer the difficulties shown by the parties' previous experience and identified by the expert.[482]

The qualifications and training for neutral evaluators and the techniques for evaluation are not standardized. Different segments of the mental health community (psychiatrists, psychologists, social workers) all play the role of neutral evaluator in different courts. Some mental health evaluators rely on psychological tests; some do not. Some interview "collateral sources" (children's teachers, doctors, day-care providers); others do not. In contrast to the *Model Standards of Practice for Family and Divorce Mediation*, which apply to all mediators regardless of profession of origin, different standards have been created by different segments of the mental health community for evaluators.[483]

The guidelines of the American Psychological Association for child custody evaluators, for example, are aspirational only, and are not intended "to be mandatory or exhaustive."[484] The *APA Guidelines* do not tell the practitioner who should be interviewed during the evaluation, whether psychological testing is appropriate, or how evaluations should be reported. They note, but do not resolve, the question whether an evaluator should be make recommendations to the court for the final custody determination.

The training and development of neutral mental evaluators is nonetheless improving as the role and profession mature. Several books from the 1990s seek to standardize and provide a more scientific basis for evaluations in child custody cases.[485] Some states, most notably California, have made an effort to create greater uniformity of training and practice of neutral evaluators by enacting appropriate court rules.[486] This effort has not yet reached a national level.

Ethics and Role Conflict

It should also be noted that whereas parents make many complaints against neutral evaluators to professional licensing boards, only 1% of those complaints result in a finding of misconduct requiring professional discipline.[487] In a small number of reported cases, evaluators have abused the authority and the confidence the court has placed in them. In one case, for example, a mental health professional served as an evaluator and also began to treat one of the children as a patient.[488] In another case, a neutral evaluator presented such a biased analysis and recommendations that the court deemed him to be an advocate for one of the parties instead of a neutral evaluator.[489] In a third case, the court criticized a neutral evaluation by child protection services for inadequate investigation of claims of child abuse in a custody dispute.[490]

The role of a neutral evaluator is an unfamiliar one to many mental health professionals, and its obligations are different from those required of a therapist, educator, mediator, arbitrator, or special master involved with a divorcing family. Mental health professionals must understand that a neutral evaluator is not a therapist for parents or children. An evaluator's job is to evaluate, not to treat or to cure a patient. The evaluator's client is the court and the child's best interests, not the parents or the child. A therapist or a mediator has an obligation of confidentiality to the parents, to the children, and to the participants in the mediation. A neutral evaluator does not have an obligation of confidentiality to the parents or anyone who participates in the evaluation process.[491] Anything a parent says to a neutral evaluator can end up in the evaluator's report to the court. It is vital that neutral evaluators make these critical role distinctions and avoid charges of breaches of professional duty, for even the smallest matters can be overblown in the emotionally charged atmosphere of a child custody dispute.

Improving Reports

Evaluation reports also need to be standardized and improved. Researchers in 2002 analyzed the content of many actual reports and, encouragingly, found that most evaluators use multiple sources to produce reports in conformity with professional guidelines. Discouragingly, the researchers also found that a small number of reports they reviewed were "adult-focused, predominantly test-oriented, or conducted by an evaluator who functioned in multiple roles (e.g., therapist and evaluator)."[492] Many evaluators do not document their discussions of informed consent and confidentiality with the parents they evaluate in their reports. Many reports do not include a child history or a discussion of how the evaluator interacted with the participants. These problematic omissions tarnish the reputation of all child custody evaluators among the legal community and parents.

The same researchers also reported that many judges and lawyers prefer shorter, focused reports to rambling discourses, thus forcing the evaluator to limit the amount of information he or she provides in an evaluation report. Some evaluators overload their reports with details, discussions of methodology, and mental health jargon in an attempt to ward off claims of malpractice by unhappy parents – the neutral evaluator's equivalent of practicing defensive medicine. Reports of this kind tend to be unreadable, and sometimes incomprehensible to parents, judges, and lawyers alike.

Responsibility for the quality of the evaluation begins with the child custody court, which should decide on its scope as part of its plan to manage the case. The court, not the evaluator, should specify the purpose of the report and the questions that the evaluator should answer. The 2001 *Wingspread Conference Report* on high-conflict custody cases discussed in previous chapters distinguishes between

a 'child custody evaluation' [which] is comparative and focuses on family relationships, parental capacities, and the needs of the children ... [and] a 'parental capacity evaluation' [which] focuses on one parent. A parental capacity evaluation should not be confused with a child custody evaluation. A child custody evaluation requires the voluntary or court-ordered participation of both parents and the children. A parental capacity evaluation can be conducted on behalf of one parent alone.[493]

A child custody court should specify whether it wants the evaluator to conduct a custody evaluation or a parental capacity evaluation. If a court wants an evaluator to report on whether a parent who abuses drugs can participate in a joint custody arrangement, the court might ask the evaluator for a parental capacity evaluation to determine the parent's fitness. If, however, the court wants a comparative evaluation between competing parenting plans presented by the mother and the father, the court should instruct the evaluator to conduct a child custody evaluation. It is up to the court, not the evaluator, to decide what information it wants, and to frame the evaluation questions appropriately. In this way, the court will regulate the scope of work of the evaluator and the expense and time of the evaluation at the outset. If the court does not specify what it wants, the evaluator should ask.

The evaluator should also remember that the court, the parents, and their counsel constitute the audience for their reports. To ensure that the report benefits the audience, the *Wingspread Conference Report* recommends that [sic]:

> Evaluation reports should be written in plain English.
> 1. Avoid technical jargon.
> 2. Accentuate positive parental attributes as well as negative ones.
> 3. Avoid adding to the family's shame by stigmatizing or blaming parents or children.
> 4. Psychiatric diagnoses should not be used unless they are relevant to parenting.
> 5. Legal terms should be used only when necessary.
> 6. ... [R]eports should provide clear, detailed recommendations that are consistent with the health, safety, welfare, and best interests of the child.[494]

Evaluators, who come from a technical, professional background, obviously need training and feedback to accomplish these goals.

Quality of the Information in an Evaluation

There is also the problem of what a neutral evaluation should include. Some divergence on this subject is desirable because different evaluators can adopt different techniques for different cases, available financial resources, and family situations. Fundamental differences between evaluators on how to perform their task, however, create concern among judges and lawyers about the underlying validity of the theory that drives the evaluation process.

There is no agreement, for example, on whether evaluators should conduct psychological testing of parents and children as part of the evaluation process. Many evaluators routinely use psychological testing as part of their evaluations. Tests can confirm data from observation and other sources and help in the diagnosis of the mental status of parents. Test results also add an air of unjustified objectivity (and greater expense) to the evaluator's report, as often the tests used are of questionable reliability and are not carefully related to the question of a parent's ability to parent.[495] There is simply no test that can tell an evaluator who is a better parent for a child or what kind of custody arrangement is in a child's best interests.[496] Most tests used in custody evaluations require "the evaluator to infer that the general characteristics measured by the test (e.g., intelligence or pathology) determine qualities of parenting."[497]

Common experience indicates that many intelligent people are less-than-stellar parents, and many people who score less well on intelligence tests or whose test scores demonstrate a degree of pathology are excellent parents. An experienced, sophisticated evaluator who relies on tests recognizes that the data these tests produce is simply part of the overall picture. Judges and lawyers, or less experienced evaluators, may, however, place excessive reliance on seemingly objective results. The fear of inaccurate generalization is what makes reliance on psychological testing in custody evaluations so controversial in the field of neutral evaluation. The tests that are specifically designed for parents and children in custody disputes are of questionable validity.[498]

Evaluators must also be careful to discriminate between the different kinds of "collateral information" they gather for a child custody evaluation. Although a judge in a custody dispute can sometimes consider hearsay testimony (statements made by people not present to testify in court), the judge is generally aware of the limitations of the quality of the information that hearsay presents. Collateral witnesses interviewed by evaluators may have a bias in one direction or another. These witnesses may not be available in court to be cross-examined. Yet their information may find its way into the evaluation and influence the evaluator's report and his or her recommendations to the court.

Mental health professionals are no more skilled than anyone else in determining whether someone is telling the truth or not. It is the court's job to separate the true from the false in a custody dispute. Evaluation reports should specifically label any reliance on hearsay testimony as such so that parents can challenge the information gathered and the court can scrutinize it appropriately. Evaluators should weigh information from neutral parties such as teachers more heavily than information from partisan witnesses identified by a parent. When relying on collateral sources, evaluators should focus on gathering behavioral descriptions of important events, not witnesses' opinions on a parent's character or who should have custody.[499] The evaluator should bring conflicting information from collateral sources to the attention of the court, not resolve them alone.

Funding and Accessibility

A neutral mental health evaluation is an extensive and expensive undertaking, and those who do it should not be expected to work without being paid. The evaluator must be adequately compensated to undertake a thorough investigation and write a careful report. An inadequate report is worse, in many ways, than none at all.

Extensive reliance on neutral mental evaluations in the child custody dispute-resolution process thus produces the same financing problems as appointing a lawyer for children or a special master/parenting coordinator. Some parents cannot afford these evaluations. If the state pays for the neutral mental health evaluations, then adequate compensation to ensure widespread availability of quality services must come from an underfunded court.

Cost considerations alone suggest that courts should not routinely use neutral mental health evaluations, but when they do, they should carefully coordinate the scope of these evaluations with other aspects of a case management plan. For example, if the court appoints a neutral evaluator, it may not also need to appoint a Guardian who performs many of the same tasks.

The Limitations of Mental Health Knowledge

Above all, both courts and evaluators must recognize that in an adversarial framework where one side wins and the other side loses, legal decisions and mental health evaluations occupy different conceptual universes. Mental health evaluations are probability judgments and risk assessments. Even after the most careful evaluation, it is impossible for even the best-trained, most competent mental health professional to guarantee that a particular custody arrangement will benefit a child. Mental health practitioners are trained in a philosophical structure that allows them to make risky or uncertain judgments. They are comfortable with the idea that their predictions and clinical judgments may turn out to be incorrect in light of greater knowledge created by the passage of time and the evaluation of experience.[500]

Despite the predictive nature of a child custody determination, lawyers and courts want as much certainty as possible in fact-finding and decision-making, and they challenge practitioners of other disciplines to produce it. They often want an expert to state definitively that a parent has a particular deficit that makes the other parent a more desirable primary residential parent, or that a child will certainly benefit from residence with one parent. "There is a danger that, because of the law's preference for certainty, experts will overreify their observations and reach beyond legitimate interpretations of the data both to appear 'expert' and to provide usable opinions. Similarly, legal decisionmakers may discard [mental health expert] testimony properly given in terms of probabilities as 'speculative' and may defer instead to experts whose judgments are expressed in categorical opinions . . ."[501]

We have no evidence that mental health professionals make better predictions of what is in a child's best interests than do courts, or vice versa. Evaluators need to be both humble and transparent in making predictions and judgments about the questions that courts must decide. The responsibility for making custody determinations still rests with judges, not with the mental health experts they appoint in order to help them get a fuller picture of family dynamics.

Neutral evaluators provide a valuable perspective into the inherently uncertain risk assessment that is a child custody determination. Given that the future of a child is at stake, the more input a court gets about the risks the child faces, the better. The neutral evaluator should, however, resist any temptation or pressure from judges, lawyers, and parents to become judges in the guise of performing their task, and judges should hold them accountable for any sloppy work. A good neutral evaluator should welcome effective cross-examination by a parent's attorney as a method of clarifying the basis of the expert's opinion. Judges, lawyers, and parents must exercise restraint and not ask for certainty in mental health evaluations. Each profession must stay within its area of expertise and assigned role if the child custody decision-making process is to function in an accountable manner. The *Wingspread Conference Report* thus recommends:

In reporting or testifying about their custody or visitation recommendations, mental health professionals should distinguish between their clinical judgments, research-based opinions, and philosophical positions. In addition, mental health professionals should summarize their data-gathering procedures, information sources, and time spent and present all relevant information on limitations of the evaluation that result from unobtainable information, failure of a party to cooperate, or the circumstances of particular interviews.[502]

If ordered with care, discrimination, and accountability, an evaluation by neutral mental health experts can play an extremely valuable role in helping to resolve contested child custody cases. It should be part of the court's overall plan for differential case management of a particular family's dispute when parent education and mediation cannot bring about a voluntary resolution. By legal standards, the profession of neutral evaluator is still in its infancy, and will develop its credentials and techniques as it grows. Until legislatures delegate child custody decision making to mental health professionals, courts remain the ultimate authority over the best interests of children. Judges should not automatically defer to the recommendations of an evaluator in order to avoid the time and trouble of hearing a case or because of the evaluator's expertise. Judges must be critical consumers of the evaluator's work to ensure that decision making for the children of divorce remains accountable to democratic values.

XIII The "Best Interests" Test and Its Presumption-Based Competitors

So far, this book has largely addressed the operating procedures and policies of the child custody court and its allied professionals. This chapter, in contrast, discusses the rules of law that a judge in child custody court applies in order to resolve parents' disputes when they cannot do so themselves.

If parents cannot agree, the legal standard the child custody court traditionally applies is the "best interests of the child" test.[503] As discussed in Chapter II, gender-biased presumptions, first in favor of the father, then of the mother, for a long time governed the way judges determined a child's best interests. Once the predictability of gender bias was eliminated from custody decision-making, our diverse society struggled to redefine the meaning of the child's best interests.

The resulting multi-factored best interests test has been heavily criticized as too discretionary and unpredictable to provide guidance to courts and litigants and too vague to guard against the risk of arbitrary judicial decision making. Mary Ann Glendon expresses a typical view:

The 'best interests' standard is a prime example of the futility of attempting to achieve perfect, individualized justice by reposing discretion in a judge . . . Its vagueness provides maximum incentive to those who are inclined to wrangle over custody, and it asks the judge to do what is almost impossible: evaluate the child-caring capacities of a mother and a father at a time when family relations are apt to be most distorted by the stress of separation and the divorce process itself.[504]

It is easier, however, to criticize the best interests test as uncertain and unpredictable than to propose a workable alternative that wins universal acceptance and acclaim. Winston Churchill once said of democracy that "it is the worst form of Government except all those other forms that have been tried from time to time."[505] The same may be said of the best interests test – it is the worst standard for child custody decision making except by comparison with all other tests.

This chapter reviews the best interest test and its alternatives by comparing with the ALI's proposals in 2002 to create a presumption of joint legal custody (decision making) and an "approximation" presumption (in fact an updated version of the primary caretaker presumption) as the rule of decision for contested physical custody (residence) cases. This chapter also compares the approximation presumption and the best interests test with another competitor – the proposed presumption that requires courts to divide a child's residence time with each parent equally. The chapter concludes by discussing proposals to make divorce more difficult for parents compared with childless couples because of the harm that divorce causes to children.

The "Best Interests" Test

It is not completely accurate to say that the "best interests" test is standardless. Courts or legislatures have articulated factors that judges should consider in making best interest determinations. Minnesota's statute is typical:

> The best interests of the child means all relevant factors to be considered and evaluated by the court including:
> 1. the wishes of the child's parent or parents as to custody;
> 2. the reasonable preference of the child, if the court deems the child to be of sufficient age to express a preference;
> 3. the child's primary caretaker;
> 4. the intimacy of the relationship between each parent and the child;
> 5. the interaction and interrelationship of the child with a parent or parents, siblings, and any other person who may significantly affect the child's best interests;
> 6. the child's adjustment to home, school, and community;
> 7. the length of time the child has lived in a stable, satisfactory environment and the desirability of maintaining continuity;
> 8. the permanence, as a family unit, of the existing or proposed custodial home;
> 9. the mental and physical health of all individuals involved; except that a disability . . . of a proposed custodian or the child shall not be determinative of the custody of the child, unless the proposed custodial arrangement is not in the best interest of the child;
> 10. the capacity and disposition of the parties to give the child love, affection, and guidance, and to continue educating and raising the child in the child's culture and religion or creed, if any;
> 11. the child's cultural background;
> 12. the effect on the child of the actions of an abuser, if related to domestic abuse . . . that has occurred between the parents or between a parent and another individual, whether or not the individual alleged to have committed domestic abuse is or ever was a family or household member of the parent; and

13. except in cases in which a finding of domestic abuse...has been made, the disposition of each parent to encourage and permit frequent and continuing contact by the other parent with the child.

The court may not use one factor to the exclusion of all others. The primary-caretaker factor may not be used as a presumption in determining the best interests of the child. The court must make detailed findings on each of the factors and explain how the factors led to its conclusions and to the determination of the best interests of the child.[506]

When scholars criticize the best interests test as arbitrary, they really criticize the great discretion it grants the trial court to apply the types of factors listed in the Minnesota statute. The factors are broadly stated and not weighted in importance. In making a custody determination, for example, the court can choose to weigh the child's preferences over the benefit of his or her having a continuing relationship with a parent. A judge in a different courtroom across the hall might not make the same choice for the same child and parents. Trial courts must articulate their reasons in applying the factors, thereby providing some protection against arbitrary decision making. But neither judge would likely be reversed on appeal, given the great discretion that trial courts have in making child custody decisions. Even if an appellate court reviewed and reversed a trial court decision, the process is slow, expensive, and frustrating.

The Benefits and Costs of the Best Interests Test

The best interests test does have a great moral virtue – it directs the child custody court to thoroughly review each child's particular circumstances without preconceptions or presumptions. The individualized nature of the inquiry is a tribute to our society's collective sense that relationships between children and parents are unique and should be judged individually. It takes time, resources, and faith in the rationality of child custody court judges to embrace the best interests test. These qualities are in short supply in emotionally wounded divorcing parents and perhaps in the academic critics of the test.

It is nonetheless fair to say that since the best interests test creates great uncertainty about the probable outcome of custody litigation, it encourages parents to litigate and to argue. As Robert Mnookin and Lewis Kornhauser point out, uncertainty in the probable outcome rewards the parent who is willing to risk litigation and has the emotional and financial resources to continue the conflict in court,[507] an incentive structure that works against the child's interest in reducing parental conflict. This is the principal motivation for those who seek an alternative to the discretion that the best interests test bestows on judges in the child custody court.

ALI Proposals

The *ALI Principles* show the influence of academic criticism of the best interests test to be uncertain and arbitrary by recommending presumptions to guide judicial decision-making if parents cannot agree. The ALI divides custody into two categories: decision-making (legal custody) and residence (physical custody). It advocates a presumption of joint decision making for major matters concerning the child (e.g., health care, education, permission to marry). "[T]he court should be required to presume that an allocation of decision making responsibility to each legal parent . . . who has been exercising a reasonable share of parenting functions for the child, jointly, is in the child's best interests."[508] The ALI makes exceptions to joint decision making for (1) day-to-day decisions while a child is in residence at the other parent's home, (2) when a parent is violent, and (3) when it is otherwise shown that joint decision making is not in the child's best interests.[509]

For physical custody, the ALI advocates an "approximation" presumption. Under this presumption, "the court should allocate custodial responsibility so that the proportion of custodial time the child spends with each parent approximates the time each parent spent performing care taking functions for the time prior to the parents' separation."[510] Professor Katharine Bartlett, the ALI's Reporter (chief drafter and researcher) for the proposed custody standards, explains how the approximation presumption operates:

In effect, it amounts to a primary caretaker presumption when one parent has been exercising a substantial majority of the past caretaking, and it amounts to a joint custody presumption when past caretaking has been shared equally in the past.[511]

The approximation presumption assumes that the parents' allocation of care-taking responsibilities before divorce is in the child's best interests after the parents' divorce. If the father was the child's primary caretaker for 60% of the time before divorce, he is awarded 60% of the child's physical custody after divorce.

The Problems with Custody Presumptions

Presumptions such as those advocated by the ALI are blunt tools to confine judicial decision making in an area as sensitive and diverse as reorganizing parent-child relationships. For some children, the presumption should not override other important factors that should shape a parenting plan. For example, let us suppose that the court presumes it should order equal physical custody, meaning the parents should share the child's residence equally each week. However, the child, a teenager, wants to spend more time with his father, who has been his primary caretaker in recent years since most of the child's friends are in the father's neighborhood. The mother lives a significant distance away and has a demanding job that requires a great deal of time and effort. She insists on joint physical custody because she wants to maintain an equal role in the child's life. It is highly unlikely that without the original presumption, the court would find that an equal physical custody plan is in this child's best interests. But under a presumption that most children benefit from equal physical custody, the court begins with just that premise until persuaded otherwise.

Furthermore, presumptions that guide custody decisions in contested cases create legal entitlements that may inadvertently influence the bargaining and trade-offs of divorce settlement negotiations. A presumption of equal physical custody, for example, generally favors men who have not taken care of their children on a day-to-day basis, whereas a presumption favoring primary caretakers and continuity of pre-divorce child care relationships generally favors women. Each can use a custody presumption in his or her favor as a bargaining chip to seek more-favorable financial terms in a divorce settlement. Because of the custody presumption, the parent who it favors may receive more economic benefits than he or she would otherwise be entitled to. Custody presumptions can thus create an incentive for parents to confuse their personal economic interests with their children's emotional needs, compounding the difficulties parents already face in focusing on the children's best interests in the turbulence of divorce.

A Presumption of Joint Decision Making?

A strong argument can nonetheless be made in support of the ALI's proposed presumption of joint decision-making, with its exceptions for day-to-day decisions and violent parents. Studies, discussed in Chapter III, indicate that children in joint custody arrangements generally do better emotionally, educationally, and economically than their counterparts in sole custody arrangements. A carefully applied presumption of joint decision-making, with exceptions for family violence, recognizes that it is in the child's best interests to have both parents play an important role in the child's post-divorce life, and encourages both of them to do so. Joint decision making may also provide some protection against child abuse in the reorganized family, as it keeps more than one parent involved in the child's life and thus provides something of a monitor for the child's treatment.

A legal standard that affirms that both fathers and mothers have equal rights and responsibilities for children after divorce is a symbolic statement of gender and parental equality. Before parents get divorced, the legal system views their responsibility to make decisions for their children as a joint one. In effect, a presumption of joint decision making after divorce simply extends that expectation to the reorganized family. Marriage is a partnership that includes making important decisions for children together. "Joint [legal] custodians of both sexes are more apt to characterize decision-making about the children as shared."[512] The important social policies behind the partnership theory of marriage suggest that the child custody court should be extremely cautious in deciding that one parent should have a greater right to make decisions for a child than the other. That caution is especially appropriate inasmuch as parental rights are constitutionally protected.

The main argument against a presumption of joint decision-making is that it will encourage continuing instability and conflict over the child. There is certainly a paradox in presuming that divorcing parents who may not respect each other should make decisions for their child jointly. As discussed in Chapter IV, the solution to the paradox is a judicial recognition that the ability of parents to make joint decisions should not be measured at the time of their most intense conflict. Dispute resolution programs, a period of parallel parenting, therapy, and the passage of time can help many parents change the level of conflict. A presumption of joint decision making should be accompanied by mandated mediation, and perhaps arbitration, for disputes about matters on which the parents cannot agree. If these interventions fail, and conflict levels do not change, the court can change joint decision making to sole custody as a last resort, awarding sole legal custody to the parent who seems to be more cooperative with the other parent in making decisions for the child.

The Approximation Presumption?

While the presumption of joint decision making recommended by the ALI is appropriate, the approximation presumption is more problematic. The approximation presumption does respond to many of the criticisms of the best interests test. It provides a predictable, gender-neutral rule based on measurable facts, such as who took care of the children in the past, rather than on speculative predictions of the child's future best interests. "One of the virtues of the past caretaking standard is that it relieves courts of making difficult determinations such as who is the best parent, who has the strongest emotional connection to the child, or who will be the best parent. The standard requires only that the courts make the kind of decisions they are accustomed to making: what happened in the past."[513]

The approximation presumption also recognizes the importance of preserving the stability of relationships and attachments for the child at a time of great stress and uncertainty. It is not a primary-caretaker standard in the sense that it does not assume that there is a single primary-caretaking parent in any family. Rather, the approximation principle preserves after divorce the relationship between care-giving and custody before it. If the parents shared care-giving responsibilities equally before divorce, they share it after divorce. If one parent provided most of the child's care before divorce, he or she receives the right to provide most of the care after divorce. The approximation principle thus reduces the risk to the child of being placed with a less experienced care-giver. The approximation presumption preserves the parenting status quo; parents neither gain nor lose any time after the divorce that they had with the child before it.

Despite its virtues, non-primary-caretaking parents, mostly men, may resent the idea that their pre-divorce or separation caretaking time with the child should determine their post-divorce or separation caretaking role. Although gender-neutral on its face, the approximation presumption was "crafted by women" as an alternative to joint custody, which they perceived as the "handiwork of men."[514] In most cases, the approximation presumption will allocate more of the child's time to the mother, as mothers do most of the pre-divorce work of caring for children. Non-primary-caretaking parents may view the unequal division of caretaking responsibilities between parents before divorce as part of an agreed-upon division of labor, and feel that they should not be penalized for working outside the home for the benefit of the other spouse and the child.[515]

Furthermore, men will likely perceive the approximation presumption as gender-biased and an incentive for women to file for divorce. Most divorce filers today are women, and most available evidence suggests that they are also the primary initiators of divorce.[516] The single strongest factor that seems to influence the rate at which women file for divorce is the probability that they will receive custody of the children. The higher that probability, the more likely a woman will file.[517]

The approximation presumption may also be looked at as a return on investment in child-rearing, the legal system's reward for the parent who spent the most time and energy caring for the child during the marriage. Child-rearing is certainly not a glamorous task, and if often goes seriously uncompensated and unrecognized in our society. A custody award to a parent, however, should not be a form of indirect compensation for time expended on child rearing. This argument is inconsistent with the partnership theory of marriage, which generally prohibits the allocation of the marital estate accumulated by the spouses according to their roles in creating the wealth. No court would recognize an argument today that the spouse who created a business (which is a marital asset) should get more of the business at the time of divorce because of a greater contribution to its development. The contributions of the other spouse in keeping the home and raising the children would be recognized in a fair division of the business even if the stay-at-home spouse made no direct contribution to its growth and development. Social policy suggests that we should not invite one partner to a marriage to argue in court that he or she did more to enhance one marital asset, and therefore deserves more of the judicial distribution of that asset upon divorce. But the approximation presumption does just that. It is inconsistent with the ideal of marriage as a lifetime partnership to which the partners make different, but equally important, contributions.

In any event, custody should be determined not by what a parent deserves but what a child needs. The approximation presumption assumes that the child's best interests are served by awarding more physical custody to the parent with whom the child has spent more time. It thus runs the risk of confusing the quantity of time spent with the quality of the interaction between parent and child. As discussed in Chapter III, contemporary theory and research supports the idea that children need secure attachments to competent care-givers for their emotional well-being. The approximation presumption assumes that there is "a reasonably high correlation between the amount of time spent in direct caretaking functions by a parent, the child's development of attachments, and the child's future socio-emotional well-being... [H]owever, in... attachment theory it is secure attachments that are predictive of future socio-emotional well-being, not simply attachments. Furthermore, the development of secure attachments is associated not only with the time spent in caregiving but also with the quality of caregiving."[518]

There is thus no reason to assume that a child's current primary caretaker is also his or her most important emotional attachment. The non-primary-caretaking parent also has significant emotional attachments to the child that are arguably as important – although more likely different – as the emotional attachment that the child has with his or her primary caretaker. The idea that the primary caretaker's emotional attachment to the child is presumptively more important than anyone else's is reminiscent of the search for a single psychological parent, a task that has been heavily discredited by modern research that suggests that children have multiple attachments and that fathers and mothers are of equal importance in children's emotional lives after divorce. As a leading interdisciplinary treatise on child custody law for judges puts it, the approximation principle does not recognize that "comparative time spent may not adequately reflect each parent's emotional relationship with the child while the marriage subsisted."[519] Children may well need two parents more than they need either one of them, no matter what role the parent played in the child's life before the divorce. We do not have enough data to address this matter with any confidence.

Moreover, the approximation presumption predicts post-divorce child care patterns based on past performance. The approximation presumption thus does not take into account the probability of post-divorce change in parenting roles. It is difficult to say with any degree of confidence that pre-divorce or separation caretaking arrangements in a particular family will remain stable after divorce or after separation. Many parents take new jobs and new partners after divorce. Some reduce their work loads to spend more time with their children. It is preferable for parents to have the flexibility to redefine their relationship to work, to their children, and to each other after divorce rather than rigidly continuing in pre-divorce patterns.

As the previously mentioned interdisciplinary treatise for judges states, the approximation principle "denies both spouses, except by mutual agreement, the right to change roles when the marriage terminates."[520]

A child's pre-divorce parenting arrangements do provide the court with important data in shaping a parenting plan, and the available evidence indicates that courts do take it into account as a major factor in contested cases. Only one state, West Virginia, has enacted a previous care-giving standard as the fundamental basis for making awards in contested child custody cases.[521] Radical change in a child's living arrangements should certainly not be made precipitously and without consideration of any potential adverse effect on the child. Adults may, however, underestimate both a child's capacity to adapt to new physical surroundings and willingness to accept change for the sake of continuing relationships with both parents. These judgments must be made on an individual basis, not on a global presumption that past parental caretaking roles should determine the future.

Finally, and perhaps most importantly, the approximation presumption does not take into account the importance of both parents in the post-divorce life of the child. The available data strongly suggests that a child of divorce generally benefits from having relationships with both parents after divorce. In making a best interests determination, courts should take into account which parent is more likely to involve the other parent in the child's life as one factor in a custody determination. Doing so creates an incentive for both parents to behave responsibly toward the other and to foster the child's interest in a continuing relationship with both. The approximation presumption eliminates that incentive by basing current entitlement to custody solely on past parenting behavior rather than on future cooperation for the child's benefit.

The Presumption of Equal Physical Custody?

The presumption that the child should spend 50% of his or her time with each parent is the principal competitor to the approximation presumption advocated by the ALI. A presumption of equal post-divorce physical custody, its advocates argue, symbolizes mother-father emotional and legal equality and encourages (some might say requires) a child to have a continuing relationship with both parents after divorce.

Whereas the approximation presumption emphasizes the parents' pre-divorce allocation of child-rearing responsibilities too much, a presumption of equal physical custody does not emphasize it enough. A fifty-fifty post-divorce residence presumption departs radically from the child-care arrangements that exist in most families prior to divorce. A corporate executive who spends little time with his or her children before divorce will have to substantially reorder life priorities to spend 50% of his or her time with them after divorce. A court administering a presumption of equal physical custody starts from the premise that this executive should have the children live with him or her 50% of the time without any evidence that he or she is willing and able to devote that much time and effort to child care.

There is little evidence that most non-primary-caretaking parents actually want 50% of the child's residence time after divorce and are willing to make the changes in their lifestyles to accommodate equal physical custody. The leading study of equal physical custody in California, admittedly with families who created their custody arrangements in the 1980s, found that only 20% of divorcing families attempted equal physical custody, and most of the children in these arrangement spent the majority of their time with their mothers.[522]

There is empirical evidence, discussed in Chapter III, that joint custody generally benefits children. There is, however, no study that shows that a rigid, equal-time division between parents, regardless of other circumstances such as a child's preferences, is generally in a child's best interests. A mandated presumption of equal physical custody takes the choice and voice out of the hands of the children about which parent's home they want to live in, and when. British researchers who interviewed children in equal physical custody found that children recognize how important this arrangement is for their parents in terms of gender equality and emotional equivalence, "but this made it particularly hard for the children to alter the arrangements if it did not suit them."[523]

Perhaps, most importantly, a presumption of joint physical custody does not take into account the risk that it may inflame the fires of already high levels of parental conflict. Joint physical custody requires a significant amount of parental interaction and may create more opportunities for highly conflicted parents to aggravate each other the wrong way and place their child in the middle.

We know too little about the possible effects of an equal physical custody presumption on patterns of behavior for divorcing parents and children to make it the social policy of choice. Here, again, a presumption that seeks to limit a court's discretion in determining the child's best interests on an individualized basis may do more harm than good.

The Parenting Plan Alternative

The circumstances of parents and children are too discrete for the best interests of the children to be served by the approximation presumption, a joint physical custody presumption, or any other presumption concerning a child's post-divorce residence time. The most appropriate rule for contested physical custody cases is to encourage parents to reach their own agreements by submission of parenting plans developed through education and mediation. As discussed in Chapter IV, a useful step to support the development of parenting plans, and one supported by the ALI, is to move away from the possessory and proprietary terms "custody" and "visitation" to more neutral legal language such as "decision-making" and "residence."[524]

The court should require all parents to submit plans for a child's residence and decision-making plans as a first step in resolving contested cases. The plans should detail a parent's proposals for the way major decisions for the child will be made, provisions for resolving disputes if they arise, and specify as to where the parent believes the child should live over a one-year period on a day-by-day basis. The parents should attempt to reconcile any differences in their plans after education and through mediation. If parents still submit competing plans, the child custody court should choose between them, or create its own, based on the factors that have traditionally been part of the "best interests" analysis. One factor in that choice should be which plan is fairer and more likely to involve the other parent in the post-divorce life of the child. Another should be the child's past caretaking arrangements.

Child Protective Divorce Laws?

Some have argued that the best way for the state to protect children from the difficulties of divorce is to make divorce more difficult for parents to obtain. As discussed in Chapter II, all states at present have some variation of a no-fault divorce law. Those who advocate a stricter standard suggest that parents should be required to prove something more in order to get divorced than childless couples.[525] If the court found that the parent seeking divorce did not meet the higher standard, the court would deny the divorce and the parents would stay married.

For example, married parents might have to show, in addition to "irreconcilable differences," that the divorce would benefit the children more than would continuation of the marriage. Other proposals, particularly those advocated by conservative family-values groups would reinstate fault grounds such as adultery and cruel and inhuman treatment.[526] These proposals are designed to prevent parents who are marginally committed to divorce from pursuing it, or at least to postpone divorce until the children reach majority.[527] It is even possible that, faced with great difficulty in obtaining a divorce, the unhappy parents will reconcile, to the benefit of the entire family unit.

Paul Amato's research divides divorcing parents into three categories: (1) those who stay together, (2) those in high conflict, and (3) those in low conflict. He found that children benefit when parents in high conflict (violence or endless disagreement) do divorce. But he believes that it is better for the children if low-conflict parents do not divorce because of the harm that the divorce causes their children. Compared with the other groups of parents, low-conflict divorcing parents, Amato found, tend to have less financial investment in the marriage, less religious devotion, and greater financial resources. Low-conflict parents had been previously divorced and had been married for a shorter time, according to Amato. Even though their marriages are tolerable, and it would probably be better for their children if they did not divorce, these low-conflict parents do so because they are unhappy, dislike some aspect of their partner's personality, or are suffering from a "mid-life" crisis. According to Amato, they leave because "barriers to leaving the relationship are weak and alternatives to the marriage are strong."[528]

The challenge with creating laws that strengthen barriers to divorce is to craft a standard that encourages high-conflict parents to divorce but discourages divorce in low-conflict parents. This is a very difficult task. Suppose a system of fault divorce were reinstated and required the spouse who wanted the divorce to go to court to prove that the other spouse was at fault (e.g., committed adultery or committed cruel and inhuman acts toward the spouse who wanted the divorce). Professor Ira Ellman provides some examples of the problems that a fault-divorce statute of this type would create:

> Consider Alice, who wants out of her marriage because her husband is an alcoholic unable to hold a job and whose drunken tantrums terrorize her children. Or Betty, whose husband often disappears for weeks at a time, coming and going with no sense of responsibility to his family. Perhaps Alice and Betty have tried unsuccessfully to help their husbands become more responsible. But now they want to end their marriage . . . [529]

Alice and Betty may be able to prove fault, but if their husbands contest their claims, they will be able do so only after an expensive, prolonged, and adversarial process. Their husbands can use the threat of contesting a divorce as leverage to get custody or financial concessions from Alice or Betty. Furthermore, and perhaps most important, it is hard to see how Alice and Betty's children are better off if their parents' divorce becomes entangled in the fault system. Social policy should encourage parents like Alice and Betty to get a divorce expeditiously, and not give their spouses grounds to hold up the process.

Resurrecting fault grounds will also bring back the procedural hypocrisy of the fault system. Most divorces, even those involving children, occur because both spouses agree to it. Any legal standard that forces two adults who agree to a divorce to stay married is extremely distasteful. In addition, a fault standard will be difficult to enforce, since parents will try to evade it. The fault-divorce system encourages consenting parents to collude and to commit perjury to satisfy the qualifying criteria for divorce. It also requires the state to devote its limited resources to detecting and punishing parental collusion, a problem that the history of the fault divorce system shows is easier for courts to decry than to eradicate.[530]

A related problem with making the grounds for divorce more stringent is that unless similar grounds are adopted in every state simultaneously, the problem of "migratory divorce" that plagued the fault divorce system might reappear. Some married couples who have children and who agree to divorce quickly, but who do not meet the more stringent criteria of their home state, could establish residence in another state with less stringent grounds. This system would discriminate against those parents not wealthy enough to move to the more permissive state.[531]

Responsible scholars such as Amato not associated with the family-values movement advocate reducing the frequency of divorce by low-conflict parents, and advance more reasonable proposals than reinstitution of fault divorce to do so. Amato believes that "dissuading low discord couples from ending their marriage is a reasonable policy goal." Instead of reinstating fault divorce grounds, Amato recommends identifying low-conflict parents through screening, and requiring them to participate in special education and counseling sessions, with the goal of keeping their marriage together.[532] Elizabeth Scott also rejects the reinstatement of fault divorce, and suggests instead that the state give parents the option of choosing either conventional no-fault divorce or divorce only after a waiting period of 2 years.[533]

The problem with these proposals, as Scott recognizes, is that they are un-likely to satisfy fierce partisans on either side of the highly polarized debate about whether divorce is too easy to obtain.[534] Some family-values advo-cates seek more restrictive divorce laws for parents as a way to return to a pre-feminist world of traditional roles for husband and wife. They do not recognize that courts should quickly grant divorces in some dangerous, high-conflict marriages. On the other hand, liberals, and particularly feminists, believe that restricting divorce traps women into male-dominated, unfulfill-ing, abusive marriages. They also fear that greater restrictions on divorce will stigmatize single-parent families. They are suspicious of the agenda of the family-values advocates, and ignore the evidence that divorce places children's well-being at great risk.

In this polarized climate, perhaps the only available compromise is leaving the current divorce laws alone, but strengthening the education and medi-ation programs of the child custody court. Those who favor and those who oppose more-restrictive divorce should be able to find common ground on this agenda. The education and mediation programs serve the counseling and educational functions that Amato and Scott seek to achieve, without the difficulties of trying to craft a law that tries to determine which par-ents should divorce and which should not. Moreover, and most important, the conflict-reduction and management programs of the child custody court benefit children whether or not their parents divorce or reconcile.

XIV Consolidating the New Paradigm

The Future of the Child Custody Court

> Judicial reform is no sport for the short-winded or for [those] who are
> afraid of temporary defeat... 'When enlisted in a good cause, never
> surrender, for you can never tell what morning reinforcements in
> flashing armor will come marching over the hilltop.'
>
> Chief Judge Arthur Vanderbilt.[535]

In the *Structure of Scientific Revolutions*, the philosopher of science Thomas
Kuhn articulated a theory of how new ways of thinking displace the old.
Kuhn defines "paradigm" as the "entire constellation of beliefs, values, techniques and so on shared by the members of a given community."[536] A
paradigm is essentially the accepted wisdom of a society as it pertains to
one area of knowledge – it is the prevailing explanation for something.

According to Kuhn, at most times science simply elaborates an accepted
paradigm. When problem-solving within that paradigm can no longer account for significant "facts," a scientific revolution may occur, involving the
birth of a new paradigm. Kuhn argues that changes in paradigms are not
evolutionary, but rather a series of peaceful interludes punctuated by intellectually violent revolutions that result in replacing one world-view with
another.

Law and judicial administration are not natural sciences, and Kuhn's
concept of "paradigm shift" may have become something of a cliché. It is,
however, a valuable shorthand way to describe what has occurred in child
custody courts since about 1980. In what for legal institutions is a remarkably
short period of time, the paradigm of the child custody court has shifted from
"sole custody" and "adversarial courtroom combat" to mediation, education,
and self-determination that aim to involve both parents in the post-divorce
life of their child.

What makes any given paradigm more attractive than another is that its
answers to the important questions of the particular field are superior to its
rivals. The adversary system paradigm assumes that one parent is more important to the child's future than another, and that a court can identify that

175

parent through courtroom combat. These assumptions do not meet the needs of parents and children in an era of mass divorce, gender equality, research establishing the importance of both parents in the life of the child, and over-crowded courts. The conflict-management paradigm, in contrast, assumes (1) that parents, not judges or mental health experts, should determine how a child of divorce is parented, (2) that both parents are important to the child's future, and (3) that carefully structured interventions can encourage parents to place their children's interests above their anger and pain. These assumptions have, in general terms, been validated by the available empiri-cal evidence and experience since they have come into public consciousness. They also are more attractive morally than the assumptions of the adversary system/sole custody paradigm in that they appeal to the better instincts of people – and parents.

Models for Interdisciplinary Coalitions

The child custody court's paradigm shift to parental self-determination and responsible conflict management now has to reach all divorcing parents and children. It also needs to become a routine part of the way the interdisci-plinary practitioners in the child custody court practice their daily work.

Interdisciplinary coalitions that support the interests of children are the key to expanding and consolidating this paradigm shift. Lawyers and judges, in particular, need to reach out beyond their profession to create alliances to support continued reform, research, and development. Judges, lawyers, mental health professionals, and advocates for children must work together to create a more humane, coordinated child custody dispute resolu-tion system that emphasizes planning for children and responsible conflict management.

Interdisciplinary coalitions should strive to create continuity between the advice that professionals give to parents outside the courtrooms of the child custody court and the advocacy and parental behavior inside those courtrooms.[537] The message that lawyers should send to parents should be similar to that that mental health professionals send to parents: Reduce your conflict, and cooperate with each other if it is safe to do so. Every at-tempt should be made to settle child custody disputes as soon as a case is filed in court, and even before, if possible. Criteria should be established through research and development for cases that need more-intensive in-terventions. The interdisciplinary reform coalitions can support legislation and the training of legal and mental health professionals to accomplish these goals.

Here are five examples of interdisciplinary reform movements from five states of different sizes and different political climates:

California. California's Center for Families, Children and the Courts is an interdisciplinary arm of the state court system that focuses on improving the quality of justice for children and families in court. The Center's aim is to bridge subject-matter divisions within family law cases and facilitate the development of a unified family court. Its vast agenda of projects includes mediation improvement, enhancement of child support enforcement, training to cope with family violence, visitation access programs, and improvement of resources for *pro se* litigants.[538]

Connecticut. In 2002, the governor appointed a multi-disciplinary Commission on Divorce, Custody and Children, which examined the available research, consulted with experts around the nation, and conducted public hearings. Its comprehensive report on Connecticut's divorce and custody system contains recommendations designed to increase the involvement of both parents in the life of divorced children and to reduce the delay, expense, and stress of the custody dispute resolution system.[539]

Florida. The mission of the Florida court system's Family Court Initiative is "to provide families and children with an accessible and coordinated means of resolving legal matters in a fair, efficient, and effective manner. In addition to adjudicating disputes and providing alternative methods of dispute resolution, the Family Court Initiative will assist in meeting the needs of families and children involved in the court system by offering appropriate court-related services and linkages to community service providers."[540] The Florida Supreme Court's Family Court Steering Committee submitted a plan for a unified family court in that state in June 2000.[541] Shortly thereafter, Florida convened an interdisciplinary Summit on Redefining Florida's Family Court in which the court's stakeholders worked on the development of a model family court. In 2001, the Florida Supreme Court adopted the recommendations of the Family Court Steering Committee and its vision of an integrated, humane approach to the problems of children in court.[542]

Idaho. Idaho's interdisciplinary bench and bar committee addressed the problems of children in high-conflict divorces. The Committee's ongoing work developed a DCM plan for management of these cases, and initiated an extensive judicial education effort.[543]

Oregon. The Oregon legislature established a Task Force on Family Law that invited all stakeholders in the family law system to sit together to discuss how the court could be improved, with the proviso that all had to be willing to admit that they might be wrong and that there might be a better way for the court to operate than the participants had previously envisioned.[544] The Task Force articulated a series of goals and values that the court should aim for, and made detailed recommendations to integrate primary, secondary, and tertiary prevention programs into coherent pre- and post-filings in court prevention programs. The Task Force has been a continuous source of helpful criticism and support for the evolution of the child custody court.[545] In 2002, it articulated a plan for a model family court.[546]

An Agenda for Consolidating the Paradigm Shift

The following 13 goals summarize the themes of this book and exemplify the way interdisciplinary reform coalitions can consolidate and continue the child custody court's continuing paradigm shift.

1. The Structure of the Child Custody Court Should Be Unified and Simplified

The child custody court should be part of a unified family court that addresses all disputes involving parents and children regardless of the legal label that their dispute receives – divorce, domestic violence, child custody, child support, child abuse and neglect. The legal label placed on a family is often arbitrary, and the problems that families present to the court are interrelated. The courts must treat families holistically, addressing both their legal disputes and the problems that underlie them.

The child custody court should be sympathetic toward families. Parents and children in crisis should be able to gain access to a judge and support services in a single location, and should not be shuttled between different courthouses because different aspects of their disputes are heard in different courts. A parent who seeks an order of protection, for example, against a physically abusive spouse should not have to go to another court to get a divorce or a child custody determination.

Families should also not be shuttled between judges. Forum-shopping for a favorable judge serves no social purpose. The court system should assign a single judge and a single support team to oversee all of the family's disputes. In this way, the number of times that family members have to tell their stories to different people is minimized, and the court can develop and implement a service plan for the family. Parents should be able to avail themselves of the support services of the child custody court without filing detailed motion papers and accusations of wrongdoing against each other. Exceptions to the one-judge, one-support team, one-family principle should be circumscribed and carefully justified.

2. Committed, Experienced Judges Should Staff the Child Custody Court

The single most important factor that determines the quality of the child custody court is the quality of its judges. They are the court's face to the public, the managers of its multi-disciplinary operations, and the decision makers of last resort for parents and children.

For too long, the child custody court has been viewed as a judicial backwater to which rookie judges are assigned; talented judges try to escape as soon as possible to the higher-status world of auto accident and business contract cases. This is a manifestation of the same point of view that pays lip service to the importance of having well-qualified teachers and doctors who serve children and families, but fails to provide them with adequate resources and the honor and compensation necessary to attract the best and the brightest.

The child custody court should be the highest rung of judicial service, not its lowest. Judges who serve on the court should want to be assigned there, and have the aptitude and background to serve in an emotionally and professionally demanding environment. Child custody court judges should serve for a substantial period of time and be honored for their dedication. They should have opportunities for professional development and advancement. In short, children and parents need child custody judges who make a professional career of service to this constituency.

3. The Child Custody Court Should Make Diversified Education Programs Available to All Divorcing Parents and Children

The importance of educational programs to the child custody court cannot be overemphasized – they prepare parents for the turbulent experience of reorganizing their relationships with their children. Most parents are *pro se*. They need help (a) to understand the court process, (b) to manage conflict for the benefit of their children, (c) to avail themselves of helping services, (d) to understand what the court system can and cannot do for them, and (e) to gain access to information in order to make responsible choices for their families.

Parents have responded well to court-affiliated programs; attendance at them should be a routine condition of divorce in every child custody court in the country. These programs should be expanded so that every divorcing parent who feels he or she needs the help of a court to resolve a parenting dispute can attend.

Courts should design diversified education programs for different segments of the population of divorcing families. A one-size educational program should not, and does not, fit all. Some families are more conflict-ridden and dysfunctional than others and thus have different educational needs from those of lower-conflict families. Short secondary prevention programs do many things well, but they do not provide intensive education in conflict management skills or therapy. They should not be weighed down with the unrealistic expectation that highly litigious parents will be able to change ingrained patterns of acrimonious interaction as a result of a few hours of lectures and discussion. Special programs need to be developed for that purpose.

Finally, the child custody court should foster primary prevention by encouraging schools to incorporate into their curriculums lessons about divorce, conflict management, and the effects of parental conflict on children.

Divorce has become a predictable event in the lives of American children. The earlier that future parents are exposed to prevention-oriented information and perspectives, the better.

For all children, their parents' divorce is a time of difficult adjustment. For a significant number of children, it is the beginning of a downward emotional, educational, and economic spiral. Educational programs can help them understand their conflicting emotions, develop coping skills, and gain access to helping services. School-based prevention programs for the children of divorce have consistently improved the functioning of those who participate in them.[547] Court-based programs show similar promise. They need to be expanded in order to serve all children who can benefit from them.

Uniform curriculum standards and rigorous evaluation should be a condition for the expansion of educational programs. Taxpayers, judges, parents, and children have the right to insist on quality control of judicial mandates, especially empirical evidence to support a claim that an educational program's curriculum provides concrete benefits to reorganizing families. Courts should seek the help of experts in program evaluation in universities and elsewhere to ensure that standards for educational programs are kept high and that programs constantly incorporate new innovations and ideas.

4. *The Child Custody Court Should Develop Special Programs to Meet the Needs of* Pro Se *Parents*

The child custody court can no longer operate on the assumption that all parents will necessarily have a lawyer. It needs to find ways to bring legal advice and information to people who cannot afford, or who do not want, the traditional full-service model of legal representation. The court needs to develop programs that advise *pro se* parents about their legal rights and the nature of the court process. Educational programs can help; so can material on the internet. More-extensive measures, such as courses for litigants and *pro se* advisor programs, can be undertaken. Unbundled legal services can meet some of the *pro se* parents' need for coaching and legal advice.

5. *The Child Custody Court Should Make Mediation, with Screening for Violence, and Safety Precautions Available to all Divorcing Parents*

Mediation is the dispute resolution process of choice for most divorce-related parenting disputes. It reduces conflict between parents and thus creates a better atmosphere for children to be able to cope with the transitions that divorce requires. It encourages parents to reach their own agreement on a parenting plan rather than having a court impose one on them. Parents like mediation – it lowers the emotional and economic costs of resolving their disputes, and their children benefit from it.

Child custody courts should require mediation as the rule, not the exception, for child custody disputes. Divorcing parents should be required to mediate before attacking each other in an adversarial courtroom proceeding. Parents who have been the victims of domestic violence should be given the option of mediating with specially trained mediators, and precautions should be taken to ensure their safety. Mediation programs need to be adequately funded and supervised to ensure that they do not sacrifice quality for quantity in the number of cases processed.

6. The Child Custody Court Should Create a Plan for Differential Management of High-Conflict Cases

A small number of families are considered to be in a high state of conflict when various interrelated indicia of serious family dysfunction show up – repetitive litigation, violence, substance abuse, mental illness, and so on. The court should develop an efficient way of identifying those families and devise a case management plan that matches their needs. A high level of teamwork and collaboration – qualities the court should encourage in its personnel and those of the agencies and lawyers it works with – between the court, court-affiliated services, counsel, and outside agencies is necessary to create and implement a DCM plan for a high-conflict family. High-conflict child custody cases should, in fact, be treated as child protection cases posing a serious risk to both children and parents.

7. The Child Custody Court Should Ensure that High-Quality Supervised Visitation Services are Available to all Families that Need Them

Supervised visitation is the single best service for reconciling safety with a child's need to have a continuing relationship with a violent (or allegedly violent) parent. Professionally supervised visitation services have proven to be of great value in preserving the relationships between parents and children while reducing the risks of violence. As the number of family violence allegations in child custody disputes increases, so should the availability of supervised visitation services. Guidelines should be developed to identify the parents who need supervision in their relationships with their children and how supervised visitation services should operate.

8. The Child Custody Court Should Ensure Accountability and Quality Control for Court-Mandated Services

The child custody court is ultimately responsible for the quality of all the services it mandates for parents and children. The court must thus create mechanisms to ensure that its interdisciplinary non-judicial personnel – educators, mediators, mental health evaluators, who are central to its operations and the welfare of the children – understand their roles in the process and are qualified and accountable. Written rules need to be developed for:

- the qualification and training requirements for all court-affiliated personnel involved in the child custody decision-making process – educators, mediators, supervised visitation supervisors, evaluators, guardians, lawyers for children, special masters, and so on;
- the content and form of neutral evaluation reports;
- asserting and resolving grievances against all court-affiliated personnel.

9. The Child Custody Court Should Encourage Lawyers Who Represent Parents to Incorporate Conflict Management and the Welfare of Children into Their Representation

A community's lawyers set the tone for whether parents perceive the child custody dispute resolution process as an adversarial proceeding or as a family reorganization. The bar and the courts should encourage parents to view their lawyers as guides to conflict management, not simply as gladiators on their behalf. Lawyers should encourage their clients to listen to the advice of mental health professionals about how best to parent their children through the time of reorganization that divorce requires. The child custody court should encourage lawyers to attend educational programs on ADR and collaboration for the benefit of children. The court should develop rules that require lawyers to discuss alternatives to litigation with parents and take the welfare of children into account in the advice they give to their clients. The court should encourage the development of law school courses that emphasize collaborative representation and the interdisciplinary knowledge necessary to effectively represent parents and children in custody disputes.

10. The Child Custody Court Should Redefine the Role of the Lawyer for the Child

The idea of appointing a lawyer for the child in custody disputes stems from humane and liberal impulses – the child's perspective and voice should be heard in critical decisions that affect its life. Implementation of the idea, however, is a subject of dispute because of ambiguity about whether the child's lawyer represents the child's best interests or the child's preferences. The child custody court should eliminate the ambiguity so that the role of the child's lawyer can be explained to parents and children with consistency. The court should ensure that those it appoints as the child's lawyer are adequately trained and compensated to perform their assigned functions, which should not overlap with those provided by other professionals in the child custody dispute resolution process. Written rules accomplishing these goals would be an important step forward. Child custody courts should consider creating a publicly funded office of lawyers to represent children in custody cases.

11. The Child Custody Court Should View Its Mission as One of Developing Parenting Plans, Not Custody Orders

Legal language is important as it sets the tone and direction of the legal process for those who participate in it. The legal term "custody" inaccurately suggests that parents are jailers of children. The term "sole custody" inaccurately suggests that one parent is more important in the life of the child than the other. Both terms encourage parents to view the custody dispute as a contest for possession. The child custody court should encourage legislatures, lawyers, and parents to use more-neutral language that encourages cooperative parenting such as decision making and residence. They should also encourage parents with disagreements to submit detailed plans for day-to-day residence, decision making, and dispute resolution to the court.

12. The Child Custody Court Should Receive Adequate Funding

The child custody court needs adequate funding for its operations and innovations. Education and mediation programs tend to get short shrift when judicial administrators and legislators think about the court's needs, focusing instead on funding for more judges and lawyers for the poor in order to deal with increasingly crushing caseloads. These are important needs, and interested stakeholders should support increased funding to meet them. Securing adequate funding for the operations of the adversary system should not come at the expense of adequate funding for conflict management programs, which are just as essential a part of the child custody court's day-to-day operations.

Obtaining adequate funding for mediation and education programs is not an impossible goal. Taxpayers, state legislators, and foundations can be convinced that such funding is a good long-term investment in their children's welfare. Hawaii, for example, has created an independent statewide children's trust fund to distribute grants to fund primary and secondary prevention efforts to strengthen families, with the aim of reducing child abuse and neglect.[548]

All states can undertake similar initiatives. Other possibilities include increasing marriage license fees and divorce filing fees to cover the costs of court services. Exceptions would have to be provided for people who could not afford the increased fees.

*13. The Child Custody Court Should Encourage Research
and Development to Refine Its Operations for the Benefit
of the Children of Divorce*

How little we know about the effect of divorce on children, what kinds
of custody arrangements are in their best interests, and how courts can best
contribute to responsible parental conflict management is a symptom of how
little we really care about children and families. Empirical research has had
a major impact on the policies and practices of the child custody court in
recent years. Nonetheless, there are significant gaps in our knowledge. We
need more, and better, research. We need to validate, for example, what
kinds of education and prevention programs have the most beneficial effect
on divorcing families. The necessary empirical research combines many disciplines, is expensive to conduct, and should be coordinated so that limited
resources are spent wisely. The need for this is so pressing that the federal
government, the states, and interested foundations should consider creating
a national institute to secure funding, promote research, and disseminate the
findings.

Margaret Mead once said, "Never doubt that a small group of thoughtful
committed people can change the world. Indeed, it's the only thing that ever
has."[549] Such people have changed the nature of the child custody court in
a very short period of time, and have thus helped redefine the nature of the
relationship between divorcing parents and children. We need to continue
that effort and make the child custody court a place a community is proud
of, not a dumping ground for families in crisis. Working together, we can
achieve that goal. We owe that to our children.

Notes

Note on Endnote Citations

Citations in the endnotes follow the *Bluebook*, more formally known as *A Uniform System of Citation*, published by the law reviews at Harvard, Yale, Columbia, and Pennsylvania law schools. Although developed primarily for published, scholarly legal writing, the *Bluebook* has for decades enjoyed the status of the leading citation system in the United States in law firms, corporate legal departments, courts, and government agencies. Competitors to the *Bluebook* do exist, but it is still the leading legal citation system.

I have made some adaptations to *Bluebook* form for clarity and for the benefit of readers who are not lawyers. The *Bluebook* does not require that a book's publisher and the city of publication be included in a citation unless the work is published by some company other than the first publisher. I have nonetheless included the publisher's name and city where I had easy access to that information. Where the publisher is not identified, readers should be able to locate the books cited in their local or university library indexes, on Amazon.com, or elsewhere on the Internet.

Readers who are not lawyers should be aware that citations to statutes and court rules change regularly. Citations are current as of December 31, 2002. Readers are advised to check for updates before relying on these citations.

Preface

1. The novelist Pat Conroy, quoted in Barbara Dafoe Whitehead, *Dan Quayle Was Right*, ATLANTIC MONTHLY, Apr. 1993, at 64.
2. The study, drafted with my co-consultant, Professor Linda Silberman, was published as New York State Law Revision Commission, *Recommendation to the 1985 Legislature on the Child Custody Dispute Resolution Process*, 19 COLUM. J. L. & SOC. PROBS. 105 (1985).

Chapter I Overview

3. Hon. Alastair Nicholson, *Setting the Scene: Australian Family Law and the Family Court – A Perspective from the Bench*, 40 FAM. CT. REV. 279, 284 (2002) (contrasting the Australian and American approaches to nationalizing divorce law).

4. Barbara Babb, *Fashioning an Interdisciplinary Framework for Court Reform in Family Law: A Blueprint to Construct a Unified Family Court*, 71 S. Cal. L. Rev. 469 (1998) (comprehensively discussing unified family courts).

5. *See generally* Julian W. Mack, *The Juvenile Court*, 23 Harv. L. Rev. 104 (1909) (describing the early philosophies of juvenile courts).

6. *In re* Gault, 387 U.S. 1 (1967) is the leading case that brought due process protections to the juvenile court. The U.S. Supreme Court majority in that case described the shortcomings of the juvenile court in great detail.

7. Robert W. Page, *Family Courts: An Effective Judicial Approach to the Resolution of Family Disputes*, 44 Juv. & Fam. Ct. J. 1, 3–5 (1993).

8. Roscoe Pound, *The Place of the Family Court in the Judicial System*, 5 Crim. & Delinquency 161, 164 (1959). *See generally* Barbara A. Babb, *Where We Stand: An Analysis of America's Family Law Adjudicatory Systems and the Mandate to Establish Unified Family Courts*, 32 Fam. L. Q. 31 (1998) (discussing the current status of unified family courts in the United States).

9. Bruce J. Winick, *The Jurisprudence of Therapeutic Jurisprudence*, 3 Psychol. Pub. Pol'y & L. 184, 185 (March 1997).

10. Stanley v. Illinois, 405 U.S. 645 (1972) (unwed father entitled to a hearing before custody rights are terminated in a child dependency proceeding).

11. Troxel v. Granville, 530 U.S.57 (2000).

12. Wilkinson v. Russell, 182 F.3d 89, 104 (2d Cir. 1999). *See also* James W. Bozzomo, *Joint Legal Custody: A Parent's Constitutional Right in a Reorganized Family*, 31 Hofstra L. Rev. 547 (2003).

Chapter II   *Kramer vs. Kramer* Revisited: The Sole Custody/Adversary System Paradigm

13. Avery Corman, Kramer versus Kramer: A Novel (Random House, New York, NY, 1977).

14. Kramer vs. Kramer (Columbia 1979).

15. Michael Asimow, *Divorce in the Movies: From the Hays Code to Kramer vs. Kramer*, 24 Legal Stud. F. 221, 222 (2000). The movie's quality has been widely recognized. Its stars, Dustin Hoffman and Meryl Streep, received Oscars® for best actor and best supporting actress, respectively. Robert Benton, *Kramer vs. Kramer's* screenwriter and director, won two Oscars® for his work. Jane Alexander was nominated for an Oscar® for best supporting actress for playing Margaret, Joanna and Ted's friend, and Justin Henry was nominated for best supporting actor for his role as Billy, Ted and Joanna's son. The film received other Oscar® nominations and other awards.

16. Curtis C. Shears, *Legal Problems Peculiar to Children's Courts*, 48 A.B.A. J. 719, 720 (1962), quoted in *In re* Gault, 387 U.S. 1, 17, n. 21 (1967).

17. *See, e.g.*, Boswell v. Boswell, 352 Md. 204, 240, 721 A.2d 662, 679 (1998) ("[L]iberal visitation" is "restricted only upon a showing of actual or potential adverse impact to the child resulting from the contact with the non-marital partner"); *In re* Marriage of Pleasant, 256 Ill. App. 3d 742, 628 N.E.2d 633 (1993) (court may not restrict parenting time merely because of sexual orientation); *In re* Wickland, 84 Wash. App. 763, 932 P.2d 652(1996) (visitation may be restricted only if the child's physical, mental, or emotional health would be endangered).

18. *See Ex Parte* Devine, 398 So. 2d 686, 688–92 (Ala. 1981) (discussing paternal preference); Richard Hurd, A Treatise on the Right of Personal Liberty and

ON THE WRIT OF HABEAS CORPUS AND THE PRACTICES CONNECTED WITH IT 465 (1858). *See also* Henry H. Foster & Doris Jonas Freed, *Life with Father: 1978*, 11 FAM. L. Q. 321–33 (1978) (summarizing the evolution of custody rights from paternal to maternal preference); Allan Roth, *The Tender Years Presumption in Child Custody Disputes*, 15 J. FAM. L. 423, 432–38 (1976–1977).

19. IRA MARK ELLMAN ET AL., FAMILY LAW: CASES, TEXT, PROBLEMS 635–36 (Lexis Law Publishing, Charlottesville, VA, 3d ed. 1998).

20. Conversely, many courts believed for a time that adolescent boys belonged in the custody of their fathers, who could prepare them for occupations in the economic world of which mothers had no knowledge.

21. Freeland v. Freeland, 159 P. 698, 699 (Wash. 1916).

22. Kreiger v. Kreiger, 81 P.2d 1081, 1083 (Idaho 1938).

23. Carol B. Stack, *Who Owns the Child?: Divorce and Custody Decisions in Middle-Class Families*, 23 SOC. PROBS. 505, 506 (1976).

24. Michael Lamb, *Fathers and Child Development: An Integrative Overview, in* THE ROLE OF THE FATHER IN CHILD DEVELOPMENT 7 (Michael Lamb, ed., 2d ed. John Wiley & Sons, New York, NY, 1981).

25. Glen W. Clingempeel & Dickon N. Reppucci, *Joint Custody After Divorce: Major Issues and Goals for Research*, 91 PSYCHOL. BULL. 102, 112 (1982).

26. Herma Hill Kay, *No-Fault Divorce and Child Custody: Chilling Out the Gender Wars*, 36 FAM. L. Q. 27, 28 (2002) citing Mary Ann Mason & Ann Quirk, *Are Mothers Losing Custody? Read My Lips: Trends in Judicial Decision-Making in Custody Disputes — 1920, 1960, 1990 and 1995*, 31 FAM. L. Q. 215, 228 (Table 2) (1997).

27. Ramsay Laing Klaff, *The Tender Years Doctrine: A Defense*, 70 CALIF. L. REV. 335 (1982); LENORE J. WEITZMAN, THE DIVORCE REVOLUTION 222 (Free Press, New York, NY, 1985).

28. ELLMAN ET AL., *supra* note 19, at 19.

29. Kay, *supra* note 26, at 32.

30. HERBERT JACOB, SILENT REVOLUTION: THE TRANSFORMATION OF DIVORCE LAW IN THE UNITED STATES (University of Chicago Press, Chicago, IL, 1988).

31. Kay, *supra* note 26, at 31.

32. Francis J. Catania, Jr. *Learning from the Process of Decision: The Parenting Plan*, 2001 BYU L. REV. 857, 858.

33. Sam Roberts, *Word for Word/Measuring a Century: America Then and Now: It's All in the Numbers*, N.Y. TIMES, Dec. 31, 2000, §4 (News of the Week in Review) at 7, col. 1, *citing* THEODORE CAPLOW ET AL. THE FIRST MEASURED CENTURY: AN ILLUSTRATED GUIDE TO TRENDS IN AMERICA, 1900–2000 (AEI Press, Washington, DC, 2000).

34. U.S. Department of Labor, *20 Facts on Women Workers*, No 96–2, Sept. 1996, available at http://www.unc.edu/~healdric/soci31/1998/assign/20facts.htm (last visited Dec. 30, 2002).

35. COMMITTEE ON CIVIL AND POLITICAL RIGHTS, REPORT OF THE PRESIDENT'S COMMISSION ON THE STATUS OF WOMEN 16–18 (Government Printing Office, Washington, DC, 1963).

36. Judith T. Younger, *Marital Regimes: A Story of Compromise and Demoralization, Together with Criticisms and Suggestions for Reform*, 67 CORNELL L. REV. 45, 64–77 (1981) (describing the partnership theory as the basis of both the community and equitable distribution systems of allocating marital assets after divorce).

37. Julia Taylor, *For Many Blue-Collar Fathers, Child Care Is Shift Work, Too*, N.Y. TIMES, Apr. 26, 1998, §3 at 11; Susan Chira, *Census Data Show Rise in Child Care by Fathers*, N.Y. TIMES, Sept. 22, 1993 at 20, col. 5.

38. *See* Margaret F. Brinig, *Feminism and Child Custody under Chapter Two of the American Law Institute's Principles of the Law of Family Dissolution*, 8 Duke J. Gender L. & Pol'y 301, 311, n. 62 (Spring/Summer 2000); John W. Jacobs, *Treatment of Divorcing Fathers: Social and Psychotherapeutic Considerations*, 140 Am. J. Psychiatry 1294, 1296 (1983) ("Within the intact family, many of these [divorced men the author treated] felt they were doing their best for their children by being the breadwinner and allowing the mothers to fulfill the nurturing role for both of them. With marital separation, some fathers no longer viewed their wives as functional extensions of themselves . . .").

39. Kay, *supra* note 26, at 36.

40. *Id*. at 40.

41. Reed v. Reed, 404 U.S. 71 (1971) (holding that the provision of the Idaho probate code that gives preference to men over women to apply for appointment as administrator of a decedent's estate is unconstitutional gender discrimination).

42. Klaff, *supra* note 27 (defending presumption on the basis that the mother has usually been the primary caretaker as well as on the basis of psychological studies based on bonding behavior); Rena K. Uviller, *Fathers' Rights and Feminism: The Maternal Presumption Revisited*, 1 Harv. Women's Law J. 107, 108–12 (1978); Mary Ann Mason, *Motherhood v. Equal Treatment*, 29 J. Fam. L. 1, 23–27 (1990–91) (supporting "tender years" presumption).

43. Orr v. Orr, 440 U.S. 268 (1979) (statute that limits alimony to women is unconstitutional gender discrimination).

44. Robert F. Cochran, Jr. & Paul C. Vitz, *Child Protective Divorce Laws: A Response to the Effects of Parental Separation on Children*, 17 Fam. L.Q. 327, 340 (1983).

45. N.Y. Dom. Rel. Law §240 1. (a) (McKinney 2002).

46. Watts v. Watts, 77 Misc.2d 178, 350 N.Y.S.2d 285 (Fam.Ct. 1973). To this day, the constitutionality of the tender years presumption has, however, not been definitively settled. No Supreme Court decision has declared the tender years presumption to be unconstitutional on the grounds that it discriminates against men, and state courts that have considered the issue are divided on it. *Developments in the Law – The Constitution and the Family*, 93 Harv. L. Rev. 1156, 1333–38 (1980).

47. Barkley v. Barkley, 60 A.D.2d 954, 402 N.Y.S.2d 228 (App. Div. 1978) (father retained custody of small child when both parents were equally fit); *In re* Vincent, 47 A.D.2d 786, 365 N.Y.S.2d 289 (App. Div. 1975) (affirming award of custody to father).

48. Asimow, *supra* note 15, at 263–64.

49. Robert H. Mnookin, *Child Custody Adjudication: Judicial Functions in the Face of Indeterminacy*, 39 Law & Contemp. Probs. 226 (1975) (discussing the indeterminacy of custody standards).

50. E.g., N.Y. Dom. Rel. Law §240 1. (a) (McKinney 2002).

51. E.g., Minn. St. Ann. §518.17 (West 2002).

52. E.g., Mich. Comp. Laws. Ann. §722.23,3 (West Supp. 2001).

53. Daniel W. Shuman, *The Role of Mental Health Experts in Custody Decisions: Science, Psychological Tests, and Clinical Judgment*, 36 Fam. L. Q. 135, 136 (2002).

54. Joseph Goldstein et al., Beyond the Best Interests of the Child 98 (Free Press, New York, NY, 1973).

55. Richard Edelin Crouch, *An Essay on the Critical and Judicial Reception of Beyond the Best Interests of the Child*, 13 Fam. L.Q. 49 (1979).

56. Nancy S. Weinfeld, *Comments on Lamb's "Placing Children's Interests First,"* 10 Va. J. Soc. Pol'y & L. 120, 121 (2002).

57. Shelly A. Riggs, *Response to Troxel v. Granville. Implications of Attachment Theory for Judicial Decisions Regarding Custody and Third-Party Visitation*, 41 Fam. Ct. Rev. 39, 41–42 (2003).

58. Michael E. Lamb, *Placing Children's Interests First: Developmentally Appropriate Parenting Plans*, 10 Va. J. Soc. Pol'y & L. 98, 108–09 (2002).

59. Richard A. Warshak, *Blanket Restrictions: Overnight Contact Between Parents and Young Children*, 38 Fam. & Conciliation Cts. Rev. 422, 429 (2000).

60. Joan B. Kelly & Michael E. Lamb, *Using Child Development Research to Make Appropriate Custody and Access Decisions*, 38 Fam. & Conciliation Cts. Rev. 297, 300 (2000).

61. Judith Areen, Family Law: Cases and Materials 488–574 (Foundation Press, New York, NY, 4th ed. 1999).

62. *Id.* at 532–33.

63. Ellman et al., *supra* note 19, at 652–53.

64. David Ray Papke, *Peace Between the Sexes: Law and Gender in Kramer vs. Kramer*, 30 U.S. F. L. Rev. 1199, 1205 (Summer, 1996).

65. The literature is reviewed in Kay, *supra* note 26, at 34–39.

Chapter III   Divorce, Children, and Courts: An Empirical Perspective

66. Pink, *Family Portrait*, on Missundaztood (Arista Records 2001).

67. Jeffrey Zaslow, *Divorce Makes a Comeback*, Wall St. J. Jan. 14, 2003 at D1, D10 (chart based on data from the National Center for Health Statistics).

68. U.S. Dept. of Health and Human Services, *Monthly Vital Statistics Report: Final Data from The National Center for Health Statistics*, May 21, 1991, at 1, 7, 9.

69. Children's Defense Fund, The State of Children in America's Union 15 (Children's Defense Fund, Washington, DC, 2002).

70. See National Center for Health Statistics, Centers for Disease Control, *Advance Report of Final Divorce Statistics, 1989 & 1990* < http://www.cdc.gov/nchswww/products/pubs/pubd/mvsr/supp/44-43/mvs43'9s.htm> (last visited Mar. 3, 2000).

71. Marsha Kline Pruett & Tamara D. Jackson, *The Lawyer's Role During the Divorce Process: Perceptions of Parents, Their Young Children and Their Attorneys*, 33 Fam. L. Q. 283, 284 (1999).

72. Rachel A. Haine et al., *Changing the Legacy of Divorce: Evidence from Prevention Programs and Future Directions*, Family Relations (forthcoming October 2003) (manuscript at 24) (on file with author).

73. *America's Children 2002: Family Structure and Children's Living Arrangements*, ChildStats.Gov., *available at* http://childstats.gov/ac2002/indicators.asp?IID=12 &id=1 (last visited Dec. 29, 2002).

74. United States Census Bureau, *Census Brief: Children with Single Parents – How They Fare* (Sept. 1997) White children are much more likely than black children, and somewhat more likely than Hispanic children, to live with two parents. In 2001, 78% of white, non-Hispanic children lived with two parents, compared with 38% of black children and 65% of children of Hispanic origin. The reasons for single-parent families are different for whites and African-Americans. Nationally, among white mothers, the major cause is divorce, although the number of single white mothers who have never married has increased rapidly. Among African-Americans, women who have never married headed 54% of single-parent families in 1991. *America's Children 2002 Family Structure and Children's Living Arrangements*,

supra note 73. Roberto Suro, *For Women, Varied Reasons for Single Motherhood*, N.Y. TIMES, May 26, 1992, at A12.

75. Jane Fritsch, *Ideas and Trends: Aspirations; A Rise in Single Dads*, N.Y. TIMES, May 20, 2001 §4 (Week in Review), at 4, col. 4.

76. Paul R. Amato, *Good Enough Marriages: Parental Discord, Divorce, Divorce and Children's Long-Term Well-Being*, 9 VA. J. SOC. POL'Y & L. 71, 72 (2002).

77. Elizabeth S. Scott, *Divorce, Children's Welfare and the Culture Wars*, 9 VA. J. SOC. POL'Y & L. 95, 95 (2002).

78. David H. Demo & Alan C. Acock, *The Impact of Divorce on Children*, 50 J. MARRIAGE & FAM. 619, 642–43 (1988); Joan B. Kelly, *Longer-Term Adjustment in Children of Divorce: Converging Findings and Implications for Practice*, 2 J. FAM. PSYCHOL. 119, 119–20 (1988); Judith S. Wallerstein, *The Long-Term Effects of Divorce on Children: A Review*, 30 J. AM. ACAD. CHILD ADOLESCENT PSYCHIATRY 349, 358 (1991).

79. Robert Bauserman, *Child Adjustment in Joint-Custody Versus Sole-Custody Arrangements: A Meta-Analytic Review*, 16 J. FAM. PSYCHOL. 91, 98 (2002).

80. Richard A. Warshak, *Who Will Be There When I Cry in the Night? Revisiting Overnights – A Rejoinder to Biringen et al.*, 40 FAM. CT. REV. 208, 215 (2002).

81. SPECIAL JOINT COMMITTEE ON CHILD CUSTODY AND ACCESS OF THE PARLIAMENT OF CANADA, REPORT: FOR THE SAKE OF THE CHILDREN 78 (1998) [hereinafter *For the Sake of the Children*].

82. Katherine T. Bartlett, *U.S. Custody Law and Trends in the Context of the ALI Principles of the Law of Family Dissolution*, 10 VA. J. SOC. POL'Y & L. 5, 52 (2002) [hereinafter Bartlett, *Custody Trends*].

83. Wallerstein, *supra* note 78, at 350.

84. Yongmin Sun, *Family Environment and Adolescents' Well-Being before and after Parents' Marital Disruption: A Longitudinal Analysis*, 63 J. MARRIAGE & FAM. 697 (2001).

85. Kelly, *supra* note 78, at 122 (citations omitted).

86. Quoted in *Family Values: The Bargain Breaks*, ECONOMIST, Dec. 26, 1992–Jan. 8, 1993, at 37–39 (reviewing research findings in the United States and Great Britain).

87. Haine et al., *supra* note 72 (manuscript at 3).

88. Sharlene A. Wolchik et al, *Six-Year Follow-up Of Preventive Interventions for the Children of Divorce: A Randomized Controlled Trial*, 288 J. AM. MED. ASS'N. 1874 (2002).

89. Mary Duenwald, *2 Portraits of Children of Divorce: Rosy and Dark*, N.Y. TIMES, March 26, 2002 at F5. *See* E. MAVIS HEATHERINGTON & JOHN KELLY, FOR BETTER OR WORSE: DIVORCE RECONSIDERED 7–8 (W.W. Norton & Co., New York, NY, 2001).

90. Lamb, *supra* note 58, at 105–06.

91. Michael E. Lamb et al., *The Effects of Divorce and Custody Arrangements on Children's Behavior, Development, and Adjustment*, 35 FAM. & CONCILIATION. CTS. REV. 393, 396 (1997) (consensus statement by experts in psychology, law, and social welfare convened under the auspices of the National Institute of Child Health and Human Development).

92. CONSTANCE AHRONS, THE GOOD DIVORCE 56 (Harper Collins, New York, NY, 1994).

93. JANET R. JOHNSTON & VIVIENNE ROSEBY, IN THE NAME OF THE CHILD: A DEVELOPMENTAL APPROACH TO UNDERSTANDING AND HELPING CHILDREN OF CONFLICTED AND VIOLENT DIVORCE 4 (Free Press, New York, NY, 1997).

94. H. Ted Rubin, *The Nature of the Court Today*, in 6 THE FUTURE OF CHILDREN 43 (David and Lucile Packard Foundation, Los Altos, CA, 1996).

95. Lamb et al., *supra* note 91, at 396.

96. CARLA B. GARRITY & MITCHELL A. BARIS, CAUGHT IN THE MIDDLE: PROTECTING THE CHILDREN OF HIGH-CONFLICT DIVORCE 45 (Lexington Books, Lanham, MD, 1994).

97. Braiman v. Braiman, 44 N.Y.2d 584, 378 N.E.2d 1019, 407 N.Y.S.2d 449 (1978). Many of the details in the description of the case are taken from the opinion of the intermediate appellate court at 61 A.D.2d 995, 402 N.Y.S.2d 976 (2d Dep't 1978).

98. Eleanor E. Maccoby et al., *Coparenting in the Second Year after Divorce*, 52 J. Marriage & Fam. 141, 142 (1990).

99. Demo & Acock, *supra* note 78, at 642.

100. Eleanor E. Maccoby & Robert H. Mnookin, Dividing the Child: Social and Legal Dilemmas of Custody 31 (Harvard University Press, Cambridge, MA, 1992).

101. Bauserman, *supra* note 79, at 97.

102. Sandford L. Braver & Diane O'Connell, Divorced Dads: Shattering The Myths 47–56 (Jeremy P. Tarcher/Putnam, New York, NY, 1998); Mel Roman, The Disposable Parent 74–75 (Henry Holt & Co., New York, NY, 1978) (noting that the intense loss a father feels at having to court his children and treat them as guests often causes him to withdraw; John W. Jacobs, *The Effect of Divorce on Fathers: An Overview of the Literature*, 139 Am. J. Psychiatry 1235, 1236–37 (1982) (citing a study that found that some fathers who were highly involved with their children before a divorce chose to avoid seeing their children altogether rather than suffer at seeing them intermittently).

103. The literature is reviewed in Robert F. Kelly & Shawn L. Ward, *Allocating Custodial Responsibilities at Divorce*, 40 Fam. Ct. Rev. 348 (2002).

104. Timothy Grall, *Custodial Mothers and Fathers and Their Child Support-Consumer Income*, in Current Population Reports, United States Census Bureau 6 (October 2002).

105. *See* Philip M. Stahl, Parenting After Divorce 28–31 (Impact Publishers, Inc., Atascadero, CA, 2000) for an excellent description of parallel parenting. I am grateful to Geri Furhmann and her colleagues at the University of Massachusetts Medical Center Department of Psychiatry and Family Services of Central Massachusetts for introducing me to the concept of parallel parenting, the basis of their educational program, *Parents Apart*. *See* Andrew Schepard, *Parental Conflict Prevention Programs and the Unified Family Court: A Public Health Perspective*, 32 Fam. L. Q. 95, 116–18 (1998) (describing *Parents Apart*).

106. Maccoby & Mnookin, *supra* note 100, at 292.

107. Braver & O'Connell, *supra* note 102, at 82–83.

108. *Id*. at 22–23.

109. For overviews of the literature, see *Family Values: The Bargain Breaks*, *supra* note 86, at 37–39 (reviewing research findings in the United States and Great Britain); David Popenoe, *The Controversial Truth: Two-Parent Families Are Better*, N.Y. Times, Dec. 26, 1992, at 21 (summarizing research evidence). *See generally* Daniel P. Moynihan, *Defining Deviancy Down*, 62 Am. Scholar. 17, 21–26 (1993) (surveying literature on single-parent families).

110. *America's Children 2002 Family Structure and Children's Living Arrangements*, *supra* note 73.

111. Nicholas Davidson, *Life Without Father: America's Greatest Social Catastrophe*, 51 Pol'y Rev. 40, 44 (1990). *See generally* Henry B. Biller, Fathers and Families: Paternal Factors in Child Development (Auburn House, Westport, CT, 1993) (discussing the importance of the father in helping his child develop socially, personally, and intellectually).

112. Sara S. McLanahan, *Father Absence and the Welfare of Children*, in Coping with Divorce, Single Parenting and Remarriage: A Risk and Resiliency

PERSPECTIVE 117–45 (E. Mavis Heatherington ed., Lawrence Erlbaum Assoc., Mahwah, NJ, 1999).

113. MARTIN SELIGMAN, LEARNED OPTIMISM 145–49 (Alfred A. Knopf, New York, NY, 1991).

114. Barbara Bloom & Deborah Dawson, *Family Structure and Child Health*, 81 AM. J. PUB. HEALTH 1526, 1526 (1991) (noting that children in disrupted families are more likely to have an accident or suffer injury); Davidson, *supra* note 111, at 41–42 (linking suicide and mental illness to single-parent homes); John Guidubaldi & Joseph D. Perry, *Divorce and Mental Health Sequelae for Children: A Two-Year Follow-up of a Nationwide Sample*, 24 J. AM. ACAD. CHILD PSYCHIATRY 531, 533 (1985) (finding that children of divorce perform more poorly on 9 of 30 mental health measures).

115. Richard H. Needle et al., *Divorce, Remarriage and Adolescent Substance Use: A Prospective Longitudinal Study*, 52 J. MARRIAGE & FAM. 157, 166–67 (1990).

116. Yongmin Sun & Yuanzhang Li, *Children's Well-Being During Parents' Marital Disruption Process: A Pooled Time-Series Analysis*, 64 J. MARRIAGE & FAM. 472 (2002).

117. Bloom & Dawson, *supra* note 114, at 1526.

118. Sheila Fitzgerald Krein & Andrea H. Beller, *Educational Attainment of Children from Single-Parent Families: Differences by Exposure, Gender, and Race*, 25 DEMOGRAPHY 221, 228 (1988).

119. EDUCATIONAL TESTING SERVICE, AMERICA'S SMALLEST SCHOOL: THE FAMILY 8–9 (Educational Testing Service, Princeton, NJ, 1992).

120. Frank F. Furstenberg, Jr. & Christine Winquist Nord, *Parenting Apart: Patterns of Childrearing After Marital Disruption*, 47 J. MARRIAGE & FAM. 893, 902 (1985) (indicating that most children have little contact with their non-resident parents, and what contact there is tends to be social rather than instrumental).

121. Brent McBride et al., *Father's Involvement in School Settings and Child Outcomes*, 15–16 (2002) (paper presented at the 2002 Annual Meeting of the American Educational Research Association, New Orleans, LA, April 2, 2002).

122. Retired California Court of Appeals Justice Donald M. King *quoted in* PAULINE H. TESLER, COLLABORATIVE LAW: ACHIEVING EFFECTIVE RESOLUTION IN DIVORCE WITHOUT LITIGATION 3 (American Bar Association Section of Family Law, Chicago, IL, 2001).

123. BRIAN J. OSTROM & NEIL B. KAUDER, EXAMINING THE WORK OF STATE COURTS, 1995: A NATIONAL PERSPECTIVE FROM THE COURT STATISTICS PROJECT 39 (National Center for State Courts, Williamsburg, VA, 1996).

124. Judith S. Kaye & Jonathan Lippman, *New York State Unified Court System Family Justice Program*, 36 FAM. & CONCILIATION CTS. REV. 144, 145 (1998) The authors are the Chief Judge and the Chief Administrative Judge, respectively, of the Courts of the State of New York.

125. UNITED STATES COMMISSION ON CHILD AND FAMILY WELFARE, PARENTING OUR CHILDREN: IN THE BEST INTERESTS OF THE NATION: A REPORT TO THE PRESIDENT AND CONGRESS 12 (Washington, DC, 1996).

126. FUTURE OF THE COURTS COMMITTEE OF THE OREGON JUDICIAL DEPARTMENT, JUSTICE 2020: THE NEW OREGON TRAIL 13 (Oregon Judicial System, Salem, OR, Jan. 1995).

127. John Sullivan, *Chief Judge Announces Plan to Streamline Family Court*, N.Y. TIMES, Feb. 25, 1998, §B at 7, col. 3.

128. JUSTICE 2020, *supra* note 126, at 14.

129. *In re* Smiley, 36 N.Y. 2d 433, 330 N.E.2d 53, 369 N.Y.S.2d 87 (1975).

130. AMERICAN BAR ASSOCIATION, LITIGANTS WITHOUT LAWYERS: COURTS AND LAWYERS MEETING THE CHALLENGES OF SELF-REPRESENTATION 8 (American Bar Association, Chicago, IL, 2002).

131. Alan W. Houseman, *Civil Legal Assistance for Low-Income Persons: Looking Back and Looking Forward*, 29 FORDHAM URB. L. J. 1213, 1233 (2002).

132. Stuart Spenser, *Middle-Income Consumers Seen Handling Legal Matters Pro Se*, N. Y. L. J., May 29, 1996, at 1.

133. Robert B. Yegge, *Divorce Litigants Without Lawyers*, 28 FAM. L. Q. 407, 408 (1994).

134. Sondra Williams & Sharon Buckingham, *Family Court Assessment: Dissolution of Marriage in Florida – Preliminary Assessment Findings* 39 FAM. CT. REV. 170, 175 (2001).

135. Nancy Ver Steegh, *Yes, No, and Maybe: Informed Decision Making About Divorce Mediation in the Presence of Domestic Violence*, 9 WM. & MARY J. WOMEN & LAW 145, 167 (2003) (citing studies).

136. Jona Goldschmidt, *The Pro Se Litigant's Struggle for Access to Justice: Meeting the Challenge of Bench and Bar Resistance* 40 FAM. CT. REV. 36 (2002).

137. Yegge, *supra* note 133, at 409.

138. William J. Howe III, *Introduction to the Oregon Futures Report*, 40 FAM. CT. REV. 473 (2002).

139. AUSTIN SARAT & WILLIAM L. F. FELSTINER, DIVORCE LAWYERS AND THEIR CLIENTS: POWER AND MEANING IN THE LEGAL PROCESS 50–51 (Oxford University Press, New York, NY, 1995).

140. Gary Skoloff & Robert L. Levy, *Custody Doctrines and Custody Practice: A Divorce Practitioner's View*, 36 FAM. L. Q. 79, 85–97 (2002).

141. Austin Sarat & William L. F. Felstiner, *Lawyers and Legal Consciousness: Law Talk in the Divorce Lawyer's Office*, 98 YALE L.J. 1663, 1682–88 (1989) (summarizing results of their observations of interviews between divorce lawyers and their clients and arguing that these conversations might contribute to the increasing view of the public that the legal process is "cynical instrumentalism").

142. Skoloff & Levy, *supra* note 140, at 93–97.

143. PARENTING OUR CHILDREN: IN THE BEST INTEREST OF THE NATION, *supra* note 125, at 38–39.

144. COMMITTEE TO EXAMINE LAWYER CONDUCT IN MATRIMONIAL ACTIONS, REPORT 1 (N.Y.S. Office of Court Administration, 1993).

145. Pruett & Jackson, *supra* note 71, at 306.

146. LYNN MATHER ET AL. DIVORCE LAWYERS AT WORK: VARIETIES OF PROFESSIONALISM IN PRACTICE 46 (Oxford University Press, New York, NY, 2001); Stephen Labaton, *Are Divorce Lawyers Really the Sleaziest?*, N.Y. TIMES, Sept. 5, 1993, §4 (Week in Review) at 5.

147. Skoloff & Levy, *supra* note 140, at 103.

148. OREGON TASK FORCE ON FAMILY LAW, FINAL REPORT TO GOVERNOR JOHN A. KITZHABER AND THE OREGON LEGISLATIVE ASSEMBLY 2 (Salem, OR, 1997).

Chapter IV   Parents Are Forever I: Joint Custody and Parenting Plans

149. Sign on a wall in an office of a mediation program in Los Angeles, California (personal observation of author).

150. H. Jay Folberg & Marva Graham, *Joint Custody of Children Following Divorce*, 12 U.C. DAVIS L. REV. 523, 529 (1979); David J. Miller, *Joint Custody*, 13 FAM. L.Q. 345, 361–66 (1979).

151. McCann v. McCann, 167 Md. 167, 172, 173 A. 7, 9 (1934).
152. *In re* Burnham, 238 N.W.2d 269, 272 (Sup. Ct. Iowa 1979).
153. *See, e.g.*, Taylor v. Taylor, 508 A.2d 964 (Md. 1986); Beck v. Beck, 432 A.2d 63 (N.J. 1981).
154. Beck v. Beck 432 A.2d 63,72 (N.J. 1981).
155. Elizabeth Scott & Andre Derdeyn, *Rethinking Joint Custody*, 45 OHIO ST. L.J. 455, 456 (1984).
156. ELLMAN ET AL., *supra* note 19, at 673.
157. Linda D. Elrod & Robert Spector, *A Review of the Year in Family Law: State Courts React to Troxel*, 35 FAM. L. Q. 577, 617, Chart 2, col. 3 (2002).
158. Catania, *supra* note 32 at 863.
159. See Kay, *supra* note 26, at 37–38 for a brief summary of this argument, with citations.
160. Bartlett, *Custody Trends, supra* note 82, at 23–24.
161. CAL. FAM. CODE §3044 (a) (West 2002).
162. Bartlett, *Custody Trends, supra* note 82, at 6–7.
163. Linda D. Elrod, *Reforming the System to Protect Children in High-Conflict Custody Cases*, 28 WM. MITCHELL L. REV. 495, 529 & n. 134 (2001).
164. WASH. REV. CODE ANN. §26.09.181(1) (West 2002).
165. COLO. REV. STAT. ANN. §14–10–105 (West 2002).
166. PARENTING OUR CHILDREN: IN THE BEST INTEREST OF THE NATION, *supra* note 125, at 36–37.
167. American Law Institute, *About the American Law Institute*, available at http://www.ali.org/ali/thisali.htm (last visited December 29, 2002).
168. AMERICAN LAW INSTITUTE, PRINCIPLES OF THE LAW OF FAMILY DISSOLUTION: ANALYSIS AND RECOMMENDATIONS §2.05 (Lexis Nexis/Matthew Bender & Co., Newark, NJ, 2002) [hereinafter *ALI Family Dissolution Principles*]; Bartlett, *Custody Trends, supra* note 82, at 6–9.

Chapter V   Parents Are Forever II: Alternative Dispute Resolution and Mediation

169. STEPHEN GOLDBERG ET AL, DISPUTE RESOLUTION: NEGOTIATION, MEDIATION AND OTHER PROCESSES 7 (Aspen Publishers, New York, NY, 3d ed. 1999).
170. L. Camille Hebert, *Introduction – The Impact of Mediation: 25 Years After the Pound Conference*, 17 OHIO ST. J. ON DISP. RESOL. 527 (2002).
171. GOLDBERG ET AL., *supra* note 169, at 7, 31 (citing Frank E. A. Sander, *Varieties of Dispute Processing*, 70 F.R.D. 111 (1976).
172. JOHN HAYNES, DIVORCE MEDIATION: A PRACTICAL GUIDE FOR THERAPISTS AND COUNSELORS (Springer Publishing Co., New York, NY, 1981).
173. O. J. COOGLER, STRUCTURED MEDIATION IN DIVORCE SETTLEMENT: A HANDBOOK FOR MARITAL MEDIATORS (Lexington Books, Lanham, MD, 1978) (unpaged introductory quote) (emphasis in original).
174. Joan B. Kelly, *Psychological and Legal Interventions for Parents and Children in Custody and Access Disputes: Current Research and Practice*, 10 VA. J. SOC. POL'Y & L. 129, 132 (2002).
175. ROGER FISHER & WILLIAM URY, GETTING TO YES: NEGOTIATING AGREEMENT WITHOUT GIVING IN (Houghton, Mifflin Co., Boston, MA, 1981).
176. Leonard L. Riskin, *Understanding Mediators' Orientations, Strategies, and Techniques: A Grid for the Perplexed*, 1 HARV. NEGO. L. REV. 7, 17 (1996).

177. Robert A. Baruch Bush & Joseph P. Folger, The Promise of Mediation: Responding to Conflict Through Empowerment and Recognition (Jossey-Bass, San Francisco, CA, 1994).

178. N.Y. CPLR §7511 (b) (McKinney 2002).

179. Stephen W. Schlissel, *A Proposal for Final and Binding Arbitration of Initial Custody Determinations*, 26 Fam. L. Q. 71 (1992); Melissa D. Philbrick, *Agreements to Arbitrate Post-Divorce Custody Disputes*, 19 Colum. J. L. & Soc. Probs. 419 (1985).

180. An excellent video introduction to mediation for parents is Gregory Firestone & Sharon Press, Mediation Works: Make It Work for You (Florida Dispute Resolution Center, Supreme Court of Florida, 1995).

181. Model Standards of Practice for Family and Divorce Mediation, 35 Fam. L. Q. 27 (2001).

182. The final text of the *Uniform Mediation Act*, including its various drafts, can be found at www.pon.harvard.edu/guests/uma (last visited Dec. 29, 2002). For an excellent discussion of the *UMA* from the perspective of the family mediation community, see Gregory Firestone, *An Analysis of Principled Advocacy in the Development of the Uniform Mediation Act*, 22 N. Ill. U. L. Rev. 265 (2002).

183. Civil Justice, An Agenda for the 1990s: Report of the American Bar Association National Conference on Access to Justice in the 1990s 40 (American Bar Association, Chicago, IL, 1989); Jessica Pearson & Nancy Thoennes, *Divorce Mediation: An Overview of Research Results*, 19 Colum. J.L. & Soc. Probs. 451, 454 (1988).

184. Morton Deutsch, *Cooperation and Conflict: A Personal Perspective on the History of the Social Psychological Study of Conflict Resolution* in International Handbook of Organizational Teamwork and Cooperative Working 24 (M.A. West et al. eds., John Wiley & Sons, West Sussex, England, 2003).

185. Susan C. Kuhn, Comment, *Mandatory Mediation: California Civil Code Section 4607*, 33 Emory L.J. 733 (1984). The mandatory mediation statute was originally enacted as part of the California Civil Code. *See* Cal. Civ. Code §4607 (West 1983). Today, it is part of the California Family Code. *See* Cal. Fam. Code §3170 (a) (West 2002).

186. Carrie-Anne Tondo et al., Note, *Mediation Trends: A Survey of the States*, 39 Fam. Ct. Rev. 431, 433 (2001).

187. Model Standards of Practice for Family and Divorce Mediation, *supra* note 181, at 28 (Overview and Definitions).

188. Hugh Mc Isaac, *Confidentiality Revisited: California Style*, 39 Fam. Ct. Rev. 405 (2001).

189. Model Standards of Practice for Family and Divorce Mediation, Standard II A 1–4, *supra* note 181, at 30.

190. Uniform Mediation Act, Prefatory Note at 1 (July 2001).

191. Uniform Mediation Act, Reporter's Notes on Sections 6(a)(3) & 6(a)(7) at 30, 32–33 (July 2001).

192. Model Standards of Practice for Family and Divorce Mediation, Standard VII, *supra* note 181, at 33–34.

193. Model Standards of Practice for Family and Divorce Mediation, Standard VII C, *supra* note 181, at 33–34. See Tarasoff v. Regents, 17 Cal.3d 425, 551 P.2d 334, 131 Cal. Rptr. 14 (1976) (psychiatrist liable for failure to warn victim of patient's threat to kill her).

194. Model Standards of Practice for Family and Divorce Mediation, Standard VI C. *supra* note 188, at 33.

195. MODEL STANDARDS OF PRACTICE FOR FAMILY AND DIVORCE MEDIATION, Standard VI.D., *supra* note 181, at 33.
196. Deutsch, *supra* note 184, at 23.
197. Frank E.A. Sander, *Some Concluding Thoughts*, 17 OHIO ST. J. ON DIS. RESOL. 705, 706–07 (2002).
198. Janet R. Johnston, *Building Multidisciplinary Professional Partnerships with the Court on Behalf of High Conflict Divorcing Families and Their Children: Who Needs What Kind of Help?*, 22 U. ARK. LITTLE ROCK L. REV. 451, 471, n. 50 (2000).
199. *Id.* at 471–72 (2000) (citing numerous studies).
200. Ver Steegh, *supra* note 135, at 176 (citing numerous studies).
201. *See* Joan B. Kelly, *A Decade of Divorce Mediation Research*, 34 FAM. & CONCILIATION CTS. REV. 373, 376–77 (1996) (describing numerous studies); CONNIE J.A. BECK & BRUCE SALES, FAMILY MEDIATION: FACTS, MYTHS AND FUTURE PROSPECTS 99–121 (American Psychological Association, Washington, DC, 2001).
202. Robert E. Emery, *Easing the Pain of Divorce for Children: Children's Voices, Causes of Conflict, and Mediation. Comments on Kelly's Resolving Child Custody Disputes*, 10 VA. J. SOC. POL'Y & L. 164, 172 (2002).
203. Ver Steegh, *supra* note 135, at 178 (citing numerous studies).
204. Peter A. Dillon & Robert E. Emery, *Divorce Mediation and Resolution of Child Custody Disputes: Long Term Effects*, 66 AM. J. OF ORTHOPSYCHIATRY 131, 132–33 (1996).
205. MATHER ET AL., *supra* note 146, at 187.
206. Craig Mcewen et al., *Bring in the Lawyers: Challenging the Dominant Approaches to Insuring Fairness in Divorce Mediation*, 79 MINN. L. REV. 1317, 1367–68 (1995) (comparing Maine lawyers who participate in that state's mandatory mediation program with New Hampshire lawyers, which does not mandate lawyer participation in mediation).
207. Williams & Buckingham, *supra* note 134, at 181.
208. Maccoby & Mnookin, *supra* note 100, at 159.
209. MATHER ET AL, *supra* note 146, at 58.
210. For a sophisticated review of the research issues see BECK & SALES, *supra* note 201, at 21–24.
211. Ver Steegh, *supra* note 135 at 171 (citing studies).
212. BECK & SALES, *supra* note 201, at 27–28.
213. *The Wingspread Report and Action Plan: High-Conflict Custody Cases: Reforming the System for Children*, 39 FAM. CT. REV. 146 (2001) (Report and action plan of national multi-disciplinary conference sponsored by the ABA Family Law Section and the Johnson Foundation).
214. KENNETH KRESSEL & DEAN G. PRUETT, MEDIATION RESEARCH 405 (Jossey-Bass, San Francisco, CA, 1989).
215. Penelope Eileen Bryant, *Reclaiming Professionalism: The Lawyer's Role in Divorce Mediation*, 28 FAM. L. Q. 177 (1994).
216. Robert H. Mnookin & Eleanor Maccoby, *Facing the Dilemmas of Child Custody*, 10 VA. J. SOC. POL'Y & L. 54, 81–82 (2002).
217. *Child Support Payments to Mothers Improved from '93–'99*, N.Y. TIMES, Oct. 27, 2002 at 22.
218. MACCOBY & MNOOKIN, *supra* note 100, at 156.
219. Elizabeth Ellen Gordon, *What Roles Does Gender Play in Mediation of Domestic Relations Cases?*, 86 JUDICATURE 135, 139 (2002).
220. *Id.* at 143.
221. BECK & SALES, *supra* note 201, at 88–90.

222. Kelly, *supra* note 201, at 377–78 (describing numerous studies).
223. Gordon, *supra* note 219, at 141.

Chapter VI   Parents Are Forever III: Court-Affiliated Educational Programs

224. Tammy Ale, Remarks at the Conference From War to P.E.A.C.E.: New Directions for New York's Child Custody Disputes (New York, NY, Apr. 24, 1993) (on file with the author).
225. Margie J. Geasler & Karen R. Blaisure, *1998 Nationwide Survey of Court-Connected Parent Education Programs*, 37 FAM. & CONCILIATION CTS. REV. 36, 37 (1999).
226. Solveig Erickson & Nancy Ver Steegh, *Mandatory Divorce Education Classes: What Do the Parents Say?*, 38 WM. MITCHELL L. REV. 889, 895–96 (2001).
227. Robyn J. Geelhoed, Karen R. Blaisure, & Margie J. Geasler, *Status of Court-Connected Programs for Children Whose Parents Are Separating or Divorcing*, 39 FAM. CT. REV. 393, 395 (2001).
228. Jeffrey T. Cookston et al., *Prospects for Expanded Parent Education Services for Divorcing Families with Children*, 40 FAM. CT. REV. 190, 199 (2002).
229. GEORGE PICKETT & JOHN J. HANLON, PUBLIC HEALTH: ADMINISTRATION AND PRACTICE 6, 81 (McGraw-Hill, New York, NY, 9th ed. 1990).
230. Haine et al., *supra* note 72 (manuscript at 20).
231. *See, e.g.*, Stewart I. Donaldson et al., *Drug Abuse Prevention Programming*, 39 AM. BEHAV. SCI. 868 (1996) (drug abuse); Caroline M. Thorton & Daniel J. Piacquadio, *Promoting Sun Awareness: Evaluation of an Educational Children's Book*, 98 PEDIATRICS 52 (1996) (skin cancer); Marianne Haenlein Alciati & Karen Glanz, *Using Data to Plan Public Health Programs: Experience from State Cancer Prevention and Control Programs*, 111 PUB. HEALTH REP. 165 (1996) (cancer); Marjorie R. Sable & Allen A. Herman, *The Relationship Between Prenatal Health Behavioral Advice and Low Birth Weight*, 112 PUB. HEALTH REP. 332 (1997) (low birthweight babies).
232. DANIEL GOLEMAN, EMOTIONAL INTELLIGENCE 256–60, 301–02. (Bantam Books, New York, NY, 1997).
233. Hattie Ruttenberg, *The Limited Promise of Public Health Methodologies to Prevent Youth Violence*, 103 YALE L.J. 1885, 1903–04 (1994).
234. PICKETT & HANLON, *supra* note 229, at 83.
235. Jessica Pearson, *Court Services: Meeting the Needs of Twenty-First Century Families*, 33 FAM. L. Q. 617, 625 (1999).
236. *Self Service Center-General Information*, available at http://www.superiorcourt. maricopa.gov/ssc/sschome.html (last visited December 29, 2002).
237. *Sample Calendars and Language for Court Orders*, available at http://www. supreme.state.az.us/dr/pdf/parenttime/parenttime9–1.pdf (last visited December 29, 2002).
238. Sanford Braver et al., *The Content of Divorce Education Programs: Results of a Survey*, 34 FAM. & CONCILIATION CTS. REV. 41, 51 (1996).
239. Kelly, *supra* note 174, at 155–56.
240. Materials describing Parents Without Conflict are available from Family Court Services of the Los Angeles County Superior Court, 111 North Hill Street, Los Angeles, California 90012-3014.
241. Sherrie Kibler et al., *PRE-CONTEMPT/CONTEMNORS Group Diversion Counseling Program*, 32 FAM. & CONCILIATION CTS. REV. 62, 63 (1994).

242. Johnston & Roseby, *supra* note 93, at 228–29.
243. Sanford L. Braver et al., *Methodological Considerations in Evaluating Family Court Programs: A Primer Using Divorced Parent Education Programs as a Case Example*, 35 Fam. & Conciliation. Cts. Rev. 9 (1997) (discussing the complexities of creating a meaningful program evaluation).
244. Haine et al., *supra* note 72 (manuscript at 6).
245. Deutsch, *supra* note 184, at 26.
246. Andrew Schepard, *War and P.E.A.C.E.: A Preliminary Report and a Model Statute on an Interdisciplinary Educational Program for Divorcing and Separating Parents*, 27 U. Mich. J.L. Reform 131, 157–158 (1993); JoAnne Pedro-Carroll et al., *Assisting Children Through Transition: Helping Parents Protect Their Children From the Toxic Effects of Ongoing Conflict in the Aftermath of Divorce*, 39 Fam. Ct. Rev. 377 (2001) (evaluating the Rochester, New York program, *Assisting Children Through Transition*); Erickson & Ver Steegh, *supra* note 226, at 895–96; Andrew Schepard, *Law and Children, Evaluating P.E.A.C.E. (Parent Education and Custody Effectiveness)*, N.Y.L.J., March 11, 2000, at 3, col. 1 (reporting on results of a study of parents who participate in P.E.A.C.E. compared with a control group of parents who did not).
247. Jack Arbutnot & Kenneth Kramer, *Effects of Divorce Education on Mediation Process and Outcome*, 15 Mediation Q. 199, 205–06 (1998).
248. Jack Arbuthnot et al., *Patterns of Relitigation Following Divorce Education*, 35 Fam. & Conciliation Cts. Rev. 269 (1997). Other studies, however, do not find any significant change in litigation behavior after attending a parent education program. Laurie Kramer & Amada Kowal, *Long Term Follow Up of a Court Based Intervention for Divorcing Parents*, 36 Fam. & Conciliation Cts. Rev. 452 (1998).
249. Robert L. Fisher, The Impact of an Educational Seminar for Divorcing Parents: Results From a National Survey of Judges, in Proceedings of the Third International Congress on Parent Education Programs 65 (Association of Family and Conciliation Courts ed. 1997) (246 of the 625 judges in the survey sample responded to the survey).
250. Wolchik et al., *supra* note 88.
251. *Evaluation of Kids' Turn*, available at http://www.kidsturn.org/others/longterm. htm. The website summarizes an ongoing study to evaluate the impact of Kids' Turn on families undergoing divorce or separation. Kids' Turn is collaborating with professors from the California School of Professional Psychology (CSPP) on the study.
252. Janet R. Johnston, Developing and Testing a Group Intervention for Families at Impasse, in Conference Proceedings Book of the Fifth International Congress on Parent Education and Access Programs, Tucson, AZ, November 2002, 9–14 (Association of Family and Conciliation Courts, ed. 2002).
253. Goleman, *supra* note 232, at 139.
254. *Id.* at 60–62.
255. *Id.* at 62.

Chapter VII   Contrasting Child Custody Court Paradigms: New York and California

256. Ellman et al., *supra* note 19, at 198, 206–07.
257. N.Y. Dom. Rel. L. §170 (McKinney 2002).

258. Pawlelski v. Buchholtz, 91 A.D.2d 1200, 459 N.Y.S.2d 190 (1st Dep't 1983); Matter of Richards v. Richards, 78 A.D.2d 943, 433 N.Y.S.2d 259 (3d Dep't 1980).

259. Kaye & Lippman, *supra* note 124, at 146–48.

260. DAVID SIEGEL, NEW YORK PRACTICE §16 at 18 (3d ed. 1999).

261. CAL. FAM. CODE §§3003–3004 (West 2002).

262. CAL. FAM. CODE §3081 (West 2002).

263. CAL. FAM. CODE §3040(a)(1) (West 2002).

264. Local Rules of the Superior Court of California, County of Tuolumne, Rule 4.0 (West 2002).

265. Local Rules of the Superior Court of California, County of San Francisco, Rule 11.20 (West 2002).

266. N.Y. DOM. REL. LAW §240.1(a) (McKinney 2002).

267. Braiman v. Braiman, 44 N.Y.2d 584, 378 N.E.2d 1019, 407 N.Y.S.2d 449 (1978).

268. Harriet Neuman Cohen, *Braiman Still Vital after All These Years: Courts Try to Keep Warring Parents Involved When Joint Custody Is Not Possible*, N. Y. L. J., July 15, 2002 at 9, col. 1.

269. Entwistle v. Entwistle, 61 A.D.2d 380, 384–85, 402 N.Y.S.2d 213, 215–16 (2d Dept 1985); Sandra C. v. Christian D., 244 A.D.2d 551, 644 N.Y.S.2d 472 (2d Dep't 1997).

270. Kaye & Lippman, *supra* note 124, at 163; Judith D. Moran, *Fragmented Courts and Child Protection Cases: A Modest Proposal for Reform*, 40 FAM. CT. REV. 486 (2002).

271. I am grateful to my research assistant, James Bozzomo, Hofstra Law School class of 2003, who created Harry, Wendy, and Cindy for a law review note he authored, and graciously allowed me to incorporate them into this book, albeit in a different context. See Bozzomo, *supra* note 12, at 551–56.

Chapter VIII   Family Violence

272. Custody of Vaughn, 664 N.E.2d 434, 437 (Mass. 1995).

273. Clare Dalton, *When Paradigms Collide: Protecting Battered Parents and Their Children in the Family Court System*, 37 FAM. & CONCILIATION CTS. REV. 273, 285–86 (1999); Catherine C. Ayoub et al., *Emotional Distress in Children of High-Conflict Divorce: The Impact of Marital Conflict and Violence*, 37 FAM. & CONCILIATION CTS. REV. 297, 300 (1999).

274. Bartlett, *Custody Trends*, *supra* note 82, at 33–34.

275. Mullin v. Phelps, 647 A.2d 714, 725 (Vt. 1994).

276. Janet Johnston, *Domestic Violence and Parent-Child Relationships in Families Disputing Custody*, 9 AUST. J. FAM. L. 12, 25 (1995).

277. Deborah Epstein, *Procedural Justice: Tempering the State's Response to Domestic Violence*, 43 WM. & MARY L. REV. 1843, 1846 (2002).

278. *Mullin*, 647 A.2d at 718. All quotations in text are from this opinion, which includes quotations from the trial court opinion.

279. Borchgrevink v. Borchgrevink, 941 P.2d 132 (Alaska 1997). All quotations in text are from this opinion, which includes quotations from the trial court's opinion.

280. Ver Steegh, *supra* note 135, at 151–52.

281. See *id.* at 152–58 (describing several different research-based classifications of different forms of domestic violence).

282. Geri S. W. Fuhrmann et al., *Parent Education's Second Generation: Integrating Violence Sensitivity*, 37 FAM & CONCILIATION CTS. REV. 24, 26 (1999).

283. MACCOBY & MNOOKIN, *supra* note 100, at 287.

284. BRAVER & O'CONNELL, *supra* note 102, at 207.

285. Jennifer P. Maxwell, *Mandatory Mediation of Custody in the Face of Domestic Violence: Suggestions for Courts and Mediators*, 37 Fam. & Conciliation Cts. Rev. 335, 335 (1999) (50–80%); Nancy Thoennes et al., *Mediation and Domestic Violence: Current Policies and Practices*, 33 Fam. & Conciliation Cts. Rev. 6, 7 (1995) (at least 50%).

286. David B. Chandler, *Violence, Fear, and Communication: The Variable Impact of Domestic Violence on Mediation*, 7 Mediation Q. 331 (1990).

287. Beck & Sales, *supra* note 201, at 29.

288. Katherine M. Reihing, Note, *Protecting Victims of Domestic Violence and Their Children after Divorce: The American Law Institute's Model*, 37 Fam. & Conciliaton Cts. Rev. 393 (1999).

289. Janet R. Johnston & Linda E. G. Campbell, *Parent-Child Relationships in Domestic Violence Families Disputing Custody*, 31 Fam. & Conciliation Cts. Rev. 282, 288–89 (1993).

290. *For The Sake of the Children, supra* note 81, at 79.

291. Carey Goldberg, *Spouse Abuse Crackdown, Surprisingly, Nets Many Women*, N.Y. Times, Nov. 23, 1999, at A1.

292. The research is reported in Karen S. Petersen, *Studies Shatter Myth About Abuse*, USA Today, June 27, 2003, available online at http://www.usatoday.com/news/health/2003-06-22-abuse-usat_x.htm (last visited June 27, 2003). This article reports on research findings from three different studies collectively presented at the 2003 Conference sponsored by the Society for Prevention Research (SPR). The studies were sponsored by the National Institutes of Health. The first study was the Oregon Youth Study, with Deborah Capaldi of the Oregon Social Learning Center as the principal researcher. The second study was conducted by the Marriage and Family Development Project at the University of Iowa, with Ericka Lawrence as the principal researcher. The third study was presented by Miriam Ehrensaft of Columbia University and consisted of results from the Dunedin Multidisciplinary Health and Development Study in New Zealand. The SPR Conference proceedings have not yet been published.

293. Brown v. Brown, 867 P.2d 477 (Okla. 1993). All quotations in text are from this opinion, which includes quotations from the trial court's opinion.

294. Bruce J. Winick, *Applying the Law Therapeutically in Domestic Violence Cases*, 69 U. Mo. K. C. L. Rev. 33, 65 (2001).

295. Wissink v. Wissink, 749 N.Y.S.2d 550 (2d Dept 2002).

296. American Bar Association, The Impact of Domestic Violence on Children: A Report to the President of the American Bar Association 1–6 (American Bar Association, Chicago, IL, 1994).

297. *Id.* at 65.

298. Joseph C. McGill et al., *Visitation and Domestic Violence: A Clinical Model of Family Assessment and Access Planning*, 37 Fam & Conciliation Cts. Rev.315, 320 (1999).

299. Janet R. Johnston, *High-Conflict Divorce*, 4 The Future of Children 169 (David and Lucile Packard Foundation, Los Altos, CA, 1994).

300. Johnston & Roseby, *supra* note 93, at 29.

301. Ayoub et al., *supra* note 273, at 309–10.

302. Children's Bureau Administration on Children, Youth and Families, National Child Abuse and Neglect Data System (NCANDS) *Summary of Key Findings from Calendar Year 2000*, U.S. Department of Health and Human Services Apr. 2002), available at http://calib.com/nccanch/pubs/factsheets/canstats.cfm (last visited Dec. 29, 2002) [hereinafter *Children's Bureau*].

303. *Id.*

304. *Id.*
305. Robin A. Rosencrantz, Note, *Rejecting "Hear No Evil Speak No Evil": Expanding the Attorney's Role in Child Abuse Reporting*, 8 Geo. J. Legal Ethics 327, 338 (1995).
306. See *id.* (citing numerous studies).
307. Linda Villarosa, *To Prevent Sexual Abuse, Abusers Step Forward*, N.Y. Times, Dec. 3, 2002 §F at 5 (chart).
308. Robin Fretwell Wilson, *Children at Risk: The Sexual Exploitation of Female Children After Divorce*, 86 Cornell L. Rev. 251, 255 n. 10 (2001) (citing numerous sources).
309. *Childrens Bureau, supra* note 302.
310. Villarosa, *supra* note 307.
311. Wilson, *supra* note 308, at 266.
312. Nicholas Bala & John Schuman, *Allegations of Sexual Abuse When Parents Have Separated*, 17 Canadian Fam. L. Q. 191, 200 (1999–2000).
313. H. Con. Res. 172, 101st Cong. (1990) (enacted).
314. National Conference of Juvenile and Family Court Judges, Model Code on Domestic and Family Violence §401 (1994).
315. E.g. Pa. Cons. Stat. Ann. §5303(a)(3) (West Supp. 2000); Colo. Rev. Stat. §14–10–124 (1.5)(a)(IX) (1999); Cal. Fam. Code §3011(b)(1)–(3) (West Supp. 2002).
316. Elrod & Spector, *supra* note 157, at 618 (chart 2) (2002) (listing 42 of the 50 states and the District of Columbia as requiring a court to consider domestic violence in the determination of a child custody dispute).
317. Lynne R. Kurtz, Comment, *Protecting New York's Children: An Argument for the Creation of a Rebuttable Presumption Against Awarding a Spouse Abuser Custody of a Child*, 60 Alb. L. Rev. 1345, 1348 (1997).
318. Wilson, *supra* note 308, at 290–310.
319. Kahre v. Kahre, 916 P. 2d 1355, 1364 (Okla. 1995).
320. See generally Stephen J. Ceci & Maggie Bruck, Jeopardy in the Courtroom: A Scientific Analysis of Children's Testimony (American Psychological Association, Washington, DC, 1995).
321. *Id.* at 4.
322. Lenderman v. Lenderman, 588 S.W.2d 707 (Ark. 1979). All quotations in the text are from this opinion, which includes quotations from the trial court's opinion.
323. Ceci & Bruck, *supra* note 320, at 32.
324. Nicholas Bala, *A Report from Canada's 'Gender War Zone': Reforming the Child-Related Provisions of the Divorce Act*, 16 Canadian J. Fam. L. 163 196–97 (1999) (citations omitted) (emphasis in original).
325. Thea Brown et al., *Problems and Solutions in the Management of Child Abuse Allegations in Custody and Access Disputes in the Family Court*, 36 Fam & Conciliation Cts. Rev. 431 (1998).
326. *Id.*
327. Nancy Thoennes & Jessica Pearson, *Summary of Findings from Child Sexual Abuse Project* in Sexual Abuse Allegations in Custody and Visitation Cases 12–17 (E. Bruce Nicholson & Josephine Bulkley, eds., American Bar Association, National Legal Resource Center For Child Advocacy and Protection, Washington, DC, 1998).
328. Ceci & Bruck, supra note 320, at 33.
329. American Academy of Child and Adolescent Psychiatry, *Guidelines for the Clinical Evaluation of Childhood and Adolescent Sexual Abuse*, 27 J. Amer. Acad. Child & Adolescent Psychiatry 655 (Sept. 1988).
330. Ceci & Bruck, *supra* note 320, at 279.

331. Bala & Schuman, *supra* note 312, at 231.
332. CECI & BRUCK, *supra* note 320, at 35.
333. Kathleen Coulborn Faller, *Child Maltreatment and Endangerment in the Context of Divorce*, 22 U. ARK. LITTLE ROCK L. REV. 429, 433 (2000).
334. FED. R. CIV. P. 11(c).
335. MINN STAT. ANN. §609.507 (West 2002).
336. ME. REV. STAT. ANN. Tit. 19-A, §1653(3)(O) (West 2002).
337. Debra Sontag, *Fierce Entanglements*, N.Y. TIMES §6 (Magazine) Nov. 17, 2002 at 52.
338. *ALI Family Dissolution Principles*, *supra* note 168 at §2.06(2).
339. *Id.* §2.11 (2).
340. *Id.* §2.07 (1) (d).
341. Bartlett, *Custody Trends*, *supra* note 82, at 32–33.
342. Schepard, *War and P.E.A.C.E.*, *supra* note 246, at 162.
343. Nancy Thoennes et al., *Mediation and Domestic Violence: Current Policies and Practices*, 33 FAM. & CONCILIATION CTS. REV. 6 (1995).
344. Schepard, *War and P.E.A.C.E.* *supra* note 246, at 170–71.
345. Fuhrmann et al., *supra* note 282, at 32.
346. Winick, *supra* note 294, at 66.
347. *ALI Family Dissolution Principles*, *supra* note 168, §2.07 Comment b.
348. Bartlett, *Custody Trends*, *supra* note 82, at 15.
349. Tondo et al. *supra* note 186, at 433.
350. *See* Ver Steegh, *supra* note 135, at 205–6 for a sophisticated chart summarizing when mediation is and is not appropriate for families in which domestic violence is present.
351. Kelly, *supra* note 174, at 140.
352. Carol J. King, *Burdening Access to Justice: The Cost of Divorce Mediation on the Cheap*, 73 ST. JOHN'S L. REV. 375, 446 (1999) (emphasis added).
353. *ALI Family Dissolution Principles*, *supra* note 168, §2.07 Comment b.
354. Ver Steegh, *supra* note 135, at 182, *citing* DESMOND ELLIS & NOREEN STUCKLESS, MEDIATING AND NEGOTIATING MARITAL CONFLICTS 61 (Sage Publications, Thousand Oaks, CA, 1996).
355. Jessica Pearson, *Ten Myths About Family Law*, 27 FAM. L. Q. 279, 289 (1993).
356. Bartlett, *Custody Trends*, *supra* note 82, at 15.
357. Jennifer P. Maxwell, *Mandatory Mediation of Custody in the Face of Domestic Violence: Suggestions for Courts and Mediators*, 37 FAM. & CONCILIATION CTS. REV. 335, 340 (1999); Alexendria Zylstra, *Mediation and Domestic Violence: A Practical Screening Method for Mediators and Mediation Program Administrators*, 2001 J. DISPUTE RESOL. 253, 278–79 (2001). Another screening protocol is contained in Rene L. Rimelspach, *Mediating Family Disputes in a World with Domestic Violence: How To Devise a Safe and Effective Court-Connected Mediation Program*, 17 OHIO ST. J. ON DIS. RESOL. 95, 107–9 (2001).
358. MODEL STANDARDS OF PRACTICE FOR FAMILY AND DIVORCE MEDIATION, Standard XC, *supra* note 181, at 27, 36.
359. MODEL STANDARDS OF PRACTICE FOR FAMILY AND DIVORCE MEDIATION, Standard X B, D 1–6, *supra* note 181, at 36.
360. CAL. FAM. CODE §3181(a) (West 2002).
361. MODEL STANDARDS OF PRACTICE FOR FAMILY AND DIVORCE MEDIATION, Standard VII C, *supra* note 181, at 34.
362. *ALI Family Dissolution Principles*, *supra* note 168, § 2.07 (2).
363. Robert Strauss & Evan Alda, *Supervised Child Access: The Evolution of a Social Service*, 32 FAM. & CONCILIATION CTS. REV. 235 (1994).

364. Ariz. Rev. Stat. Ann §25–410 (West 2002).

365. EVS is described in Jessica Pearson & Jean Anhalt, *Enforcing Visitation Rights*, 33 Judges J. 3, 4 (1994).

366. Mitchell Baris et al. Working With High-Conflict Families of Divorce: A Handbook for Professionals 252–74 (Jason Aronson, Inc., North Vale, NJ, 2001) (reprinting the *Massachusetts Supervised Visitation Task Force, Supervised Visitation Risk Assessment for Judges*).

367. Bartlett, *Custody Trends*, *supra* note 82, at 33.

368. Barbara Flory et al, *An Exploratory Study of Supervised Access and Custody Exchange Services*, 39 Fam. Ct. Rev. 469 (2001).

369. Baris et al. *supra* note 366, at 145.

370. Martha Bailey, *Supervised Access: A Long-Term Solution?*, 37 Fam. & Conciliation Cts. Rev. 478 (1999).

371. Pearson & Anhalt, *supra* note 365, at 39.

372. The Committee on Family Court and Family Law, *Court Ordered Supervised Visitation: Documenting an Unmet Need*, 50 The Record of the Association of the Bar of the City of New York 1, 99 (1995).

373. Nancy Thoennes & Jessica Pearson, *Supervised Visitation: A Profile of Providers*, 37 Fam. & Conciliation Cts. Rev. 460, 474 (1999) (describing a "public perception that supervised visitation programs serve dysfunctional adults who are undeserving of charity rather than children").

374. Robert B. Straus, *Supervised Visitation and Family Violence*, 29 Fam. L.Q. 229, 235–36 (1995); Fla. Stat. Ann §753.002 (West 2002); Conn. Gen. Stat. Ann. § 17a-1011 (West 2002); Kan. Stat. Ann §75–720 (West 2001); N.J. Stat. Ann. §2A:12–9 (West 2002).

375. *Wingspread Report*, *supra* note 213, at 152.

376. Fed. R. Civ. Pro. 53.

377. Patricia M. Wald, *'Some Exceptional Conditions' – The Anatomy of a Decision under FRCP 53(b)*, 62 St. John's L. Rev. 405, 406 (1988).

378. The work of the special master in high-conflict cases is described in detail in Baris et al., *supra* note 366.

379. Okla. Stat. Ann tit. 43 §120.2 (West 2002).

380. Janet M. Bowermaster, *Legal Presumptions and the Role of Mental Health Professionals in Child Custody Proceedings*, 40 Duq. L. Rev. 265, 272 (2002). See *In re* Olson, 17 Cal. Rptr. 2d 480, 485–86 (Cal. Ct. App. 1993).

381. *In re* Matthews, 161 Cal. Rptr. 879 (Cal. Ct. App. 1980).

382. Glauber v. Glauber, 192 A.D.2d 94, 600 N.Y.S.2d 740 (2d Dep't 1993).

383. Michigan is an example. See Mich. Comp. Laws §600.5071 et seq. (2002).

Chapter IX   Differentiated Case Management

384. Kaye & Lippman, *supra* note 124, at 163.

385. Ember Reichgott Junge, *Business Courts: Efficient Justice or Two-Tiered Elitism?* 24 Wm. Mitchell L. Rev. 315, 318–19 (1998).

386. *See generally* Hildy Mauzerall et al., *Protecting the Children of High Conflict Divorce: An Analysis of the Idaho Bench/Bar Committee to Protect Children of High Conflict Divorce Report to the Idaho Supreme Court*, 33 Idaho L. Rev. 291 (1997).

387. Andrew Schepard, *Law and Children: Introduction to Unified Family Courts*, N.Y. L. J., Apr. 16, 1997, at 3 (describing history and rationale of the movement for unified family courts).

388. Barbara Babb, *Where We Stand Redux: Another Look at America's Family Law Adjudicatory Systems*, 35 Fam. L. Q. 628, 632 (Chart 10) (2002).

389. *See Developments in the Law – The Law of Marriage and Family, Unified Family Courts and the Child Protection Dilemma*, 116 Harv. L. Rev. 2099, 2100 (2003).

390. *In re* Report of Family Court Steering Committee, 794 So.2d 518 (Fla. Sup. Ct. 2001).

391. Colorado Judicial Branch, Court Improvement Committee, Colorado Courts' Recommendations for Family Cases: An Analysis of and Recommendations for Cases Involving Families 9 (May 2001).

392. Catherine J. Ross, *The Failure of Fragmentation: The Promise of a System of Unified Family Courts*, 32 Fam. L. Q. 3 (1998).

393. Anne H. Geraghty & Wallace J. Myniec, *Unified Family Courts: Tempering Enthusiasm With Caution*, 40 Fam. Ct. Rev. 435 (2002).

394. Jay Folberg, *Family Courts: Assessing the Trade-Offs*, 37 Fam. & Conciliation Cts. Rev. 448, 451 (1999).

395. *For the Sake of the Children, supra* note 81, at 78.

396. For a similar view on the evolution of family law procedure in Canada, see D.A. Rollie Thompson, *The Evolution of Modern Canadian Family Law Procedure: The End of the Adversary System? Or Just the End of the Trial?*, 41 Fam. Ct. Rev. 115 (2003).

397. See sources cited in *supra* note 357.

398. William G. Austin, *A Focus on Child Custody Evaluations: Guidelines for Using Collateral Sources of Information in Child Custody Evaluations*, 40 Fam. Ct. Rev. 177 (2001).

399. Thea Brown, *Magellan's Discoveries: An Evaluation of a New Program for Managing Family Court Parenting Disputes Involving Child Abuse Allegations*, 40 Fam Ct. Rev. 320 (2002) (reporting findings of Project Magellan).

400. Brown et al., *supra* note 325.

401. Paul Adams & Susan Chandler, *Building Partnerships to Protect Children: A Blended Model of Family Group Conferencing*, 40 Fam. Ct. Rev. 502 (2001) (describing Family Group Conferencing).

402. John A. Martin & Steven Weller, *Mediated Child Protection Conferencing: Lessons from the Wisconsin Unified Family Court Project*, 41 Judges J. 5 (2002).

403. Nancy A. Flatters, *Family/Child Judicial Dispute Resolution (JDR): An Overview of One Canadian Court's Settlement Conference Approach to the Pretrial Resolution of Family and Child Welfare/Protection Matters*, 40 Fam. Ct. Rev. 182 (2003).

404. Winick, *supra* note 294, at 39–43.

405. *See* Gregory Firestone, *Dependency Mediation: Where Do We Go from Here?* 35 Fam. & Conciliation Cts. Rev. 223 (1997) for an excellent discussion of the future of mediation in child protection disputes.

Chapter X   Lawyers for Parents

406. Abraham Lincoln, *Notes for a Law Lecture*, in Life and Writings of Abraham Lincoln 329 (Modern Library, New York, NY, Philip V. D. Stern, ed., 2000) (paperback ed.).

407. M. K. Gandhi, An Autobiography: The Story of My Experiments With Truth 134 (Beacon Press, Boston, MA, 1993) (paperback ed.).

408. Mather et al., *supra* note 146, at 106, 114, 121.

409. Lewis Becker, *Ethical Concerns in Negotiating Family Law Agreements*, 30 Fam. L. Q. 587, 624 (1996).

410. Janet Weinstein, *And Never the Twain Shall Meet: The Best Interests of Children and the Adversary System*, 52 U. MIAMI L. REV. 79, 86 (1997).

411. Judy Mann, *Rudy Runs Amok in Manhattan Melodrama*, WASHINGTON POST, May 25, 2001, at C 9.

412. Stephen Seplow, *Giuliani's Divorce Juicy Grist for Media Mill*, PHILADELPHIA INQUIRER, May 28, 2001 at A02.

413. Kathy Kinser, *Representing the High Profile Client and Celebrity*, American Academy of Matrimonial Lawyers, Spring Seminar (March 3–10, 2001), available at http://www.aaml.org/Articles/2001–03/KinserCelebrity.htm (last visited Dec. 20, 2002).

414. Andrea Schneider, *Shattering Negotiation Myths: Empirical Evidence on the Effectiveness of Negotiation Style*, 7 HARV. NEGO. L. REV. 143, 167 (2002).

415. MODEL CODE OF PROFESSIONAL RESPONSBILITY DR 7–101 (1969).

416. MODEL RULES OF PROFESSIONAL CONDUCT, Rules 1.1 & 1.3 (2002).

417. MODEL RULES OF PROFESSSIONAL CONDUCT, Preamble ¶'s 1 & 9 and Rule 1.3 cmt.1 (2002).

418. Mike France, *More Big Businesses Ask: Can We Talk, Not Sue?*, NAT'L L. J. Mar. 13, 1995 at B1.

419. Andrew Schepard et al., *Preventing Trauma for the Children of Divorce Through Education and Professional Responsibility*, 16 NOVA L. REV. 767 (1992).

420. Nicole Pedone, *Lawyer's Duty to Discuss Alternative Dispute Resolution in the Best Interest of the Children*, 36 FAM. & CONCILIATION CTS. REV. 65 (1997).

421. AMERICAN ACADEMY OF MATRIMONIAL LAWYERS, BOUNDS OF ADVOCACY: GOALS FOR FAMILY LAWYERS RULE 6.1 (2000) ("An attorney representing a parent should consider the welfare of, and seek to minimize the adverse impact of the divorce on, the minor children"); Rule 6.2 ("An attorney should not permit a client to contest child custody, contact or access for either financial leverage or vindictiveness").

422. FED. R. CIV. P. 11.

423. TESLER, *supra* note 122.

424. TEX. FAM. CODE ANN. §153.0072 (a) (West 2003).

425. TEX. FAM. CODE ANN. §153.0072(b) (West 2003) (emphasis added).

426. John Lande, *Possibilities for Collaborative Law: Ethics and Practice of Lawyer Disqualification and Process Control in a New Model of Lawyering*, 64 OHIO S. L. J. (2003) (forthcoming Nov. 2003) (manuscript at 70) (on file with author).

427. ROBERT H. MNOOKIN ET AL., BEYOND WINNING: NEGOTIATING TO CREATE VALUE IN DEALS AND DISPUTES 93–96 (Belknap Press of Harvard University Press, Cambridge, MA, 2000).

428. TESLER, *supra* note 122, at 9, n. 3.

429. *Id.* at 9.

430. *Id.* at 165.

431. *Id.* at 169.

432. Lande, *supra* note 426, manuscript at 30.

433. MODEL RULES OF PROFESSIONAL CONDUCT Rule 1.16 (2002).

434. FORREST S. MOSTEN, UNBUNDLING LEGAL SERVICES: A GUIDE TO DELIVERING LEGAL SERVICES A LA CARTE (Law Practice Management Section of American Bar Association, Chicago, IL, 2000).

435. Forrest S. Mosten, *Unbundling: Current Developments and Future Trends*, 40 FAM. CT. REV. 15 (2002).

436. MOSTEN, *supra* note 434, at 91–103; Richard Zorza, *Discrete Task Representation, Ethics and the Big Picture*, 40 FAM. CT. REV. 19 (2002).

437. See Law Competitions for Law Students (last visited Dec. 15, 2002) < http://www.law-competitions.com/>.
438. They read, for example, Mnookin et al., *supra* note 427, and jointly discuss the divorce case study that is contained in the last third of the book.
439. Deborah Weimer, *Ethical Judgment and Interdisciplinary Collaboration in Custody and Child Welfare Cases*, 68 Tenn. L. Rev. 881 (2001).

Chapter XI   The Voice of the Child, the Lawyer for the Child, and Child Alienation

440. Alanna's essay is quoted in Richard Ducote, *Guardians Ad Litem in Private Custody Litigation: The Case for Abolition*, 2002 Loyola J. Pub. Int. L. 106, 107.
441. Kelly, *supra* note 174, at 149.
442. Barbara Bennett Woodhouse, *Talking About Children's Rights in Judicial Custody and Visitation Decision-Making*, 36 Fam. L. Q. 105, 116 (2002).
443. Parham v. J.R., 422 U.S. 584, 602–03 (1979).
444. Woodhouse, *supra* note 442, at 123.
445. Florida Stat. Ann. §61.13(3) (i) (West Supp.2002) (emphasis added).
446. Ellman et al., *supra* note 19, at 652.
447. Woodhouse, *supra* note 442, at 122.
448. Ellman et al., *supra* note 19, at 653–54.
449. National Interdisciplinary Colloquium on Child Custody, Legal and Mental Health Perspectives on Child Custody Law: A Deskbook for Judges §23.10 at 298 (West Group, New York, NY, 1998).
450. Kelly, *supra* note 174, at 153–54.
451. *Id.* at 157–61.
452. *Id.* at 160–62. The Australian pilot study is described in Jennifer McIntosh, *Child-Inclusive Divorce Mediation: Report on a Qualitative Research Study*, 18 Mediation Q. 55 (2001).
453. Model Standards of Practice for Family and Divorce Mediation, Standard VIII E, *supra* note 181, at 35.
454. Model Standards of Practice for Family and Divorce Mediation, Standard VIII D, *supra* note 181, at 35.
455. There is a rich scholarly literature on this subject that is too complex to summarize and cite here. A good starting place is Martin Guggenheim, *A Paradigm for Determining the Role of Counsel for Children*, 64 Fordham L. Rev. 1399 (1996), and the other articles in the symposium issue of the *Fordham Law Review* devoted to the subject. *See* Bruce A. Green & Bernardine Dohrn, *Foreword: Children and the Ethical Practice of Law*, 64 Fordham L. Rev. 1281 (1996) for a description of the background to the symposium and the authors who wrote for it.
456. Theodor S. Liebmann, *Confidentiality, Consultation and the Child Client*, 75 Temple L. Rev. 821 (2002) (discussing confidentiality issues for attorneys who represent children).
457. N.Y. Fam. Ct. Act §241 (McKinney 2002) (emphasis added).
458. 273 A.D.2d 753, 710 N.Y.S.2d 149 (3d Dep't 2000).
459. *Id.* at 273 A.D.2d at 755, 710 N.Y.S.2d at 153.
460. *Id.* at 273 A.D.2d at 755, 710 N.Y.S.2d at 152–53.
461. American Bar Association Family Law Section, Standards of Practice for Lawyers Representing Children in Custody and Visitation Cases (Committee Final Draft April 4, 2003).

462. Note, *Lawyering for the Child: Principles of Representation in Custody and Visitation Disputes Arising from Divorce*, 87 YALE L.J. 1126, 1132–33 (1978).

463. ALISON A. BEYEA & FRANK D'ALESSANDRO, A VOICE FOR LOW-INCOME CHILDREN: EVALUATING GUARDIANS AD LITEM IN DIVORCE AND PARENTAL RIGHTS AND RESPONSIBILITIES CASES (2002) (Report of the Edmund S. Muskie Fellowship for Legal Services Guardian *ad litem* Project).

464. Ducote, *supra* note 440, at 119.

465. Laura Morgan, *Malpractice Liability of Guardians Ad Litem*, 7 DIVORCE LITIGATION 107 (1995); Dana E. Prescott, *The Liability of Lawyers as Guardians ad litem: The Best Defense is a Good Defense*, 11 J. AM. ACAD. MAT. LAW. 65 (1993).

466. Ducote, *supra* note 440, at 111.

467. For a discussion of fees to Guardians in New York representing children of high-income parents, see Joel R. Brandes, *Law and the Family: Compensation of Law Guardians*, N.Y.L. J., July 28, 1998, at 3. For a discussion of the need to adequately fund Guardians for poor children, see BEYEA & D'ALLESSANDRO, *supra* note 463, at 13–15.

468. Ducote, *supra* note 440, at 113–14.

469. FLORIDA BAR COMMISSION ON THE LEGAL NEEDS OF CHILDREN, FINAL REPORT 24–25 (June 2002).

470. Kathleen Murray, *When Children Refuse to Visit Parents: Is Prison an Appropriate Remedy?* 37 FAM. & CONCILIATION CTS. REV. 83 (1999).

471. *In re* Marshall, 663 N.E.2d 1113 (Ill. App. Ct. 1996). The facts of the case are taken from the court's opinion.

472. *Id.* at 663 N.E.2d at 1118.

473. Editorial, *The Judge Is Unclear on the Concept*, CHICAGO TRIBUNE, July 28, 1995 at 18.

474. Joan B. Kelly & Janet R. Johnston, *The Alienated Child: A Reformulation of Parental Alienation Syndrome*, 39 FAM. CT. REV. 249, 251 (2001) (emphasis added).

475. RICHARD A. GARDNER, THE PARENTAL ALIENATION SYNDROME: A GUIDE FOR MENTAL HEALTH AND LEGAL PROFESSIONALS (Creative Therapeuties, Inc., Creskill, NJ, 1992). It is important to note that this book is self-published.

476. James R. Williams, *Should Judges Close the Gate on PAS?*, 39 FAM. CT. REV. 267 (2001); Lewis Zirogiannis, *Evidentiary Issues with Parental Alienation Syndrome*, 39 FAM. CT. REV. 334 (2001).

Chapter XII Neutral Mental Health Evaluators

477. PHILIP M. STAHL, CONDUCTING CHILD CUSTODY EVALUATIONS: A COMPREHENSIVE GUIDE (Sage Publications, Thousand Oaks, CA, 1994).

478. Philip M. Stahl & Gregory Firestone, *Guest Editors' Introduction to the Special Issue on Child Custody Evaluations*, 38 FAM. & CONCILIATION CTS. REV. 292, 294–95 (2000).

479. Shuman, *supra* note 53, at 159.

480. Young v. Young, 212 A.D.2d 114, 628 N.Y.S.2d 957 (2d Dept. 1995); Rosenblitt v. Rosenblitt, 107 A.D.2d 292, 486 N.Y.S.2d 741 (2d Dept. 1985).

481. Shuman, *supra* note 53, at 155–57.

482. *In re* DuRoque, 74 Cal. App. 4th 1090, 1096, 88 Cal. Rptr. 618, 622 (1st Dist. Ct. App. 1999)

483. AMERICAN ACADEMY OF CHILD & ADOLESCENT PSYCHIATRY, SUMMARY OF PRACTICE PARAMETERS FOR CHILD CUSTODY EVALUATION (available at http://www.aacap.org/clinical/Custody~1.htm) (last visited May 14, 2002); ASSOCIATION OF

Family and Conciliation Courts, Model Standards of Practice for Child Custody Evaluation (available at http://afccnet.org/docs/resources_model child.htm) (last visited Dec. 17, 2002); Committee on Ethical Guidelines for Forensic Psychologists, *Specialty Guidelines for Forensic Psychologists*, 15 L. & Human Behavior 655 (1991).

484. American Psychological Association, *Guidelines for Child Custody Evaluations in Divorce Proceedings*, 49 Am. Psych. 677 (1994) (available at http://www.apa.org/practice/childcustody.html) (last visited Dec. 20, 2002).

485. Stahl, *supra* note 477; Jonathan W. Gould, Conducting Scientifically Crafted Child Custody Evaluations (Sage Publications, Thousand Oaks, CA, 1998).

486. Cal. Court R. 1257.3–4 (2002).

487. Karl Kirkland, *The Epistemology of Child Custody Evaluations*, 40 Fam. Ct. Rev. 185, 185 (2002).

488. Azia v. DiLascia, 1999 WL 989561 (Conn. Sup. Ct. Oct. 18, 1999).

489. *In re* Rebouche, 587 N.W.2d 795, 799 (Iowa Ct. App. 1998).

490. Wilkinson v. Russell, 182 F.3d 89, 106 (2d Cir. 1998).

491. Gary B. Melton et al. Psychological Evaluations for the Courts: A Handbook for Mental Health Professionals and Lawyers 75 (Guilford Press, New York, NY, 2d ed. 2000).

492. James N. Bow & Francella A. Quinnell, *A Critical Review of Child Custody Evaluation Reports*, 40 Fam. Ct. Rev. 164, 172 (2002).

493. *Wingspread Report*, *supra* note 213, at 148.

494. *Id.* at 149.

495. Shuman, *supra* note 53, at 142–54.

496. Stahl, *supra* note 477, at 54 .

497. Randy K. Otto et al., *The Use of Psychological Testing in Child Custody Evaluations*, 38 Fam. & Conciliation Cts. Rev. 312, 334 (2000).

498. Shuman, *supra* note 53, at 150–54.

499. William G. Austin, *Guidelines for Utilizing Collateral Sources of Information in Child Custody Evaluations*, 40 Fam. Ct. Rev. 177 (2002).

500. Bowermaster, *supra* note 380, at 299–300.

501. Melton et al., *supra* note 491, at 11.

502. *Wingspread Report*, *supra* note 213, at 149.

503. N.Y. Dom. Rel., §240 1 (a) (McKinney 2001).

Chapter XIII   The "Best Interests" Test and Its Presumption-Based Competitors

504. Mary Ann Glendon, *Fixed Rules and Discretion in Contemporary Family Law and Succession Law*, 60 Tul. L. Rev. 1165, 1181 (1986).

505. The Oxford Dictionary of Modern Quotations 55 (Oxford University Press, Oxford, U.K., Tony Augarde, ed., 1991) (quoting Winston Churchill's Address at the House of Commons in Nov. 1947).

506. Minn. Stat Ann. §518.17 (West 2002).

507. *See generally* Robert Mnookin & Louis Kornhauser, *Bargaining in the Shadow of the Law: The Case of Divorce*, 88 Yale L.J. 950 (1979).

508. *ALI Family Dissolution Principles*, *supra* note 168, at §2.09 (2).

509. *ALI Family Dissolution Principles*, *supra* note 168, at §2.09 (2) & (3).

510. *ALI Family Dissolution Principles, supra* note §168, at 2.08 (1).
511. Katharine T. Bartlett, *Child Custody in the 21st Century: How the American Law Institute Proposes to Achieve Predictability and Still Protect the Individual Child's Best Interests*, 35 WILLIAMETTE L. REV. 467, 480 (1999).
512. Pearson, *supra* note 355, at 297.
513. Katherine T. Bartlett, *Preference, Presumption, Predisposition and Common Sense: From Traditional Custody Doctrine to the American Law Institute's Family Dissolution Project*, 36 FAM. L. Q. 11, 25 (2002).
514. Kay, *supra* note 26, at 38.
515. Brinig, *supra* note 38, at 311, n. 62.
516. See Williams & Buckingham, *supra* note 134, at 174 (women are petitioners in 58% of marital dissolutions, men in 42%, in survey of Florida court filings).
517. Margaret F. Brining & Douglas W. Allen, *"These Boots Are Made for Walking": Why Most Divorce Filers Are Women*, 2 AM. L. & ECON. REV. 126 (2000).
518. Kelly & Ward, *supra* note 103, at 357.
519. DESKBOOK, *supra* note 449, §2:3 at 13.
520. *Id.*
521. Bartlett, *Custody Trends, supra* note 82, at 17.
522. MACCOBY & MNOOKIN, *supra* note 100, at 112, 149–53.
523. Carol Smart, *From Children's Shoes to Children's Voices*, 40 FAM. CT. REV. 307, 314 (2002).
524. The ALI uses the terms "custodial responsibility" and "decision-making responsibility" for essentially physical and legal custody. *ALI Family Dissolution Principles, supra* note 168, at §2.03(3)–(4).
525. JAMES Q. WILSON, THE MARRIAGE PROBLEM: HOW OUR CULTURE HAS WEAKENED FAMILIES 172–74 (Harper Collins, New York, NY, 2002); Cochran, Jr. & Vitz, *supra* note 44, at 344–49; Younger, *supra* note 36, at 67.
526. JUDITH WALLERSTEIN ET AL., THE UNEXPECTED LEGACY OF DIVORCE xxiii (Hyperion, New York, NY, 2000); Whitehead, *supra* note 1, at 47.
527. WILSON, *supra* note 525, at 172–74.
528. Amato, *supra* note 76, at 90.
529. IRA MARK ELLMAN ET AL., TEACHERS MANUAL FAMILY LAW: CASES, TEXT, PROBLEMS 29 (Lexis Law Publishing, Charlottesville, VA, 3d ed. 1998).
530. CALEB FOOTE ET AL., CASES AND MATERIALS ON FAMILY LAW 954–57, 1004 (Little, Brown & Co., Boston, MA, 2nd ed. 1976) (describing techniques to make divorce appear uncontested in court under a fault system, and describing experience in England with Queen's Proctor, whose job it was to investigate divorce cases at random for signs of perjury).
531. MICHAEL WHEELER, NO-FAULT DIVORCE 10–11 (Beacon Press, Boston, MA, 1979) (describing the problem of migratory divorce under the fault system).
532. Amato, *supra* note 76, at 91.
533. Scott, *supra* note 77, at 105.
534. *Id.* at 107–114.

Chapter XIV Consolidating The New Paradigm: The Future of the Child Custody Court

535. Arthur T. Vanderbilt, *Introduction* to MINIMUM STANDARDS OF JUDICIAL ADMINISTRATION xix (Law Center of New York University, for the National Council of Judicial Councils, New York, NY, Arthur T. Vanderbilt, ed., 1949).

536. Thomas S. Kuhn, The Structure of Scientific Revolutions 175 (University of Chicago Press, Chicago, IL, 3d ed. 1996).

537. Forrest S. Mosten, *Mediation and the Process of Family Law Reform*, 37 Fam. & Conciliation. Cts. Rev. 429 (1999).

538. Christopher N. Wu, *Making Families and Children a High Priority in Courts: California's Center for Families, Children and the Courts*, 40 Fam. Ct. Rev. 417 (2002).

539. Report of the Governor's Commission on Divorce, Custody and Children, State of Connecticut, Governor John G. Rowland (Dec. 2002) (available at http://www.opm.state.ct.us/pdpd1/CCDC/draftrec.htm) (last visited Dec. 15, 2002).

540. The Family Court Initiative: Mission, available at http//www.flcourts.org/osca/divisions/family/index.html (last visited Nov. 11. 2002).

541. Recommendations of the Florida Supreme Court's Family Court Steering Committee: A Model Family Court for Florida, available at http//www.flcourts.org (June 2000) (last visited Dec. 20, 2002).

542. *In re* Report of the Family Court Steering Committee, 794 So.2d 518 (Fla. 2001).

543. Elizabeth Barker Brandt, *The Challenge to Rural States of Procedural Reform in High Conflict Custody Cases*, 22 U.Ark. Little Rock L. Rev. 357, 370–74 (2000).

544. Forest S. Mosten, *supra* note 537, at 432–34.

545. *See generally* William Howe III & Maureen McNight, *Oregon Task Force on Family Law: A New System to Resolve Family Law Conflicts*, 33 Fam. & Conciliation Cts. Rev. 173 (1995).

546. Futures Subcommittee of the Statewide Family Law Advisory Committee, *The Integrated Family Court of the Future-Final Report*, 40 Fam. Ct. Rev. 474 (2002).

547. Joanne Pedro-Carroll, *The Children of Divorce Intervention Program: Fostering Resilient Outcomes for School-Aged Children, in* 6 Issues in Children's and Families' Lives: Primary Prevention Works 312 (George W. Albee & Thomas P. Gullotta eds., Sage Publications, Thousand Oaks, CA 1997).

548. Haw. Rev. Stat. §3052B-1 – B-7 (West 2001).

549. Quoted in Tesler, *supra* note 122, at 214.

Index

Ahrons, Constance, 31
Alexander, Jane, 9
alienated child
    definition of, 147, 149
    differentiated case management required
        for courts to deal with, 150
    In re Marshall as illustration of, 148
    should not be treated as criminal, 151
    see also In re Marshall; Parental Alienation
        Syndrome (PAS)
alternative dispute resolution (ADR)
    arbitration as, 54, 55
    continuum of different processes for, 51–2
    court-affiliated education is not, 52
    custody disputes as natural fit for, 50, 51
    definition of, 50–1
    duty of lawyer to advise client of, 130
    expert evaluation as, 53
    mediation as, 52–3
    negotiation as, 52
    Pound Conference, major influence on
        development of, 50
    processes can be combined with others, 54
    processes of, illustration comparing, 54–7
    trial, compared with, 56
    see also arbitration; expert evaluation;
        mediation; special master
Amato, Paul, 172–4
American Academy of Matrimonial
    Lawyers (AAML), *Bounds of Advocacy*,
    130
American Law Institute (ALI)
    described, 49, 101
American Law Institute, *Principles of the Law
    of Family Dissolution* (*ALI Principles*)
    "approximation presumption" advocated
        by, 165, 167–70

description of, 101
disadvantages of presumptions to resolve
    custody disputes, 165–6
domestic violence and child custody,
    general position on, 101
educational programs affiliated with
    courts, support for mandated, 101
joint decision-making, presumption of,
    165–7
mandatory mediation, opposition to,
    102
parenting plans, support of 49
see also best interests of the child; custody,
    joint legal; custody, joint physical;
    custody, physical; mediation; parenting
    plan; violence, domestic
American Psychological Association,
    Guidelines for Child Custody Evaluators,
    155
approximation presumption (proposed
    standard for determining child's
    residence)
    ALI Principles advocate of, 165, 167–70
    definition of, 165
    gender neutrality of, 167
    incentive for women to seek divorce may
        be created by, 168
    joint custody, "crafted by women" as
        alternative to, 168
    one state-enactment of, 170
    parents, locked into pre-divorce child care
        roles by, 169–70
    parents' willingness to cooperate with
        other parent, not taken into account by,
        170
    preserving stable parent-child
        relationships and, 167–8

211